STARKWEATHER
A STORY OF MASS MURDER ON THE GREAT PLAINS

Jeff O'Donnell

J & L Lee Publishers

© 1993 Jeff O'Donnell

ISBN 0-934904-31-6

Photos are from the Nebraska State Historical Society and the files of the *Lincoln Journal*.

J & L Lee Co.
P.O. Box 5575
Lincoln, NE 68505

INTRODUCTION

On Tuesday, January 29, 1958, KMTV's veteran anchorman, Bill Talbott, opened his noon news program with the following lead story:

> Police in Nebraska and five other states continue to search for two missing teenagers wanted for questioning in the triple murders discovered in Lincoln yesterday. Lincoln Policeman Joe Carroll said that nineteen-year-old Charles Starkweather and fourteen-year-old Caril Ann Fugate are being sought for what light they might shed upon the case.

By the time Starkweather and Fugate were run down and captured on a lonely, windswept highway in Wyoming three days later, eleven people lay dead, murdered in cold blood. At the time, it was the second worst case of multiple murder in United States history; only Howard Unruh's killing of 13 people in 1949 topped Starkweather's feat.

People in Nebraska today have vivid memories of exactly what they were doing when it became known a mass murderer was on the loose. My dad, an elementary school principal in a town just south of Lincoln, remembers sending children home early in the afternoon with the armed fathers. There was no telling when and where Charlie, along with his female accomplice Caril Fugate, would show up to murder again.

Residents of eastern Nebraska hastened to defend themselves. Sporting goods stores quickly sold out of handguns, shotguns, and rifles. Farmers carried guns on their way to and from their normal chores and field work. In Lincoln itself, where six bodies were found, there was near panic as National Guard troops were called out by Governor Anderson and were ordered to patrol the streets in troop trucks and jeeps. They carried riot guns, machine guns and rifles.

Fear of the unknown gripped all of Nebraska and parts of the Midwest as body after body was discovered. Starkweather and his female accomplice appeared indiscriminate in both their choice of victims and the locations of the crimes. It was thought they could be lurking anywhere at any time.

Exasperated lawmen, conducting the largest manhunt in the history of the midlands, remained always a corpse behind. When finally caught in Wyoming, the murderous duo had left behind the following victims:

> Robert Colvert, 21, gas station attendant
> Marion Bartlett, 57, Caril Fugate's stepfather
> Velda Bartlett, 36, Caril's mother
> Betty Jean Bartlett, 2½, Caril's stepsister
> August Meyer, 70, farmer near Bennet

INTRODUCTION

>Robert Jensen, 17, of Bennet
>Carol King, 16, of Bennet
>C. Lauer Ward, 48, prominent Lincoln businessman
>Clara Ward, 46, his wife
>Lillian Fencl, 51, the Wards' maid
>Merle Collison, 37, shoe salesman

Starkweather and Fugate were finally stopped near Douglas, Wyoming, following a wild car chase, with officers pursuing them at speeds exceeding 110 miles per hour. Charlie and Caril were eventually returned to Lincoln where they stood trial. Charlie was convicted of murder and electrocuted on June 25, 1959. Caril Fugate was convicted of second-degree murder and sentenced to life imprisonment.

Charles Starkweather was a model of cooperation with the police, sheriff's officers, and lawyers for the prosecution from the beginning. Confessions and statements flowed from the onset, often unsolicited and always contradictory. One of his statements was written on the wall of the jail in Gering, Nebraska, the overnight stop of the two-car caravan returning Starkweather to Lincoln from Wyoming. He wrote:

> Caril is the one who said to go to Washington State. by the time any body will read this i will be dead for all the killings. then they can not give caril the chair to. from Lincoln Nebraska they got us Jan 29, 1958
> 1958 kill 11 persons
> Charles kill 9 all men
> Caril kill 2 all girls
> They have so many cops and people watching us . . . I can't add all of them up.

On the wall was an arrow-pierced heart with Charles' and Caril's names in the center. Starkweather had drawn the traditional symbol of sweethearts in a message accusing his girl friend of two murders. He later excluded Caril from any part in the crime and then brought her back as an active participant.

Starkweather was represented by two court-appointed Lincoln attorneys, T. Clement Gaughan and William F. Matschullat. The plea they entered on his behalf immediately put them in disfavor with Starkweather and his entire family. To kill eleven people was one thing, but to plead not guilty by reason of insanity was quite another. They felt this reflection on the family was unbearable, and the two attorneys were discharged because of the plea after the first appeal was ruled on and refused.

Throughout the trial, Starkweather hampered his own defense by refusing medical tests when there were indications he might be suffering brain damage, as well as generally refusing to cooperate with his attorneys. He was supported by his family, and at one point accused his attorneys of being intoxicated during a visit to the penitentiary.

Neither of Starkweather's parents did a good deal to aid in the defense. Mrs. Starkweather said in court she had raised "six problems and one catastrophe," a statement she later explained in detail to the newspapers.

The Starkweathers had more communication with the prosecution and newspapers than with the defense counsel, at one point being given a lecture by the prosecution that it might be better if they took their revelations to those persons charged with keeping their son alive, not those seeking to kill him.

Starkweather was a spectator's delight during the trial. He fell asleep often; he tugged playfully at the chains with which he was attached to a deputy; and at one point he struck a news photographer in the face with his steel-shackled wrists.

The jury of eight women and four men took little more than six hours to find Starkweather guilty. Starkweather's reaction was to turn to defense counsel Matschullat and yawn. His father suggested minutes after the verdict, "Let's all go out and get a steak."

Meanwhile, Caril Fugate was quietly awaiting trial for the murder of Robert Jensen. Starkweather was called to testify against her and accused her in court of the murder. Caril was convicted and sentenced to life imprisonment. Repeated prison-to-prison pleas that Starkweater "tell the truth" went unheeded, and Caril became more desperate as Starkweather's execution date neared. Ultimately, she sent what she thought was an "eleventh hour" telegram to President Eisenhower. The wire of May 21, 1959, was as follows:

> President of the United States
> White House
> Washington, D.C.
>
> I am 15 years old. About a year and a half ago on a day when I was in public school, 19 year old Starkweather who I had told several days before in front of my mother never to see me again went into my home and killed my 2 year old baby sister, mother, and stepfather. Starkweather first confessed I had nothing to do with his murder which is true. Later he changed his story and said I helped him do his murder which is not true. He forced me to go with him when I got home from school against my will. Starkweather will be executed tomorrow (Friday). I have been denied by Governor Brooks a request to see him and see if he will tell the truth.
>
> Thank you
> Caril Ann Fugate

The reply from the President's special counsel, David W. Kendall, was as follows:

> The Starkweather case is entirely a state matter. The President has no jurisdiction or authority in any way to comply with your request.

INTRODUCTION

This reply came three days after Starkweather was to have died. Presumably, a positive response would have arrived in time. Starkweather did not die on May 21; he had received another delay in his execution date, one of five postponements. In the meantime, he worked on an autobiography and developed an interest in religion.

Charles Starkweather was executed on June 25, 1959. With his death went the last hope of that final "confession" exonerating Caril Fugate. If she was not guilty of a capital crime, only she and Starkweather knew it. If she was innocent, he may have lost sight of that fact during his months in prison, for facts to Charlie were subject to change.

PROLOGUE

It was the time of year most Nebraskans dreaded. The Indian summer had come and gone, its warm days and cool nights giving way to the bitter cold of yet another prairie winter. Lincoln's tall, majestic oak trees were bare now, naked and trembling before winter's relentless presence. The crimson and golden leaves marking another autumn season had long since spiraled in silent agony to the frozen earth below. Raked up into huge piles, they were burned in countless incinerators hidden in alleys behind Lincoln's houses.

One more season of Nebraska football had been played. The Cornhuskers had struggled through another poor year full of frustration and losing. Grown men prayed to the football god for a deliverer who would lead them to the promised land. Someone who would turn the losing seasons into winning ones, maybe even a bowl game. Was it too much to ask, they wondered?

Nebraska's farmers finished the fall harvest and cascades of golden corn filled tall white elevators in towns called Lexington, Fremont, and Fairmont. Yields were good, but like every harvest, not good enough for these tough second-generation sons of prairie pioneers. From Falls City to Pierce, from Hastings to Chadron, these hardworking men of the soil prepared for another winter.

Four-row corn pickers needed oiling and were stored in grey steel quonsets. Black and white Holstein cattle and dark brown Herefords were brought in from the short grass pastures and secured in hundred-year-old barns. Farm houses needed to be prepared for winter's heavy blows; replacing furnace filters, tacking plastic over north-facing windows, and stacking thick bales of prairie hay around foundations were just a few of the jobs yet to be done.

Businessmen working at Lincoln Electric System and Dorsey Laboratories pulled winter overcoats from musty basement storage closets. Gloves, scarves and winter hats had to be located before the first blizzard blew down from the Dakotas. Department stores, such as Miller and Paine's or Gold's, laid out new winter stocks of woolen sweaters, long underwear, and multicolored flannel shirts in anticipation of another winter season.

Pheasant hunters cleaned and oiled their 12-gauge pumps, waiting for the opening of another bird season. Nebraska is known far and wide for its quail and pheasant hunting. Out-of-state hunters from Missouri and Oklahoma migrate to Nebraska's cornfields and hedgerows every year at the end of October and the beginning of November. They fill small-town motels, and when opening morning arrives they eat hearty breakfasts of eggs, sausage, and pancakes while their Brittanies, pointers and Labs wait impatiently outside in old pickups.

PROLOGUE

It was a time of rebellion in the nation's youth. Movie star James Dean had become the symbol of the rebel teenager, and kids all over the country were caught up in decisions of whether to conform or rebel. Girls used more makeup, trying to look older than they were. Boys wore their hair slicked back in "ducktails" and let their sideburns grow. Just having sideburns was enough to label you a "hood." Parents shook their heads whenever the radio played "rock and roll" songs, especially when sung by a southern boy named Elvis Presley. They were convinced their sons and daughters would be corrupted by this new music, which featured a "jungle beat."

It seemed to be an innocent time, but violence and danger lurked below the surface, even in Lincoln, Nebraska. No one in the sleepy, midwestern city of Lincoln suspected that the city, and ultimately the entire state, would experience a reign of terror and uncertainty in the coming month which would never be equaled again.

This is the story of Charles Starkweather and Caril Ann Fugate.

CHAPTER ONE

December 1, 1957
2:45 a.m.

1

Nineteen-year-old Charlie Starkweather sprawled across the battered, cloth-covered couch. Empty Schlitz bottles littered the barren wood floor, and the room smelled of stale beer and unwashed clothes. Charlie crinkled his nose in disgust. He usually took his work clothes home for his mom to wash, but he had not done so for a week or two. No sense in getting into another fight, he thought. The last time he went home, his dad got mad and threw him through a bedroom window. Piss on him! He glanced at the table sitting next to the couch. On it was a half-empty bottle of Wild Turkey and a small, dirty glass.

Charlie grabbed the bottle and poured himself three fingers. He drained the glass with a quick movement, coughing as the fiery liquid burned his throat. Staggering over to the front picture window, he tried to look outside. The opening was covered with a milky-looking plastic that was supposed to keep out the cold, drafty wind but didn't.

Taking his right forefinger, he poked a hole the size of a baseball in the plastic, big enough to look through. He shivered as the cold air poured in. The street outside was deserted. Tiny flecks of powdery snow drifted in and out of the soft glow thrown out by a solitary street light. For the first time, Charlie knew he was really alone. No one, not even Caril, knew what it was like and how the loneliness burned deep into his soul. Yes, he was alone, and nobody gave a damn. He turned his back to the window.

He looked around the dimly-lit room. There was little in the way of furniture, but that was okay with Charlie. He didn't much care as long as he had a place to sleep. Besides, it would not be long before he would have plenty of money, and fame, too. He'd show everybody once and for all he was someone to respect. He had it all figured out.

It was the end of November, and Nebraska's cold winter winds were starting to sift through the cracks of the ramshackle tenement at 425 North 10th. He had moved into the three-story rat-trap four months earlier, near the end of July. Money was tight. Even though his brother had helped him get a job on Niederhaus's garbage route, it only paid $42.00 a week—hardly enough for a 19-year-old to live on.

He was cold.

Cold and sweating.

CHAPTER ONE

His head pounded with a deep, throbbing pain, but that was normal. The headaches were coming almost every other day now, and they were not the kind you could chase away with a couple of Anacin. In fact, his dad had asked about his headaches just the other day. Charlie told him they had gone away. He lied. What did his dad care anyway? Charlie had asked, "Since when do you give a shit what happens to me?"

There had been no reply.

The headaches always started in the back of his head, working slowly to the front of his face. The white-hot pain usually settled in just above his left eye. At times, the headaches seemed almost too much for Charlie to handle. He would lay on the couch moaning, trying to wish it away. Often he wondered why he got these awful headaches.

It didn't really matter; all he knew was that the headaches hurt like hell, and they usually lasted the better part of a day. Tossing down a couple of Schlitz seemed to give him some relief, but even that quit helping after a while.

Taking off his glasses, he rubbed his bloodshot eyes and stared across the room. Charlie was as blind as an old bull. He had been wearing the thick, heavy-looking spectacles since he was 16 and was used to them. He wished he could have had them when he was younger, but his parents didn't seem to think he needed them. That was bullshit. He couldn't see the chalkboard starting in the second grade, and it became worse as he grew older. He had a lot of trouble with the other kids, but now nobody called Charlie four-eyes. He made sure of that.

He laid back and watched the TV. "Gunsmoke" was on the old Zenith crowded into the corner. It was his favorite show. Watching every Saturday night, he never missed the opening, the part when Marshal Dillon draws and shoots some unknown villain in the streets of Dodge City. Charlie got a kick out of that every week. He often wondered what it would be like to shoot someone. It couldn't be that big of a deal, he thought.

Charlie's eyes wandered around the stark room. The flickering lights of the television sent shadows dancing crazily across the walls and ceiling. Each one, darting and jumping, seemed to whisper Charlie's name.

"Charlie, Charlie," they called.

Maybe he was dreaming. He suddenly sat upright, startled. Was Death in the room?

"Is that you?" he whispered. "Are you coming to see me again?"

The house was silent except for Kitty telling Doc Adams to have a beer. Doc Adams was always mooching a beer.

Beads of sweat formed on Charlie's forehead. He stretched and stood up. His friend had been there; he was sure of it. But now the house was empty, and Charlie was disappointed.

He shuffled into the darkened kitchen and flipped on the light switch.

DECEMBER 1, 1957

Nothing happened. He tried again. Now he remembered. The bulb had burned out a week before, and even though he planned to get a new one, he kept forgetting. He opened the refrigerator door and took out the last bottle of Schlitz. Grabbing an opener from the filthy, dish-piled counter, Charlie popped the cap and threw it on the floor. He stood fascinated and watched as it rolled around and around. The cap eventually joined the other twenty or so that had accumulated in a pile on the dirty linoleum.

Taking a deep swig from the long-necked bottle, he slowly walked back into the front room. Was he trying to get drunk? He didn't think so. He didn't want to be drunk for what was going to happen that night. Being drunk would only dull his reflexes. A hunter had to have sharp reflexes. This was something he knew.

He glanced at his friend Sonny's 12-gauge pump shotgun standing upright in the corner, covered by a pair of dirty, blue chinos. Charlie found himself walking over and picking up the gun. He chuckled as he thought about how yesterday he had "borrowed" it from Sonny Von Busch's garage. Sonny was Bob Von Busch's cousin. Charlie had been good friends with Bob for years, since their hell-raising days together at Irving Junior High. Charlie didn't think Sonny would miss the shotgun. Besides, by the time he finished what he wanted to do, it wouldn't make any difference anyway.

The Remington 12-gauge pump was a little dirty, and its walnut stock had a couple of dings in it, but Charlie liked the gun all the same. He liked all guns. There was something about the naked power of a gun and what it was capable of doing that gave him a real sense of power and control in his life. Nobody could tell him what to do when he held a gun in his hands. People would respect him even if he was bowlegged and had four eyes.

Charlie worked the shotgun's action once, then twice. He liked the sharp clicking sound it made. Where were those shells? He bought two boxes of 6's just the other day at Greely's Hardware Store. Charlie was always losing things.

Opening one of the boxes, he took out three yellow shells, placing them on the couch's arm. Carefully, he loaded one shell at a time into the magazine. With a quick movement only hunters know, Charlie pumped a shell into the chamber. Putting the gun to his right shoulder, he looked down the front sight at the TV. After a moment, he again worked the well-oiled pump, ejecting each shell—one, two, three—until they all lay on the living room floor.

Walking back to the closet, Charlie found a pair of old leather work gloves stuffed onto the lower shelf. He took the gloves and threw them on the couch. He also grabbed an old hunting cap that was hanging from a nail on the closet wall.

A strange feeling burned deep in his gut, and Charlie's bones ached with the knowledge of what had to be done.

CHAPTER ONE

2

Cornhusker Highway wound in and around Lincoln's north side, its black asphalt surface covered with a light dusting of snow. Although there were several filling stations located up and down the highway, the Crest Service Station was by far the newest. It attracted a good number of travelers all year long: businessmen on their way east to Omaha, locals on their way to Havelock, and traveling salesmen crisscrossing the state. They liked to stop, get gas, and maybe even a cup of hot, black coffee.

Drivers watched expectantly for the giant, round Crest sign looming up on the horizon, signaling a chance for them to stop and stretch their legs. Crest's well-lit driveway also offered a safe place to stop and fill their gas tank. A sweeping, red arrow on the sign pointed to the current gas price—28.9¢ per gallon. Small, red, diamond-shaped flags fluttered from Crest's two light poles.

A small cardboard sign sat by itself on one of the shiny new gas pumps. "FRUIT CAKE 98¢" was written in large letters across its front. A large billboard stood to the west of the station itself, reading "IN ALL 48 STATES GET THE BEST! ASK FOR ETHYL!"

The Crest Service Station had concrete block walls and two garage doors in the front. A triangular canopy extended out from the main building to a double row of shiny new gas pumps, giving the attendants protection from the elements while servicing their customers. A nude pin-up girl calendar hung on one of the office walls, and a box of snow scrapers sat on the main counter—blue ones and red ones—the kind with the brush on one end. A special display of Firestone Christmas records sat in one corner, while a supply room filled with toilet paper, antifreeze and a couple of old tires sat just a few feet from the main office.

Twenty-one-year-old Robert Colvert was working the eleven-to-seven shift that night. Recently discharged from the Navy, Colvert was happy to find a job he liked. He stood 5-feet-6-inches tall and weighed 150 pounds, although his swept-back, pompadour hair style made him look even taller. Nicknamed "Little Bob" by his friends, Colvert had a nineteen-year-old wife at home expecting their first child. He had not worked long at the Crest station, having been hired just two weeks before. Bob McClung, the attendant at the time, approached him about the job and wondered if Colvert was interested. Colvert told him he was, so McClung quit in the middle of November.

Colvert didn't really mind working the late shift. It gave him plenty of time to work on the cars since there weren't too many customers coming in that late at night. Robert liked his job of attendant-mechanic and was proud of his white Unionalls, or "monkey suit."

Robert was sure it would be a slow night—it was too cold for most people to be out. He walked over and read the thermometer attached to the outside wall. It showed six degrees below zero. He glanced up at the big clock over the water cooler and saw it was not quite 3:00 a.m. He'd better get with it; the '56 Olds needed to be finished by Monday morning, and he was only half done rebuilding the carburetor.

3

Charlie liked hanging out at the Crest Service Station. In fact, he came almost every night, staying four or five hours, talking about comic books and cars. He was disappointed Bob McClung had quit working at the station, especially since he thought they were getting to be friends.

Charlie liked to sleep in the back seat of his car outside the filling station, waiting to start his garbage route about 4:30 every morning. Bob had always walked outside and tapped on the car's window, waking Charlie so he wouldn't be late to work.

Charlie liked to corner Bob and brag about how he was rebuilding a car or about how great a drag racer he was down at the Capitol Beach racing strip. Bob thought Charlie was a big talker and hated it when Charlie bummed a quarter for cigarettes or a dime for a soda pop. Didn't he have his own money? Charlie also had a bad habit of talking in circles, and Bob had trouble following what he was saying. Charlie would even sometimes fall asleep at the counter—one moment he'd be talking, and the next moment he'd be fast asleep.

There were other times when Charlie really scared Bob, like the other night when Charlie made him walk outside and touch his car. He'd just painted the body a beautiful eggshell color and insisted Bob go outside and see it. Bob was busy counting money, but Charlie got so worked up that Bob decided he'd better go out and feel the newly-painted surface. It was the wild crazy look in Charlie's eyes that convinced him.

Then there was Charlie's fascination with money, bordering on fanaticism. He liked to stand near Bob and watch him count the night's receipts. Bob should have told him to leave, but having Charlie there made the night go faster so he let him stay. Besides, he was quitting anyway—who cared what happened after he left?

Throwing Sonny's 12-gauge, a pair of leather hunting gloves, a greenish-blue plaid hunting cap and a red handkerchief onto the front seat of his car, Charlie got in and turned the ignition key. The engine sputtered, then coughed into life, followed by a deep, powerful roar as Charlie held his foot down on the accelerator. Grasping the column stick shift with his right hand, he jammed the car into reverse, backing crazily out of the driveway.

Once onto 10th Street, he changed gears, letting out the clutch with his left foot. The squealing tires sent out a spray of gravel in all directions as he

CHAPTER ONE

clamped his foot down hard on the gas pedal. Speeding down the deserted street, he happened to glance up and see his face in the rear-view mirror. It was like someone else was staring back at him, someone he knew yet didn't. Charlie smiled, his eyes glowing with excitement. He was ready for the grand adventure as he roared down 10th Street directly toward the Crest Service Station.

Charlie turned west on Cornhusker. The highway was virtually deserted, although one or two ice-covered cars passed him on their way out west. Each time they passed, Charlie dimmed his headlights, shielding his face with his left arm.

He glanced down at the front seat, making sure his disguise was all there. He had everything planned out to the last detail. There would be no need to case the station since he knew when the money was counted and where it was kept. He was sure the local police would suspect a transient coming off the highway before they would a local person.

Charlie laughed out loud. This was going to be a piece of cake. Lincoln cops were so stupid.

Charlie didn't know the new attendant very well, only that his name was Colvert. Several days earlier he had a run-in with Colvert that angered him. He and Caril had gone into the station to look for Christmas presents, and the Colvert kid had refused Charlie when he tried to buy a stuffed toy dog on credit. Embarrassed, Charlie backed off and left the store.

The humiliation he felt walking out of the station still pissed him off. He began to sweat, and his heart began to race. He knew all he needed was a few minutes to get in and get out. If Colvert somehow recognized him through his disguise, well, that would be too bad for him.

It was only a few minutes before Charlie saw the Crest sign loom into sight. He drove past once, then turned around and came back a second time—only this time much slower. It was a good set-up—no cars on the highway and no cars at the station. He pulled onto the brightly-lit driveway and sat for a few minutes, letting the car engine idle. Wanting to check out the filling station a little closer, he drove up, got out, and walked briskly up to the front door. He looked around for Colvert but couldn't see him.

"Is anyone here?" Charlie yelled, straining to see where the attendant might be.

After a few minutes, Colvert walked in from the garage, wiping his greasy hands with a towel. Tired and not in the best of moods, he asked, "What can I do for you?"

"Give me a pack of Camels."

Charlie threw a quarter down on the counter, took the cigarettes, and walked out. He got into his car and drove away.

He drove down Cornhusker and a few minutes later turned around. Once again he pulled up in front of the station, stopped the car and got out. Running up to the door, he could see Colvert through the front window standing behind the counter.

"What's the problem?" Colvert snapped as Charlie came in the office. He was in no mood for this shit.

Charlie glared at the attendant and then glanced out through the frost-edged front window. No one was in sight.

"Give me a pack of Beechnut, will ya?"

Colvert looked at Charlie and then reached under the counter for the gum.

"That'll be five cents."

Charlie reached into his pocket, pulled out a nickel, and handed it to the attendant.

"Thanks again," he replied, walking out the door.

Charlie got into his car and drove away. This time he turned onto Cornhusker, drove a couple hundred feet, and stopped the car. He quickly pulled on the leather gloves and jammed the hunting cap down over his head. He took the red bandana and wound it tightly over his face, leaving just his eyes and forehead showing. He wasn't wearing his glasses. Leaning over to the right, he pulled the dark brown canvas money bag he had found on his garbage route from its hiding place under the seat. He loaded the 12-gauge and set it on the seat.

Charlie drove back to the station and pulled up in front of the shiny new gas pumps. He got out of the car, carrying the shotgun in his left hand and the money bag in his right. Back at work on the Olds, Colvert never heard Charlie enter through the front door.

Charlie looked around the station a couple of minutes, then decided Colvert was in the shop. Colvert never realized someone had snuck up behind him until he felt the barrel of the shotgun against the back of his head. Startled, Colvert jerked around to find himself staring down the business end of a 12-gauge shotgun held by a masked intruder.

Charlie motioned for him to proceed toward the office. Nodding his head in agreement, Colvert walked into the office with Charlie following close behind.

It was deathly quiet in the filling station, and Colvert was scared. Charlie stood in the middle of the office, opened the canvas money bag and watched as Colvert started emptying his pockets of loose change. Charlie glanced through the window and saw the bright floodlights. The lights bothered him—what if someone could see in?

"Turn off those damn lights!" he barked.

Colvert turned around and walked shakily to the supply room and flipped the only switch he saw on the wall. His knees felt weak, and his stomach was turning. Two of the lights darkened but the others remained on, reflecting off the ice-covered drive.

"You only got two!" Charlie yelled. "Turn the rest of 'em off!"

"I, I . . . don't know where the other switches are."

CHAPTER ONE

"You've got to be shittin' me!"

Charlie thought for a minute.

"Okay, forget the lights; just get me all the money. Fast!"

Colvert began to scoop loose change, bills, and checks from the open counter drawer and shoved them into Charlie's bag. He dumped 11 five-dollar bills, a ten-dollar bill, and 31 ones into the bag as fast as he could. He also grabbed a small metal money changer containing about twelve dollars in silver, throwing it into the open bag.

"This isn't going to cover it, punk!" Charlie snarled. "There can't be more than a hundred bucks here!" He pointed the barrel of the shotgun down at the large metal safe below the counter and tapped the metal combination lock a couple of times.

"Open the goddamned safe!"

The color drained from the terrified attendant's face. McClung had neglected to give him the combination before he left, and the owner hadn't had time to teach it to him either.

"I don't know the combination! The boss hasn't taught me yet." At the terrible look on Charlie's face, Colvert hastily added, "Honest, mister—if I could open it, I sure as hell would! It's not my money!"

Charlie glared at Colvert for a full minute, then began to think maybe Colvert was telling the truth. But he certainly didn't have time to stand around all night. What if someone stopped in?

"Okay, let's get the hell out of here! You're coming with me. We're going for a little ride."

Shoving Colvert with the shotgun, Charlie steered the frightened attendant out to the car and around to the passenger side. "Get in. You're driving." Charlie knew he wouldn't be able to steer and hold the shotgun on Colvert at the same time.

Colvert opened the door, slid across the front seat and got behind the steering wheel. He kept thinking, stay calm, stay calm. Maybe he'll just take you out to the country and let you go.

They pulled out on Cornhusker Highway and turned northeast. Colvert tried desperately to stay within the speed limit as he turned left on 27th. He was nervous and wasn't used to driving Charlie's car. Reaching the intersection of 27th and Superior, Charlie made him take a left.

The headlights of Charlie's Ford pierced the black night, reflecting off several speed-limit signs sitting on the roadside. It was a good thing the weather had turned cold, freezing the dirt-covered road; getting stuck on Superior Street was not what Charlie had in mind.

"Where are we going?" Colvert choked.

Charlie stared straight ahead, pointing the shotgun at Colvert's belly. He said nothing.

DECEMBER 1, 1957

They raced past Bloody Mary's dilapidated farmhouse sitting east of Salt Creek bridge. Charlie knew the area well—every Lincoln teenager knew where Bloody Mary lived. She had the reputation of being just a little bit crazy. It seemed she liked to fire a shotgun filled with rock salt at any and all intruders. Charlie had been out here many times on dares to see who could touch her front door and run away before she came out to fire her gun.

It was deathly quiet in the car as Colvert tried to concentrate on the road, and Charlie nervously fingered the shotgun's trigger. When they approached a set of railroad tracks about three-quarters of a mile east of Bloody Mary's house, Charlie leaned over and told Colvert to stop the car.

"Get out; get out on your side," Charlie ordered, waving the shotgun in Colvert's face.

"What are you gonna do?" Jesus, I'm a dead man for sure, thought Colvert.

"Just get your butt out of the car."

Colvert opened the driver's side door and stepped outside. Charlie slid across the front seat and got out the same side. The two men stood facing each other.

The frigid night air cut through Colvert's Union coveralls. He started to tremble. Terrible thoughts raced through his mind—he knew Charlie had brought him here for only one reason. It was now or never.

Lunging in desperation, Colvert succeeded in grabbing the barrel of Charlie's shotgun.

Charlie struggled, trying to wrench the gun away from Colvert's iron grip but couldn't. White clouds of breath vapor rose into the black night. Silently the men fought, each desperately trying to get the advantage over the other.

Hoping to get in a shot, Charlie cocked the gun while Colvert stepped this way and that, trying to stay away from the gun's lethal barrel. Mustering his strength, Colvert jerked with all his might. The crisp, loud report of the blast shattered the winter night's stillness. Colvert flew backward, landing face down on the frozen dirt several yards away.

Charlie ejected the spent shell and reloaded, watching all the time to see if Colvert was dead. He didn't think so because of the low, animal-like moans coming from the fallen man. Walking to where Colvert lay sprawled on the ground, he saw a large pool of dark blood spreading across the graveled road.

Charlie was curious to see how anyone could survive a point-blank blast from a 12-gauge. Unbelievably, Colvert was trying to get up on his hands and knees. Charlie placed the shotgun barrel on Colvert's skull. He squeezed the trigger, blowing off the entire back of his head.

Charlie leaned over and picked up his hunting hat. It had fallen off during his struggle with Colvert. Leaving the body lying in the road, Charlie threw the shotgun in the car and headed east.

Reaching Bloddy Mary's house, Charlie suddenly realized he had left the

CHAPTER ONE

spent shell from the first shot on the ground. Wheeling the car around, he roared back until his headlights illuminated the crumpled body on the road. Jumping out, he ran over and picked up the shotgun shell.

Back in his blue Ford, Charlie headed west toward 27th Street. Turning onto Cornhusker Highway, he barely noticed the solitary pickup sitting at the Crest Service Station waiting to be serviced as he whizzed past.

He had other things on his mind.

4

That is how the killing began. Charlie would have been the first to say that he killed Bob Colvert in self-defense. Didn't he try to grab the shotgun from his hands? What would have happened if Bob had gotten possession of the gun? Why, he was just defending himself, that's all.

Charlie's concept of the world around him definitely influenced his behavior. He believed if he killed all the people on earth he would live in peace with the animals. He didn't belong to the world as it was then. Charlie's ideal world was one of nature. He thought about this many times. Charlie felt that trees were supernatural and that if he looked between the jagged limbs and greenish-brown and yellow foliage he would see for miles and miles into the undiscovered and the unknown. At such moments, an irresistible feeling swept over his soul—entering a dream-like state, he somehow seemed to acquire a new self-awareness. But something, an approaching animal or person, always snapped him back to reality.

He experienced this feeling the night he killed Bob Colvert. He had been drinking at a bar close to his apartment, and as he walked home, the trees came alive before his eyes. The branches and limbs swayed to music only Charlie could hear. It was preparing him. Charlie knew he was about to enter a contest, an adventure that would only end one way.

5

About 5:00 that same morning, members of the Lincoln Police Department drove past the Crest Service Station on Cornhusker and saw that it was open but unattended. They radioed in a report regarding the incident and searched the premises. At the same time, an operative for the Nebraska Detective Agency, contracted by several large businesses in the locale to keep an eye on their property, was making his rounds. It was this man who found Bob Colvert's body lying in Superior Street. Since the murder happened outside the Lincoln city limits, he called the Lancaster County Sheriff's office. The adventure had begun.

CHAPTER TWO

December 2, 1957
9:00 a.m.

1

"Did you hear about the shooting last night?" Charlie asked, grinning slyly.

"Who hasn't?" fourteen-year-old Caril Fugate yawned. "It's been on the news and in the *Star*." She turned around and took a newspaper from the back seat and read the front page headline out loud: "Lincolnite slain: theft motive seen."

"I wonder who could have done such a terrible thing?" Charlie mocked.

"You and I both know who did it, don't we, Charlie?"

Charlie looked over at his girl friend sitting next to him. Caril, although only fourteen, was well developed for her age. She wore her dark brown hair in a ponytail and liked wearing tight-fitting jeans. She was quick-tempered and rebellious, just like Charlie. He admired that in a girl, and that's why they had gotten along so well in the beginning. She liked to cuss and was driving cars before most of her friends.

Charlie rembered the first day he met Caril. A friend of his, Bob Von Busch, was dating a girl named Barbara Fugate, who lived in the Belmont section of Lincoln. One day he got Charlie to come with him and meet Barb's younger sister. Caril was barely thirteen at the time but looked more like eighteen. They all went to the Nebraska Theater together; and from then on, Caril only had one other date with another boy. Charlie found out about it, hunted the boy down, and threated to kill him if he ever saw Caril again. It had been over a year now that Charlie and Caril were a couple and considered "going steady."

"Maybe," Charlie replied. "By the way, do something with these will you?" Charlie put his hand in his front jean pocket, dug out a handful of coin wrappers, and tossed them across the car onto Caril's lap.

Caril stared at Charlie, a questioning look on her face.

"Keep 'em or throw 'em away; I don't give a shit what you do with them."

Caril took the wrappers and stuffed them in her coat pocket. "These are from the gas station, aren't they?" she accused.

"Naw, I just found them lying around," Charlie laughed.

"You were there, weren't you?" she quizzed persistently. "You killed that Colvert guy, didn't you?"

CHAPTER TWO

"Maybe. You just never know. He probably deserved it anyway. Guys like that always deserve it. Let's talk about something else, okay?'

Charlie was nervous. He had been driving the last twenty-four hours with Sonny's shotgun tucked under the seat, and he figured he'd better dump it. He was staring out the window when Salt Creek came into view. Looking out at the water, he got an idea. Crossing the South Street bridge near Neihoff's junkyard, he pulled over and stepped out. Making sure no one was looking, he pulled the shotgun out from under the seat and threw it as far as he could into the creek. There was a loud splash as the gun disappeared under the water. He took the coin changer and ground it under his foot, then covered it with some loose dirt.

Satisfied he had gotten rid of the murder weapon in a safe place, he said to Caril, "Let's go down to that clothing resale place on North 12th. You know the place. I need to get some clothes; it's too damn cold for what I got." She nodded her head and said nothing.

Charlie's mind wandered as he drove. He glanced over at Caril and suddenly felt a surge of happiness. Things were going just right. Now that he had killed, he was well into his plan. He never felt closer to Caril, knowing he would be with her now. Hell, killing someone wasn't as hard as he thought.

People would wonder how he could kill, but he didn't give a shit what they thought. He always knew he would die young, but now he had something to accomplish before death came and took him to the other side. He would be with Caril, and they could do what they wanted. He would leave his mark on the world. He would show everyone they had made him into a killer. It wasn't his fault.

He started a new way of thinking when he met Caril. Being with her was something to live for. At the end of each day, after he said goodbye to Caril, he knew that another day of garbage lifting and hating the world would have to come and go before he could see her again. It was during this time by himself that the surroundings would take on frightful, bizarre shapes and the voice of the wind would terrify him. But he always knew she would be there for him.

Caril never cared what he looked like, and she never cared that he lived in a cockroach-infested tenement building. She thought everything he did was good, and she liked that Charlie could shoot a gun. He was cocky and seemed invincible when he carried a gun. And Charlie felt better after being with Caril. He stopped hating himself, at least for the moment, because Caril made him quit thinking about his bow-legs. She liked his legs . . . the more bowed they were the better she liked them. He loved her.

He snapped out of the daydream and looked down at his clothes. The blue Levis had holes in both knees, and his flannel shirt was definitely ready for the trash. Why did he always have to wear clothes that someone else had thrown away, clothes they left in a "used-clothing" store? It really pissed him off that he had to cover his nakedness with clothes people who hated him had thrown away. It was like wearing another man's skin, only the people who wore these clothes weren't dead. Maybe it was time he did something about it.

2

December in Nebraska usually brought people to shop in Mrs. Kamp's used-clothing store. The cold north wind was always a motivating factor, so Mrs. Kamp was surprised sales had been so slow that day. She looked up when Charlie and Caril entered the store. Although she did not know the teenage boy's name, she had seen him come in many times in the past year and a half. He would stop in and pick up a change of underwear or a shirt, always something under $2.00. She was struck by his appearance, his fiery red hair and bow-legs weren't something a person could miss very easily.

She watched out of the corner of one eye as the couple walked over to the men's clothing section. They looked over a rack of clothes, then a few minutes later came over to the counter with several items of clothing.

"Will that be all?" she asked, her eyes searching Charlie's face.

"Yeah, that's it," Charlie replied, his voice edged with boredom.

She quickly totaled the items on an adding machine and said, "That will be $9.55."

Charlie smiled and started pulling handfuls of coins from both pockets. He slapped the money down on the counter and watched the old lady's face, anxious to see her reaction.

Mrs. Kamp stared at the dimes, quarters, and nickels piled on the counter and frowned. Just what she needed, ten dollars worth of change to count.

"Don't you have any bills?"

Charlie's face flushed with anger. "No, I don't. If I did, I would have given them to you. It's money, ain't it?"

Upset with his smart-aleck answer, Mrs. Kamp counted out the coins using as many quarters as she could in order to save time until it totaled $9.55. Putting the coins in a bag from under the counter, she placed the clothes in a sack and handed it to Charlie.

She stared at the couple as they walked out of the store and drove away.

3

Lancaster Sheriff Merle Karnopp was not a happy man. His initial investigation into the Colvert murder was leading nowhere. First of all, it happened that two airmen from the Lincoln Air Force base were riding with the detective who found the body, and one of them didn't want to get involved. To avoid

CHAPTER TWO

some unexplained "personal embarrassment" for the airman, the detective and the other man made the report to Karnopp's office without mentioning him. It became clear during their questioning that a third man was involved and that they were witholding information. Several days were wasted before they decided none of the three were involved with the murder.

If that wasn't enough, a habitual criminal named Philmon Immenschuh confessed to Colvert's murder. At first Karnopp felt he might be the man. Immenschuh was being held in the Omaha city jail on another charge; so one of Karnopp's deputies drove the forty-five miles to Omaha, picked him up, and brought him back to Lincoln. Not until Immenschuh failed a lie detector test did they finally get the truth out of him. He hoped the food would be better in Lincoln, and if he was going to be in jail, he wanted it to be there.

Initially, the sheriff's office thought the murderer to be a transient. Because the Crest Service Station was on such a major highway, it seemed plausible that someone could have easily stopped into the station, taken Colvert, killed him, and continued on his way east or west on Cornhusker Highway. Sheriff deputies even conducted spot traffic checks and called all of the local motels but were unable to gain any leads.

They inspected the Crest Station for clues and asked the employees if there had been any suspicious-looking people hanging around the station the last couple of months. One ex-employee named Robert McClung mentioned a red-haired teenager who was a frequent visitor to the station. In fact, he would stay and talk to him for hours on end about cars. The short, red-haired teenager sometimes fell asleep reading comic books in the station but always made sure McClung woke him up at about 4:15 a.m. so he could make his garbage route. Unfortunately, the whole time McClung talked to Charlie he never once asked him his name. This slight on McClung's part would play a significant part in the days to come.

4

Mrs. Kamp heard about the robbery-murder at the Crest Service Station at noon the same day Charlie and Caril stopped into her store. Suspicious, she immediately called the Lincoln Police Department; that afternoon a detective named Davis came out to visit with her.

She described how Charlie came in and bought almost ten dollars worth of clothes and paid the bill with coins. Did she know that a lot of coins were taken at Crest's? Yes, she did. She did not know Charlie's name but described him as being about 5'4" tall and having bow-legs. His fiery red hair was badly in need of a haircut, and his sideburns needed trimming. His face was blotchy with freckles, and he wore a broken pair of horn-rimmed glasses held together with a piece of white adhesive tape.

The detective wrote down his description and came back several days later with three or four mug shots for her to look at. None of them were Charlie.

5

While the Lancaster Sheriff's Department and the Lincoln Police Department were searching for clues regarding Colvert's death, Charlie had been busy. Although convinced the Lincoln Police Department was made up of a bunch of incompetents and would never catch him, he wanted to be careful at the same time.

As a kid, he liked going downtown to the State or Stuart movie theaters and watching gangster movies. He now used some of the things he saw in those movies to help hide his trail. The first thing he did was change the tires on the Ford. The Crest station's driveway was part concrete and part dirt, and he figured that changing the tires would make it impossible for them to trace his vehicle in case he left some tracks.

He painted the Ford black, removed the grille, and painted the interior of the grille area red. One of his friends aked Charlie why he painted his car. He replied, "I had to paint it. A bunch of boys got drunk the other night and spotted it with a lot of different-colored paint."

Charlie had another problem. Frightened that the authorities might find it, Charlie went back to Salt Creek and recovered Sonny's shotgun. He cleaned the weapon and put it undetected back in Sonny's garage. Charlie's timing was excellent, as two deputies and two jail trustees were working their way down the creek from the murder scene, using rakes to search for a murder weapon.

On December 3, Charlie stopped at his landlord's and paid up his back rent. Mrs. May Hawley and her husband, Orlin, were certainly happy to see Charlie pay up. They noticed his recent change of clothes and asked if he'd suddenly become rich. He told them, "I took it out of my savings."

From the Hawley's, he went to see his dad and mom. Over breakfast, they chatted about the Colvert murder. Wasn't that a terrible thing? Charlie agreed that it was a tragedy; and the last thing he said was, "I wonder what sort of a person it would take to do such a thing?"

Concerned that his sudden absence from the Crest station might arouse suspicion, he and Caril went there on December 10, and he bought her a stuffed poodle. No one there suspected Charlie was the killer. That same day, Charlie stopped at the Western Paper Company warehouse where he worked before he began hauling garbage. The employees kidded him about what he was going to do with the robbery money. He laughed along with them and then left.

CHAPTER TWO

Charlie and Caril spent most of this time together. They went to the movies on several occasions, picking from "The Parson and the Outlaw" or "Escape from San Quentin" at the State, "Man in the Shadow" at the Stuart or "Last of the Badman" at the Nebraska.

Caril spent long hours with Charlie in his apartment, practicing knife-throwing with him, playing 45s on the record player, and eating snacks her step-dad wouldn't let her have at home. Most importantly, they had each other and that was enough.

It had now been fifty days since the Colvert killing, and Charlie was still free. He sensed he had been lucky. At the same time, the confusion Lincoln's law enforcement community was experiencing only made Charlie feel more invincible.

Charlie told Caril, "Up till now, I ain't done much out of the ordinary, what most anybody would do . . . now it's time for something different to start."

January 19, 1958

6

Charlie tossed and turned on the cold, hard, cement floor. A week had passed since Mr. Hawley tossed him out of his apartment for not paying the rent, and it had been a struggle. The money from the robbery was gone, and he was broke. With the temperature hovering in the high 20s and low 30s, the unheated garage on Woodsdale Boulevard was the last place he wanted to sleep; but he had no choice.

He sat up and hacked a huge wad of phlegm from deep in his throat. Leaning over, he spat into a corner of the small wooden garage. He felt terrible. He had a cold and a cough and probably should have taken some kind of medication, but he was broke. If he could only get a good night's rest, then maybe he would feel better. He laid back down, rearranged the gunny sack he was using as a pillow, and after a few minutes, drifted off into a fitful sleep.

It was after midnight when he heard the whistle. It wasn't the first time he heard the eerie noise. In fact, he had heard it many times before. It meant one thing, that he was going to have a visitor. He was ready. Now a barely-audible tapping noise filled the small garage. Charlie smiled. The tapping sound continued, tap . . . tap . . . tap . . . until the clouds parted and a burst of moonlight flooded the side of the garage opposite the front window. Charlie knew who was outside. It was his friend. He sat up and motioned for him to come into the garage. The door opened very slowly, and a half man–half bear shuffled inside.

JANUARY 19, 1958

It had no arms or ears, no neck, just a big chest tapered upward to a small rounded head. It made a low, rasping sound.

"Hi, Charlie," it said. "I see you're not feeling very well. That's too bad."

Charlie blew his nose on his shirt sleeve. "Yeah, got a damn cold; maybe worse."

"Aren't you taking care of yourself, Charlie? You know what happens if you don't take care of yourself in this weather, don't you Charlie?"

"Didn't have the money to pay old man Hawley; so he threw me out."

Death sat undisturbed in the shawdows and didn't answer.

Finally, it said, "I've got something for you, Charlie. It's outside. I'll get it if you want. I think you'll like it."

"Sure, go ahead," Charlie replied. "It's not like I've got a lot of other things to do tonight."

The apparition shuffled out the door and, a second later, came back lugging a big, black box shaped like a coffin. It placed the coffin on the cement floor in front of Charlie.

"Get in, Charlie. Don't be afraid. I want to show you something."

Charlie wasn't afraid. Death was his friend. He had come to love Death. They had known each other for a long time. How about the time when he played car chicken with the other guys? One time he considered yanking the steering wheel and plunging his car into a ravine, but Death came into the car and told him to wait. There would be another time he said; so Charlie waited. Charlie trusted Death to take care of him.

Charlie nodded his head and stepped into the coffin. He layed down and waited quietly. He wasn't scared. There was something peaceful about the coffin, soothing and relaxing.

Suddenly, they were flying through the air. He could see the earth below, but it hurt his eyes to look down. They flew through the air for what seemed only a brief time before Charlie saw a hugh fire buring on the distant horizon. The flames arched and leaped high into the sky. A reddish glow illuminated a bleak and barren landscape in all directions.

He braced himself as they rapidly approached the blazing inferno. Before he knew it, the coffin plunged into the middle of the fire. Charlie watched as the flames burned away the wood, leaving him standing on a street with flames shooting up on either side. Charlie thought he was in hell. It had to be hell; where else would he go? But something was wrong. He always thought hell would be unbearably hot and the flames would torture him for eternity, but that wasn't the case. The flames were soothing and more beautiful than anything he had ever seen or experienced on earth. He wished he could stay there forever.

Then Charlie woke up and found himself back in the garage on Woodsdale. Had his trip been nothing more than a dream? He didn't know; but he was certain now, more than ever, that Death was his friend. He knew life with his

CHAPTER TWO

friend would be much better than his life on earth. As he sat reflecting on what had just happened, he heard the low, mournful whistle once again. He got up and looked out the frosted-over garage window.

It was his friend, and he was calling to Charlie.

"Charlie, Charlie. Don't be in a hurry. Your time will come; and, when it does, Caril will be with you. Remember that."

Then it was gone. Charlie felt better. He knew what he had to do.

CHAPTER THREE

January 21, 1958
1:10 p.m.

1

"Crap!" Charlie muttered under his breath as he saw the padlock on the apartment door. He tried to pull the padlock off the hinge, but it was no use. He turned to walk away when he heard someone coming down the hallway.

"What are you doing, Charlie?" the woman asked. It was Barbara Von Busch, Caril's sister.

"Just trying to get into my apartment, Barb," he replied. "You don't know where old man Hawley is, do you?"

"No I don't, but, if I can help, let me know."

"Okay, see ya later."

Charlie was pissed. Nothing was going right. He left the house and got into his car. He drove over to his brother Rodney's house and borrowed his .22 rifle. Charlie told him he'd bring it back when he was done with it. It seemed he and Marion Bartlett were going hunting, which surprised Rodney. Marion hated Charlie and almost never went hunting. Charlie assured him that the plans had been made a week earlier, and Marion was eager to go. "Don't worry about it," he finally said. Charlie left and decided to go over to Caril's house.

As he drove through the small Lincoln suburb known as Belmont, Charlie couldn't help but notice the slum-like conditions. Much of Belmont had a squalid look about it, especially where Caril lived. Most of the houses were run-down, and the Bartlett house was no exception.

He pulled up in front of Caril's house and sat there for a few minutes, finishing a cigarette. The Bartlett house was a tiny, single-story, five-room shack covered with an asphalt imitation-brick siding. He could not remember a time when the house was not in some state of disrepair. Caril's old man was one for starting a lot of projects but pretty lax about finishing them.

Flicking the cigarette butt onto the snow-covered street, he stuck two boxes of .22 shells in his motorcycle jacket and grabbed the rifle and the two pieces of carpet he found at a junkyard that Mrs. Barlett wanted. He got out of the car and walked slowly across a yard littered with trash, building materials and automobile parts. A double row of warped 1×12s serving as a sidewalk stretched along the driveway to the front door. In the back sat an old outhouse and what passed for a chicken coop. Near the kitchen door at the back of

CHAPTER THREE

the house was a wooden clothesline pole with a mop dangling from it, the mophead frozen over the crossbar.

The Bartlett dog, a black mongrel named Nig, growled until he recognized Charlie. Wagging his tail, he dragged his chain over to greet the teenager. Charlie smiled, reached down, and petted him behind the ears.

Charlie walked up to the back door, knocked, and waited until Mrs. Bartlett came to the door. She looked at the red-headed teenager with disgust as he pushed his way into the kitchen.

"I brought the rugs you wanted," he announced, while at the same time ignoring her dirty look. He brushed past the older woman and took the rugs to the living room. The small room was cluttered with a piano, the couch, a television, a portable clothes closet and a few chairs. Four or five pieces of rope used as clotheslines were stretched from wall to wall on nails. He sat down on the ratty counch, untiled the carpets, and rolled them out on the bare tile floor.

Velda Bartlett followed him into the living room, glared at the teenager for a minute or two, and then left. Marion Bartlett, Caril's stepdad, was in the kitchen with Caril's 2½-year-old stepsister, Betty Jean. Charlie could hear the girl crying. Whatever happened to her served the little monster right, he thought to himself. He didn't like the youngster and knew Caril couldn't stand her either. She was a spoiled little snot and wouldn't mind anyone. How many times had she told her mom and dad that Charlie hit her just to get him in trouble. Just once he would like to give her something to really tell on. And Caril didn't like her because both Marion and Velda treated her far better than they did her.

Charlie sat on the couch and fiddled with the bolt of his rifle. He snapped it in, then pulled it out. In and out. After several minutes, he got up to see what everyone else was doing. Walking through the small house, he saw the old man lying down in one of the bedrooms; Velda and Betty Jean were sitting on Caril's bed listening to the radio. He wished it was time for Caril to get out of school.

Finally, he asked Velda, "Does Marion still want to go hunting?"

"I don't think so," she replied curtly.

Charlie glared back at Caril's stepmother. "Why not?"

"Don't ask me. I guess he just doesn't want to go, that's all."

Charlie propped the rifle against the wall and sat down on a wooden crate in the corner of the kitchen.

Mrs. Bartlett stared at Charlie, a frown on her lined face, and said forcefully, "You have to leave, and I don't want you ever to come back."

"How come?" Charlie asked, sensing her anger.

"I don't want you to see Caril any more. You've caused enough trouble around here."

"What do ya mean—trouble?"

"You know exactly what I'm talking about!"

"No, I don't! Why don't you tell me?"

Velda Bartlett stood up and slapped Charlie twice across the face. The sound of flesh against flesh reverberated through the room.

"You got Caril pregnant, and I hate you for it!" she shouted and tried to slap Charlie again.

"You go to hell!" he shouted as he blocked another blow with his right arm. He turned around, ran out the back door and jumped into his car. Slamming it in gear, he drove away. He needed a few minutes to think. He drove around the block several times until he remembered he left his rifle in the kitchen. Determined to get the rifle, he returned once again to the house.

He stomped up to the back door, knocked and waited until Caril's mom answered it. He shoved his way past Velda and went into the kitchen where Marion Bartlett stood waiting. Marion weighed about one hundred and sixty pounds packed on a powerful frame. He was older but was strong from years of manual labor.

"Get the hell out of my house!" he shouted at the teenager.

"That's okay with me, you son of a bitch!" Charlie retorted as he walked through the living room and headed for the front door. Without warning, Marion ran up and gave him a powerful kick in the butt.

"That ought to help you on the way out!" he roared.

Charlie stopped and clenched his fists. He was tempted to turn around and confront the old man; but, for some reason, he decided to keep going. There were more permanent ways to get even.

2

Marion Bartlett sat at the kitchen table, nursing a lukewarm cup of coffee. He was shook up. It was that damn Charlie Starkweather. Hate was a pretty strong word, but Marion hated the cocky teenager and wished he could get Caril to stop seeing him. For one thing, he was nineteen and she was only fourteen, and that was too much difference in age to his way of thinking. Pretty soon he would be hearing that Caril was pregnant, and then what would happen?

"Well, what are we going to do? You probably really made him mad this time," Velda said, a worried look creasing her worn face. She had come into the kitchen and sat down to talk to Marion.

"So what! I'm glad I kicked his butt out of here. He's got a lot of nerve, shoving his weight around here like that." Marion was so mad he was shaking. "No punk teenager is going to come into my house and give me shit!"

CHAPTER THREE

"I agree," Velda replied. "But something else is bothering me."

"What's that?" Marion asked.

"I think Charlie's got something to do with that Colvert kid getting killed out at the Crest station."

Marion sat down his coffee cup and stared at his wife.

"Why do you think that?"

"Think about it for a second. It makes sense. Charlie used to hang out there all the time. I even heard him talk to Caril about the time they embarrassed him. You have to admit, Charlie's not the type to forget a slight. Don't forget he got fired from his job, and I'll bet he's broke. No money to spend. It all fits. Don't forget the empty coin wrappers I found in Caril's room. The paper said a lot of coins were stolen."

"I guess that's true enough, but do you think he could actually kill someone?"

"He's got a terrible temper, and he's always carrying around some kind of gun. I think he's capable of killing someone if he got mad enough. I wish he'd never come back."

"Maybe we should talk to Caril about all this. What do you think?" Marion asked.

"I was thinking the same thing. When she gets home from school, I'll have a talk with her. Maybe I can get her to see what's happening."

"It's worth a try, I guess," Marion agreed. "I just hope he stays away from the house. He's gonna push me too far one of these days, and there's no telling what I'll do."

3

Charlie was burning! He didn't like what just happened, and he would have his revenge! The Bartletts were like everybody else in the world; they didn't care for him, and he didn't care for them. He needed to do something about it. He drove down to Hutson's Grocery. He went straight to the pay phone, fished a dime out of his pocket and called Watson Brothers Transportation Company.

"Is this Watson Brothers?" he asked the person who answered the phone.

"Yes, it is. How may I help you?"

"I'm calling to let you know that Marion Bartlett won't be in to work for a couple of days. He's sick."

"I hope it's nothing serious," the voice replied.

"Nah, it's not that bad. He wanted me to call."

"Thank you."

Charlie hung up the receiver and smiled. It would all fall into place shortly.

4

The Safeway store located on North 27th Street was usually filled with customers. Since it sat halfway between Vine and Holdrege Streets, it was convenient for most people who lived in the Belmont area to slip in and do their grocery shopping.

Virginia Robson, a switchboard operator at Watson Brothers Transfer Company, decided to use part of her lunch hour to drive over to the Safeway store and pick up some bread and other items. The store was nearby, and it would save her time later in the day.

She was walking down the bread aisle when she recognized Marion Bartlett standing at the meat counter. Marion was the night watchman at Watson's, and he would often stop in the office and say hi to the employees after he worked his shift.

"Nice to see you, Mr. Bartlett," Virginia said, as she walked over to where he stood waiting for the butcher to slice some thick pieces of bologna.

He looked up and smiled.

"Hi, Virginia. I see you have the same idea I do. Need to pick up some things?"

"That's right. We go through more milk and bread in a week than I'd care to say. Hated to use my lunch hour, but stopping now will save me later."

"Sounds fine," he replied. He took the package of meat the butcher laid on top of the counter and turned to leave. "I'd better get going," he replied. "Need to get some lunch before I come to work this afternoon."

"See you later," Virginia offered, and continued to do her shopping.

Virginia Robson left the Safeway store and drove into the Watson Brothers parking lot a little before two o'clock. She went inside and waited while her lunch replacement, Mrs. Vivian Buess, stood up and prepared to leave.

"Anything I should know about, Vivian?"

"I don't think so," was the reply. "Oh, wait a minute, there was a call from someone who said Marion Bartlett wouldn't be in for several days. Said he was sick."

Virginia sat down, a puzzled look on her face.

"What's the matter?" Mrs. Buess asked.

"That's strange. I just saw Marion at the Safeway over on 27th. He looked fine to me, never mentioned being ill."

Mrs. Buess looked perplexed. "That doesn't make much sense. Oh, well, I don't have time to worry about it now. I gotta go; see ya later."

Virginia wrote a note about Mr. Bartlett's absence and made sure her manager got it. She was still wondering about the strange call when the afternoon calls started to come in and she got busy.

CHAPTER THREE

5

Charlie returned to the Bartlett house and tried to get in, but the Bartletts wouldn't let him. Angry, he sat out in the backyard playing with Nig for about an hour and a half, waiting for Caril to come home from school. Finally, at three o'clock, he got back into his car and decided to drive over to Whittier Junior High and pick her up.

He started the car and shifted gears. He grimaced as a savage grinding sound in the transmission broke the afternoon silence. He frowned. Now the transmission was acting up. He drove over to the Griggs house about a block away and left the car sitting in front along the curb. Then he walked back over to the Bartletts' and waited on the back porch for Caril to come home.

Suddenly, he heard voices shouting in the house. It was Caril and Velda Bartlett screaming at each other. He let himself in the back door and ran into the kitchen. Caril and Velda were standing in the kitchen doorway having a shouting match. Caril saw Charlie and ran into the bathroom, slamming the door behind her.

"You back again?" Velda shouted. "Why don't you leave?"

"You don't have the right to talk to Caril like that!" Charlie shouted.

Velda ran over to Charlie and slapped him once, then twice. "I hate you! Not only that, but I'll bet you killed the Colvert boy! It sounds like something you'd do, and we're gonna call the police department and tell them if you don't get out of here!"

"You bitch!" Charlie balled up his fist and hit the old woman, knocking her back several feet against the counter. She swayed and fell to her knees, blood trickling from her mouth.

Marion ran to the kitchen doorway just in time to see Charlie knock his wife to the floor. He surged into the room and picked Charlie up by the neck and slung him over his back like a sack of potatoes. He carried the teenager kicking and screaming as far as the front door. He tripped, and they fell heavily to the floor. Charlie grappled with the old man, trying desperately to get an advantage as they rolled around the living room floor. They knocked over a lamp and several chairs in their furious thrashing. Caril saw the fight and ran screaming into her bedroom.

Suddenly, Charlie broke free of the older man's grip. He stumbled into Caril's bedroom. He saw the .22 rifle, took a shell from his pocket, and in one quick motion loaded it. He looked up just in time to see Marion run into the room, a claw hammer raised over his head. The old man had a crazed look on his face.

Charlie quickly raised the rifle and fired, only half aiming. Marion went down heavily and lay on the bedroom floor, a pool of blood forming under his head.

JANUARY 21, 1958

Velda heard the shot and ran in from the kitchen, holding a foot-long, black-handled butcher knife.

"I'm gonna chop your head off!" she screamed at Charlie.

Charlie loaded the rifle once again, pointed it directly at her, and said, "Don't come any closer, or I'll blow your head off!"

She took a step, and Charlie fired. The force of the bullet spun her around, and she fell heavily against the wall. Charlie watched as she struggled to regain her balance. She staggered into the living room, blood streaming from a jagged wound in her face. Barely able to see through the blood, Velda leaned over and attempted to pick up Betty Jean, blood dripping down her face and onto the floor.

Charlie ran over, took the rifle, and struck Velda full in the face with the butt—once, twice—until she gasped and fell to the floor in a bloody heap. Betty Jean was screaming and clutching at her mother when Charlie hit her with the gun butt again and again until she finally quit making sounds.

Charlie panted with exertion. He was sweating. A moment later, he heard a groan come from the bedroom. It was a long drawn-out sigh from a dying man. Leaning over Velda, Charlie picked up the butcher knife laying next to her hand and walked into the bedroom and stood over the old man. Marion groaned once again and tried to crawl away from the teenager. Charlie took the knife and plunged it into the old man's neck but grimaced when it hit something hard. The knife wouldn't go in like he thought it should. Taking a strong grip on the knife and placing it on the man's neck, he hit the top part of it with his other hand. Finally it went in, and the man went limp. Charlie felt better.

He sat down on the bed and stared at the body. After a few minutes, he got up, walked into the kitchen, and got a drink of water.

Caril walked in behind him and asked, "What do you think we ought to do now?"

Charlie didn't answer. He brushed past her and went into the living room and flopped down on the couch.

Caril pursued him into the room, "What's the matter?"

"Nothing! Nothing's the goddamn matter!"

"We sure got ourselves in a helluva mess," she gasped.

"Well, isn't this what we wanted? Just you and me against everyone else. At least we don't have to worry about your dad and mom anymore. They were going to blackmail me, and you know it. Your mom was going to turn me in for killing Colvert, sure as hell!"

Caril stared vacantly across the room.

Finally, she gestured toward the bodies and said, "We better get them out of here."

"Don't worry about it; I'll do it," Charlie replied as he reloaded the rifle. He set the rifle against the couch, then got up and turned on the television. He

CHAPTER THREE

wanted some noise, any kind of noise, in the house. He reached up and yanked down some of the clothesline strung up in the living room. He went into the spare room and gathered some rugs, rags, bedclothes, and building paper. He tied the clothesline around Velda's knees, then wrapped her up in a quilt and a green rug.

Betty Jean was still bleeding when he picked her up; so he put the pathetic, little body in the kitchen sink until he could find a quilt to wrap her in. He took most of the garbage out of a cardboard box and replaced it with Betty Jean's body. He put the box on the back porch and then dragged Velda's body out into the porch.

He looked out the back porch window, then half-drug, half-carried Velda's body across the muddy ground and out to the privy. He took her limp body and stuffed it down the toilet as far as it would go. Returning for Betty Jean, he laid the small child on the toilet seat.

He walked back into the house and stared at the large amounts of blood still on the floor. Grabbing some rags, he got down on his hands and knees and cleaned up all he could.

Finally satisfied, he leaned back and figured he'd better get the old man out of the house. He dragged Marion's heavy body into the kitchen and wrapped it in a blue sheet, tying it with clothesline around the ankles, knees, chest, and head. Grabbing one of Caril's scarves from the bedroom, he tied it around the head and then wrapped an army blanket around that. Then he rolled the whole body up in heavy green building paper.

He tugged the body to the back door and tried to get it to go through. It was no use. The body was too wide. Rummaging around the back porch, he finally found a screwdriver and used it to take off the screen door. Using the door as a litter, he and Caril carried the heavy corpse out to the chicken coop and put it inside on the ground next to the north wall. Charlie took the screen door and covered the body.

He walked back to the house and began cleaning up. As he straightened up the overturned furniture, he said to Caril, "I need some perfume. Where do you keep it?"

"There's a bottle on the commode in the bedroom. What do you want it for?"

Charlie went into the bedroom and found the small bottle. He came back into the living room and sprinkled the perfume around the room in hopes of getting rid of the blood smell.

He found a rug and replaced the one in Caril's room he'd used to wrap up Mrs. Bartlett. He checked under the bed and found a box of .410 shells and loaded a shotgun belonging to the old man. He also found a .32 pistol Mrs. Bartlett kept in the kitchen, but it wasn't loaded.

It was getting dark, and Charlie was hungry. He looked in the kitchen but there was very little to eat. He decided to walk down the block to Hutson's Grocery. He left and returned a half hour later with three bottles of Pepsi and a large bag of potato chips. They ate until Caril fell asleep in the chair and Charlie dozed off in the rocker. He woke up during the night to a humming sound and saw the test pattern on the TV set. He sat and stared at the set, then finally turned it off and laid down next to Caril.

He thought about Caril as he lay next to her on the couch. Being alone with her was like owning a little world all their own. He liked lying next to her, kind of squeezing her, listening to the wind blow or looking at the same star and moving their hands over each other's faces. He knew the world had given them to each other. Now if only the world would quit getting in their way. Each time something got in their way, he knew it must be eliminated at whatever cost. He would live with Caril and die with her. He put his arm around her and fell asleep. It had been a long day.

CHAPTER FOUR

Wednesday, January 22, 1958
6:30 a.m.

1

Charlie was awakened by a soft knocking on the front door. He struggled off the couch, grabbed the shotgun off the floor, and stumbled into the bathroom. He checked to make sure the gun was loaded, then whispered "Caril, Caril," from behind the door. "Get up and see who's here."

Caril woke up and rubbed the sleep from her eyes. She got off the couch and picked her way across the room to the front door. Unlocking the door, she opened it a crack and saw it was her girlfriend, Bonnie Gardner.

"Aren't you ready yet?" the girl asked.

"Oh, gee Bonnie, I'm not feeling too good today. I think it's the flu or something so I'm not going."

"Are you sure?" the girl asked.

"Yeah, I'm not sure when I'll be ready to go back, but when I am I'll call you, okay?"

"Okay," Bonnie agreed. She turned around and walked down the walk, while Caril closed the front door.

Charlie came out and plopped down on the couch.

"You did a great job."

"Yeah, I don't think she'll be back for a few days."

"That's good. We need to buy some time. I think as long as we say everyone's sick they should go away."

Caril nodded her head in agreement and laid back down on the couch. Charlie went about washing his face and brushing his teeth while Caril tried to get a little more sleep.

A half hour later there was another knock, but this time at the back door.

Charlie grabbed the rifle and slipped into the bedroom. He made sure the weapon was loaded as he strained to hear the muffled voices coming from the kitchen, but he was too far away and couldn't make out what was being said.

A few minutes later, Caril walked into the bedroom looking for Charlie, "You can come out now."

Charlie got off the bed and followed Caril into the kitchen, "Who was it?"

"Don't worry, it was just the milkman. I took a couple of bottles. He didn't want anything else."

"Good, we could use the milk." Charlie stretched and smiled, "God, I'm starved. Let's fry up some eggs and bacon."

CHAPTER FOUR

2

This began a familiar pattern Charlie and Caril would go through for the next six days. To Charlie, being alone with Caril was great. They were living like kings; at last no one was at her house who could order them around. He felt absolutely no guilt or remorse for what he had done to the Bartlett family. Why should he? In his mind, he killed everyone in self-defense. They were either trying to kill him or turn him into the cops, weren't they? He was just protecting his freedom. As for the little girl? Well, he killed Betty Jean because she screamed too much and it got on his nerves. Besides, she never would have kept her mouth shut about what happened. He didn't have a choice.

Late afternoon of the second day, Charlie walked down to Hutson's Grocery and bought a sackful of groceries. He purchased Pepsi, potato chips, chewing gum, ice cream, candy, and sunflower seeds. He chuckled to himself the whole time he paid for the items. Old man Bartlett would shit if he knew what they were buying. He never let Caril eat that type of food. Not only that, but he'd really be mad to find out they were using his money. What goes around comes around, Charlie thought to himself, and he loved every minute of it.

By the middle of the week, people began stopping over to the house more frequently. A neighbor and long-time friend of the Bartletts, Mrs. William Yordy, came by to pick up her eggs. The Bartletts bought eggs for her when they got their own and she wondered if they were in. Caril told her they hadn't gotten their eggs yet that week, and to come back another time.

On Thursday afternoon Marion Bartlett's boss stopped, but Nig's growling and barking kept him from coming to the door. Caril saw him and yelled out that her father was still sick and he would not be in to work for awhile. Bartlett's landlady came over to talk about Marion buying the house but was told the Bartletts were not home. Caril's schoolmate Bonnie Gardner stopped every morning, and finally Caril stopped answering when the girl knocked.

Charlie and Caril lived like husband and wife for six days. Caril took care of her two parakeets and the family dog, as well as a new collie puppy named Kim. Charlie had bought the puppy several days earlier at Pet Paradise for five dollars and given it to her. They played gin rummy and watched television most of the time. Caril even went to the mailbox every afternoon just to make sure the mail didn't pile up in the box.

Charlie spent a lot of his time planning their "getaway" and practicing his knife throwing. On the third day, he got a hacksaw from a box in the back porch and sawed off the barrel on Marion's shotgun so the shells would spread more when he fired it.

Whenever someone stopped at the house, Charlie took the guns and hid in the bathroom or one of the bedrooms. He tried to stay close enough to hear what was being said. There wasn't a time in those six days that he did not feel totally in control.

Charlie thought a lot about Caril that week. They made love every night and morning, and he felt lucky to have her. Why shouldn't he? She never cared what he looked like. She never criticized him like his parents and the teachers at school did. He looked good to her, and she liked him despite the fact he was a garbage man and lived in a cockroach-infested tenement.

Saturday, January 25, 1958
5:00 p.m.

3

Barb Von Busch sat at the kitchen table, sipping a cup of coffee. Her husband Bob sat across from her reading the *Lincoln Star*. Barb was worried. It wasn't like her mom to stay out of touch so long. It had been a week since Velda had promised to stop by with some pictures she took of Barb's new baby and Barb had not heard a word from her.

"You know, Bob, I haven't talked to mom for almost a week," she said, a worried look on her face.

"So what?" he replied. "It's not that big a deal, is it?" he murmered, keeping his face buried behind the paper.

"Maybe not, but all the same she said a week ago she was going to bring over some pictures of the baby for us to look at. She just got 'em back and was excited for us to see them. I took that to mean right away."

Bob grimaced and put the paper down on the table, "Maybe they got busy or something. She could have forgot, you know."

Barb stirred her coffee, "I don't think so. That's not something mom would put off. I don't know, I feel a little uneasy about it."

Bob thought for a minute, "I have to admit that when your mom says she's going to do something, she usually does it. If it would make you feel any better, I suppose we could go over there and check it out."

A smile broke over Barb's face, "Thanks, Bob. It would make me feel a whole lot better. Why don't you call a cab while I get the baby ready."

He nodded and picked up the phone.

4

The Yellow Cab driver pulled into what constituted the Bartlett driveway and parked behind Mr. Bartlett's Packard. Barb and the baby got out and

CHAPTER FOUR

Bob was paying the driver when the front door of the Bartlett house opened and Caril yelled through the screen door, "Stop, Barb! Don't come any further! Mom, dad and the baby are sick. You wouldn't want your baby to get it," she instructed.

Barb was startled at Caril's appearance. Her hair was messed up and she looked like she had not slept in a week. She wore a house coat and looked very pale.

"I want to see mom," Barb yelled back.

"Go away! Go away, if you know what's best! You need to go away so mother won't get hurt," Caril persisted.

That was a strange thing to say, Barb thought. She didn't know what to reply.

Bob leaned out the car window and said, "What's she talking about?"

Barb replied, "I don't know, but she's really upset. Maybe we better go."

"Okay, get back in the car and we'll go home. We can always come back later; right now doesn't look good."

Barb climbed back into the back seat. She rolled down her window and was going to wave to her sister when suddenly Caril came running out of the house and over to the car.

"I'm sorry I'm so cranky, but I have to be."

"Why?" Barb asked.

Caril stared down at her sister, "I can't say. Just go home and stay there. If you don't, mom will get hurt."

She turned and ran crying back to the house.

Barb and Bob reluctantly told the cab driver to take them home. Something was very wrong, but they did not know what to do next.

5

"Something's going on over there, I know it," Bob Von Busch said to Rodney Starkweather as they drove back to the Bartlett house. Barb had been upset all evening and wanted him to go back and talk to Caril. He picked up Rodney and together they drove over to Belmont.

They went up to the front door and knocked. Caril opened the door a few minutes later.

"Caril, I need to pay Velda for doing my laundry. If they're sick, the money will come in handy. Can't I come in?" Bob asked.

Caril shook her head from side to side, "They're asleep. You can't see them."

Bob tried to push the door open enough so he could slip inside, but Caril leaned against it with all her weight. Bob was getting angry. There was no reason why she shouldn't let him into the house. He didn't care if anyone was sick or not. Finally, Bob grunted, "I'm coming in!"

Caril struggled even harder to keep her brother-in-law from coming in, "Please don't try to get in, my mom's life will be in your hands if you try to get in!"

Bob ignored her pleas and forced his way a little further into the doorway.

Caril was desperate! She shoved with all her might and somehow kept Bob from forcing his way in any further, "Please go away and don't come back until Monday!" she pleaded.

Bob saw the fear in her face and stopped, "Okay, we'll go, but I don't like it." The two men turned and walked back to their car.

6

Officer Frank Soukup had worked for the Lincoln Police Department for a little over two and a half years. A responsible officer, he liked living and working in Lincoln, and hoped he would have a long career in this growing midwestern city. Even though Lincoln had its share of problems, overall he liked what the city had to offer, and was proud to serve on its police force.

On Saturday, January 25, his shift ran from 3:30 in the afternoon to midnight. He and partner Donald Kahler were used to working with one another. It had been a fairly routine night when an 813 (call the station) came over their radio about 9:25 p.m. They called back to the station and listened while Captain Joseph Harbaugh told them to check out a problem in Belmont. When Soukup asked what the problem was he said that certain people were not being allowed to enter a residence at 924 Belmont. Soukup acknowledged the call and turned the patrol car around. They would be there within five minutes.

As the patrol car turned down Belmont Street and moved closer to the house, Officer Soukup noticed that although an outside light was on, the interior of the house appeared dark and deserted. He parked the patrol car along the curb in front of the house and both he and Officer Kahler got out.

A nearby streetlight cast a feeble glow of light across the half-frozen front yard as the two officers walked slowly up to the house. After making sure it was the correct address, Officer Soukup knocked on the front door. There was no answer. He knocked a little harder and still no answer. Finally, he tried the handle and found it was unlocked. He opened the door and attempted to do the same with the inside screen door, but it was locked.

"There must be someone home because the screen door's locked from the inside," he told Kahler.

"You're right," his partner replied. Before he could say another word, they

CHAPTER FOUR

heard a metallic click, and a young girl opened the screen door. She wore a light-colored nightgown covered with a flower print and looked as if she had just awakened. Her face looked tired and her hair needed combing.

"We're from the Lincoln Police Department. Has there been some trouble here?" Soukup asked, his eyes searching the face of the young girl.

"Well, there isn't any trouble," Caril replied. "Who said there was trouble?"

"We got a call that some people weren't allowed to enter this house. Is that true?"

Caril thought for a minute, then replied, "Oh, that was my sister, my brother-in-law and a little baby."

"Well, how come they couldn't come in?" Soukup persisted.

"I told them my mother and father and little sister had the flu, especially my sister. My mother said my sister had a little baby and she didn't want her to come into the house and catch the flu."

"Is there any trouble between you? Did you have an argument or something?"

"No, we didn't. They just left after I told them they couldn't come in."

"What's your name?" Soukup asked.

"My name's Fugate, but my mother's name is Bartlett. She's been married a second time."

"How old are you?"

"Fourteen."

"Well, Caril, it seems awful funny that your brother-in-law would call us down here just because you wouldn't let him in to try to keep him from getting the flu."

"Oh, we don't get along with our brother-in-law, and he don't like us very well. He probably called you here just because he didn't like us."

Officer Soukup studied the girl's face. The whole time he had been talking to her, Kim, a small collie puppy, had been jumping up and down on his pant leg. Its paws were muddy and they were making a mess on his pants. He tried to push the puppy away but it was persistent in wanting his attention. Caril finally unlocked the screen door and let Kim run past her into the living room.

Soukup figured there wasn't anything more to say, so he thanked Caril for her time and, motioning to Kahler, they walked back to the patrol car. The two policemen drove away and a few minutes later stopped at a call box on the corner of 10th and Oak. From there, Soukup called the station and told the captain on duty their conversation with Caril. Captain Herbaugh asked if they found out the name of the Bartlett doctor. They said no and asked if they should go back. Harbaugh said no, it wouldn't be necessary.

7

The entire time Soukup and Kahler questioned Caril, Bob Von Busch and Rodney Starkweather watched with great interest from just down the street. When the two officers left, they followed them to the police station. They went in and asked what Caril had said. The two men were told that nothing was wrong at the house, nothing except that the Bartletts had the flu and they should leave them alone.

Bob returned home and told Barb what the police had said. She listened, then informed him that Charlie had called twice while he was gone and wanted Bob to know he left Rodney's .22 rifle at Griggs'. He also said that he was stranded at Tate's Conoco Station on south Highway 77. He needed a ride home—could Rodney come and get him? Then he called back fifteen minutes later and said the Bartletts all had the flu, that he had taken them groceries, and that everybody should stay away.

Bob called Rodney and they went to Griggs' and were told Charlie had left the rifle there but had left. Bob and Rodney drove out to Tate's Conoco but Charlie was not there. It was evident Charlie was playing games, possibly to divert attention from the Bartlett residence. Neither Bob nor Rodney reported this new information to the police department. They figured the police wouldn't care one way or the other.

CHAPTER FIVE

Monday, January 27, 1958
9:00 a.m.

1

Caril's sixty-two-year-old grandmother, Pansy Street, was concerned. She was used to seeing her daughter, Velda Bartlett (she called her Betty) almost every day, but it had been almost a week since she heard the family was sick and it bothered her. It wasn't like her daughter not to call and visit about what was happening. Sensing something was wrong, she decided to see for herself. Calling a Yellow Cab, she told the driver to go to 924 Belmont Avenue. The whole way there she had a terrible sense of foreboding and just could not shake the feeling that there was a serious problem.

Since Belmont Avenue was only partially graveled and it was so muddy, the cab driver decided not to try to get into the driveway, so he let Pansy out near the curb. As she picked her way through the dirty snow and slush, she noticed the front door was slightly open. She saw Caril standing about two feet into the front room. Immediately, Pansy knew something was wrong with her granddaughter. Caril looked agitated and was white as a ghost.

Before Pansy could greet her granddaughter, Caril blurted out, "They're all sick, Grandma! Go away, Grandma, go home! Oh, Grannie, go away! Momma's life's in danger if you don't go away!"

Caril slowly backed up until she was almost directly against the gas heater sitting against the far wall. Suddenly, she put a hand against her mouth and pointed toward one corner of the room with two fingers as if she was pointing toward someone or something.

Pansy was terrified. Something was dreadfully wrong and she didn't know what to do. Never had she seen Caril act this way.

Mrs. Street pleaded, "I want to see Betty! Please let me see Betty!"

Caril stood silent in the living room.

Pansy yelled again, but louder this time, "Betty, if you can't speak so I can hear you, just come to the door where I can at least see you!"

Again, no sound came from within the house.

Now, Pansy was getting angry! She suspected someone was in the house and was holding her daughter and granddaughter as hostages. "Well, if you won't let me in here I'm going to leave and get a search warrant. I'll get in here one way or the other!" she warned.

CHAPTER FIVE

Pansy abruptly turned and walked briskly back to the cab. The front door at the Bartlett house slowly closed.

2

Charlie tossed the half-eaten plate of bacon and eggs on the bed. Caril's grandmother said she would be back with a search warrant and he believed the old crone. Pansy was not one to make idle threats. He knew the old biddy well enough to know if she said she would get a search warrant, that's exactly what she'd do. It was time to leave.

"Pack up your stuff, Caril! We're leaving!" he ordered.

Caril, startled at the urgency in Charlie's voice, nodded and began packing things in her record player case. Deciding the case was too big and bulky, she threw it down and picked up a red swim bag from behind her bed. She took her photo album and grabbed several photos to take along. There was a snapshot of Betty Jean playing with a plastic tea set at Christmas time; Velda, Barbara and Caril washing clothes together; and one of Charlie holding a demolition derby crash helmet against his hip. She stuffed them into the bag and took a quick glance around the room.

"You got everything you want?" Charlie asked as he put on his jacket.

"Yes, that's all," Caril replied.

Charlie picked up the bag, the .32 pistol and the hunting knife. He wrapped the sawed off .410 in a blue blanket and the two teenagers slipped out the back door and ran down the alley to the Griggs house.

Charlie was glad he had spent some time thinking through his getaway plans. He had a good plan and he was confident it would work. They would head toward Bennet and stop at August Meyer's house. He had hunted there plenty of times and always got along pretty decent with the old farmer. Here was their chance to hide out, just him and Caril. The stupid cops would never think to look for them out there.

Charlie threw the shotgun in the front seat and Caril's red bag into the back. They were ready to leave when Charlie noticed the car had a flat tire.

"Son of a bitch!" he muttered beneath his breath. "Wait in the car Caril, while I fix the flat. It won't take long."

Charlie was almost done when Mrs. Griggs and her daughter pulled up along the curb and parked behind them. They got out and stopped for a few minutes to visit.

"Everything okay, Charlie?" she asked. She hoped he wasn't in a real talkative mood. The grocery bags were heavy and it was cold. She didn't want to stand out there all day passing the time.

"Just a flat tire. I'm almost done now," Charlie replied.

"Good, I'll see you later." The older woman replied as she and her daughter shuffled up the walk and into the two-story house.

Charlie was glad he had a spare to put on, but as he rolled it over to the car, he saw it had a bent rim and the tube was sticking out. Unfortunately, the spare would have to do. It was still early in the morning so they would have time to stop at a service station on their way out of town and get it fixed, and maybe get the transmission worked on, too.

3

After leaving her daughter's house, Pansy Street made her presence known immediately at the Lincoln Police Station. She wanted to have an officer go back with her, but this time she would go inside and look for herself. Only then would she be satisfied that nothing was wrong. She insisted until two detectives, George Hansen and Ben Fischer, agreed to drive her back to Belmont.

Upon arriving at the Bartlett house, all three went up to the front door. The detectives waited while Pansy pounded on the door several times. There was no answer. She tried again, and still no answer.

"Can you try to get into one of the windows?" Street asked.

Fischer thought for a minute. "Maybe, but we don't have a search warrant."

"So?"

"So, that means we would be getting in illegally. Will you take responsibility?"

Pansy didn't hesitate, "Yes, go try to get in."

Fischer found the south window unlatched and crawled in. He came through the house and let the other two in the front door. They searched the house thoroughly but found nothing. No one was there and nothing appeared to be out of place. At no time did anyone think to check the two wooden buildings in back. The two men were satisfied they had gone out of their way to help the old woman, but they had other things to do.

Despite her pleas that something was still wrong, they took Pansy back to her tenement house on North 10th, but not before lecturing her about minding her own business, and how she should not be sticking her nose in her children's affairs.

Pansy sat down in her kitchen and began to cry. She knew something terrible had happened to Velda and resigned herself to finding out exactly what it was on the KOLN-KGIN ten o'clock news. Actually, she would not have to wait that long to find out what happened to her daughter.

CHAPTER FIVE

4

Bob Von Busch was fit to be tied! He had waited almost a half hour to see Police Captain Harbaugh and was almost ready to leave when he was told to go into the captain's office.

"What's the problem now, Bob?" Harbaugh asked wearily from behind his desk.

Bob noticed the policeman's disinterest. "I want to know if anything's happened yet!" he demanded.

"You mean about the Bartletts?" Harbaugh leaned back in his chair and put his hands behind his head. "Let me see, we called Watson's and they said Marion's nephew or someone called in, and said he was sick and wouldn't be in for a few days."

He stopped for a few minutes, then continued.

"You know what I think, Bob? I think they went on vacation for a few days and forgot to tell you. Maybe they went on a trip somewhere and decided to leave Caril home by herself. Then what did she do? She called her boyfriend, this Starkweather guy, over to stay with her. Obviously, they didn't want anyone to know what was going on. That's what I think happened."

Bob angrily replied, "No way would Marion go on some trip without his car! It's still sitting in the driveway! And he wouldn't leave no thirteen-year-old girl in a house all alone out in Belmont; she goes every place they do."

Harbaugh waved his hand in the air. "I'm getting tired of this. I'm telling you to leave them alone. This isn't the first time you've had trouble with them, is it?"

"What are you talking about?"

"I mean you've had trouble before with the Bartletts. I've seen the reports."

Bob let the last statement sink in. Suddenly it struck him, "You must be mistaking me for Sonny Von Busch. He ain't no relation to me."

Harbaugh shook his head, "I've never heard of Sonny Von Busch, just Bob Van Busch and that's you."

Bob knew he was fighting a losing battle with the officer. Finally, he just shook his head and got up, "I gotta go. I can see you ain't gonna be much help."

"I'm sorry."

CHAPTER SIX

Monday, January 27, 1958
11:00 a.m.

1

Dale's Champlain Service Station sat on the corner of 17th and Burnham. Situated forty blocks south of 'O' Street, it was only a block from the Nebraska State Highway Patrol Administration Building.

It had been a slow morning for business. Every once in a while someone stopped to fill their gas tank, but for most of the morning business had been sporadic. The owner, Dale Smallcomb, stood off to one side of the main office room and admired the floor he and employee Lee Lamson had just finished washing and waxing. He stood there admiring the shine when a black 1949 Ford pulled up in front of one of the service bays.

He called to Lamson, "Lee, can you go out and see what he wants? I don't want anyone walking on this floor before it has time to dry. I didn't spend the last hour working my butt off to see someone track it up with muddy shoes," he added in a grumpy voice.

Lee nodded his head and walked outside to see what the customer wanted.

He walked around to the front of the Ford, glanced in the windshield, and recognized the driver right away. It was a friend of his from school, Charlie Starkweather. Lamson crouched down and looked in the driver's side window. A young, attractive girl sat next to Charlie wearing a white bandana tied tightly around her head and chin.

"It's been a while since I've seen you. How are you doing, Charlie?" Lee asked, smiling.

"Huh . . . fine, I guess fine," Charlie replied hesitantly. The station attendant looked halfway familiar to him, but he really didn't care who the guy was. He had other things on his mind.

"What can I do for ya?" Lamson asked.

Charlie lit a Camel and tossed the smoldering match out on the pavement. "Got a problem with the transmission. How 'bout packing it for me?"

"Sure, no problem. I'll open the door, and you can drive right in. We'll put the car on the hoist and have it done before you know it."

Lamson opened up the overhead door and guided Charlie as he drove the Ford over the hoist. Waving for him to stop, he adjusted the arms of the X-frame hoist until they were completely under the car.

CHAPTER SIX

Charlie stepped out of the car, leaned over, and asked Caril, "Aren't you getting out?"

"No, I think I'll just sit here. Can you get me a pop?"

"Yeah, I'll get you one. What kind do you want?"

"How 'bout a grape Nehi?"

Charlie nodded, "Okay."

He turned and asked Lamson, "Where's the pop machine?"

Lamson pointed to the narrow hall that led from the service bay to the front officeway.

Charlie thanked him and walked out of the service area. He found the pop machine and bought himself a Coke and Caril a grape Nehi. He took the bottles and walked back around the corner to the car. Before Lamson hit the lift button, he handed a bottle to Caril through the passenger side window. He stepped back as Lamson hit the lift button, engaging the hydraulic hoist and watched as the Ford was lifted eight feet above the floor.

Charlie walked nonchalantly down the hallway and into the front office area. He stopped and stared out the front window. From there, he could see the State Patrol Building and the State Penitentiary. He smiled at the thought of being so close to both buildings. They didn't have any idea what he was doing. What a bunch of idiots.

Halcomb watched the teenager carefully. There was something about the young man wearing a black leather jacket that really bothered him, but he couldn't put a finger on it. Maybe it was the tight purple Levis he wore or the blue and white cowboy boots. No doubt part of his uneasiness stemmed from Charlie's attitude. He seemed cocky, and when he came into the office he walked with an arrogant swagger. Halcomb watched the red-headed teenager like a hawk. No sense ignoring potential trouble.

Back in the service bay, Lamson worked quickly. He had packed a hundred transmissions before and was good at it. While Lamson worked on his car, Charlie finished his Coke, set the bottle in the crate near the machine, and bought another.

Taking a long swig, he called out, "You got a bathroom in here?"

"Yeah, over there," Lamson replied pointing to a door in one corner of the garage.

Charlie nodded and headed toward the closed door. Lamson finished up, and as he let the car down, the hoist gave out a tremendous rush of air. He went into the front office and made up a ticket for the work. He laid the paper on the counter for Mr. Holcomb to approve.

Charlie came out of the restroom and walked down the hallway into the office area. He stopped for a second when he noticed the new shine on the floor, then smiled, and tracked over it anyway. Charlie glared at Holcomb standing behind the counter, "How much?"

Holcomb looked down at the ticket, "Let me see. It took three pounds at forty cents a pound. I guess that makes $1.20."

Charlie nodded his head and pulled out his wallet from his back pocket. "Can you change a twenty?"

Holcomb stared at the teenager. That was a lot of cash to carry around. Besides, he still had the feeling Charlie was up to no good. He felt the redhead might even try to rob him, especially if he knew he carried enough money to change a twenty.

"No, I don't think I can," Holcomb replied nervously.

Before Charlie could say anything, another customer walked in through the front door.

"Hi, Dale; how 'bout changing this ten for me?"

Charlie watched carefully as the owner cleared his throat. "Sorry, don't have it today. You'll have to go someplace else."

The man looked puzzled with Holcomb's reply but turned around and walked out the front door.

Charlie was satisfied Holcomb was telling the truth, so he rummaged through his pockets until he came up with the money. He handed a couple of dollars to the older man and left.

Holcomb watched with relief as the couple drove away.

"You know that guy?" he asked.

"Yeah, I know him from school. He always seemed a little crazy to me."

"Well, I'm just glad he's gone," Holcomb said, a look of relief on his face. "Seems like he wanted to make trouble."

"Maybe so."

2

It was quiet in the car. Charlie stared down the highway while Caril looked out the window and watched the bleak winter landscape flash by.

"That went pretty smooth, but we still gotta stop and get air in that tire. How 'bout we go to Tate's?" Charlie offered.

"Okay—besides, I'm kind of hungry. We could pick something up at Brickey's."

Charlie nodded, and they continued south on Highway 77. It was not quite 12:30 p.m.

3

Robert Tate had owned the Conoco Gas Station on south Highway 77 for over twenty years. Located eight miles south of Lincoln on the west side of the

CHAPTER SIX

blacktop, it was only a block away from the Turnpike Ballroom. A service station and a cafe combined into one building, it was a popular stopping spot for motorists traveling back and forth between Lincoln and Beatrice.

It was a little after 12:30 when Bob Tate heard a car engine and looked up from behind the counter. He watched as a black 1949 Ford pulled in from the north and stopped at the second-to-last pump in front of the cafe. "Wouldn't you know it," he muttered out loud, "It never fails." Why did his customers always pull into those pumps instead of the ones directly in front of the station, especially when it was cold outside?

He walked over to the dirty Ford and began cleaning off the windshield. After giving the window a clean sweep, he went around to the driver's side and waited for a tough-looking teenager with bright red hair to roll down the window. Tate peered into the car and noticed a gun butt, half hidden by a light blue blanket, lying wedged in the front seat. It sat between the teenage boy and a young girl. No big deal, he thought to himself. They're probably going hunting or something. It was the time of year when a lot of people stopped to top off their gas tanks before they went hunting pheasant or quail.

He looked at the teenager and asked, "Need some gas?"

"Fill it up," Charlie grunted.

Tate nodded, took the gas hose, and began to fill the tank. He had no more than turned on the hose when it rang full. He glanced at the pump and saw it registered 45 cents. Hardly seemed worth the trouble.

Charlie slowly stepped out of the car, stretched his legs, and then opened the back door. He pulled out one of two tires sitting in the back seat. "Where's the air hose? I think I got a leak in this damn tire."

Tate studied the worn-out tire and replied, "You got a leak all right, son. The hose is right over there; but that's okay, you don't have to mess with it. I'll take care of it for you."

Charlie continued to examine the tire while the middle-aged man tried to put air in it. "Do you think it's coming out between the tire and the tube?" he asked.

"Could be," Tate replied. "Normally, I put in fifty pounds in order to check it; but I can't get this one up over twenty-eight."

Several moments later, he concluded, "Hate to say it, but you got a pretty bad leak."

"Shit! Can you fix it?"

"Sure, but it'll take about ten to twenty minutes."

Charlie thought for a moment. He ran his fingers through his thick, greasy hair. "Go ahead. I'll move the car while you get started."

The young girl leaned over across the seat and asked the redheaded youth, "Do you want anything to eat?"

"I guess so."

"Well, then, what do you want? I can't read your mind," she snapped.

"Just get me whatever you think is good. I don't care."

Caril got out and hurried over to Brickey's Cafe while Charlie hopped into the Ford and drove around to the back of the service station. He parked, got out, and walked in the south entrance of the building.

4

Juanita Bell had been waiting tables since 8:00 a.m., and she was tired. Waitressing at Brickey's Cafe was hard work, and her day was lengthened by having to drive in from Roca each morning. Mr. Brickey ran a brisk business in the cafe attached to Tate's Service Station. Most days there was a constant stream of traffic between Beatrice and Lincoln of people who wanted to stop and eat breakfast, lunch or dinner.

The young waitress stood behind the counter, wiping off its surface, when she glanced out the front window and noticed a girl hurrying across the lot. The girl was dressed in a blue jacket, white kerchief, and what appeared to be majorette boots. She hurried up to the front door, entered, and sat down on a stool in the west end of the cafe.

Juanita grabbed her order pad, took the pencil out from behind her right ear, and walked down to where the girl was waiting.

"Can I get you a menu?" the waitress asked.

Caril glanced around at the filled cafe, then answered, "No, that's okay. I'm in a hurry. What can I get that's quick?"

Juanita looked across the counter at the girl who seemed nervous and anxious.

"We could fry up some hamburgers pretty fast, the griddle's always hot. How's that?"

"Sounds good. Give me four hamburgers."

Juanita nodded her head, jotted down the order on her pad, and shuffled back toward the kitchen.

Leaning across a counter separating the main cafe from the kitchen, she ordered, "Four burgers to go."

Satisfied the cooks got the order, she went back to waiting on other customers.

CHAPTER SIX

5

By 1:00, Marv Krueger, one of Tate's employees, had returned from lunch and was working the main gas station counter. Charlie walked up to the young man, balancing a .32 caliber pistol in his right palm.

"Got any shells for this kind of gun?" he asked nonchalantly, while spinning the cylinder.

"What caliber is it?" Krueger asked.

"It's a .32; haven't you ever seen one before?"

Marv frowned and yelled into the garage bay, "Hey, Bob, we got any .32 shells? This guy's got one and needs some shells for it."

"No, we don't carry .32s," came the muted reply from back in the service bay.

Marv turned and faced Charlie, "I guess not."

Charlie grimaced and replied, "That's okay, how 'bout .410s or .22s?"

Krueger smiled, "Those we got. How many do you want?"

Charlie stared at the shelf where the boxes were stacked one upon another. "Give me a box of those Remington 3s—the ones in the red and green box. I might as well take three boxes of those Remington .22 longs. And I need a pair of gloves."

Krueger grabbed a paper sack and busied himself filling the order. When he got all the items sacked up, he turned and asked Charlie, "Is that all?"

"Yeah, that'll do it."

Marv rang it up on the cash register, and Charlie handed him a five-dollar bill.

Marv took the money and made change. He handed the money to Charlie and watched the red-haired youth walk outside.

Several minutes later, Tate emerged from the garage, rolling the tire toward the black Ford. He saw Charlie leaning up against the building, smoking a cigarette. "All done," he said.

"Good. I guess I've already paid for it; so I'll go get my girlfriend, and we'll leave."

Tate nodded his head, "Thanks for the business."

6

Caril nervously drummed her fingers on the counter. She glanced down at her watch and then looked over at the waitress. What was taking so long? Didn't she say it would only be a few minutes? Finally, Mr. Brickey emerged from the kitchen with four hamburgers piled on a paper plate. While Juanita sacked up the burgers, Charlie walked briskly through the front door. He took his half-smoked cigarette and stubbed it out in an ashtray sitting on the counter. He walked up to Caril and stopped a few feet behind her.

"How much is it?" he asked. "Do you think a dollar will cover it?"

Juanita replied, "No problem." She watched while Charlie pulled a crumpled dollar bill from his jean pocket and tossed it on the counter. Caril took the bill and shoved it closer to Juanita.

Juanita picked it up, "I'll be right back with the change."

A few seconds later, she returned and handed the coins to Caril, who got off the stool and started for the front door. Suddenly, Charlie hurried ahead of her and stopped between Caril and the front door.

"What do you want, Charlie?" Caril asked, her voice edged with anger.

He pointed to the waitress. "Everything go all right with her?"

"Sure, fine. Why shouldn't it have? All I did was order some burgers. You said you were hungry, didn't you?"

Charlie searched Caril's face with his eyes. He was pissed off but didn't really know why. Maybe it was because they kept getting delayed from what he really wanted to do. He didn't know. The only thing he knew for sure was that he was anxious to get going.

"Let's go!" Caril finally said angrily. She bumped into Charlie, only to be thrown back a step.

"Goddamn it, Charlie," she said under her breath, looking around at the other people in the cafe. "Everybody's watching. What are you doing?"

When he didn't answer, Caril shoved him as hard as she could, and only then did he turn around to let her by. Together they walked out the front door.

Juanita watched the scene with curiosity. It was obvious the two knew each other and just as obvious they were mad about something. She watched as they passed in front of the window. Her eyes widened as Caril stared back at her. Juanita thought it strange that the girl would look at her so intensely. It was as if Caril wanted to say something to her, to communicate in some way. She kept up the eye contact until they disappeared around the corner of the building. Finally, Juanita shrugged and went back to wiping down the counter. She still had a couple of hours until she was off work. Then she could go home and relax.

7

Charlie shoved the Ford in gear and smiled as they screeched down the driveway and out onto a windswept Highway 77. Caril took a hamburger out of the paper sack and took a bite. "Ugh! This tastes like dog food. Let's take them back!"

CHAPTER SIX

"We're not going back anywhere," Charlie growled.
"Well, we ought to go back and shoot them for serving junk like this," she whined.
"Why don't you just shut the hell up?" Charlie barked. "You're really starting to bug me, you know that?"
No one spoke as they munched their hamburgers. Charlie's mind turned to other things. They would go to old man Meyer's farm. Yeah, that's what they would do. He liked going there to hunt; and nothing compared to being out in the fresh air, away from the city. He would feel revived, reborn with his lover next to him. He would get away from the world of people and all the bitterness that went with it.

8

Charlie took the main road past the Bennet Cemetery into town, turned east onto a farm road at the Bennet Community Church, traveled about a mile, then turned north onto another dirt farm road. Several hundred yards down the road he saw the bullet-ridden mail box that marked the entrace to August Meyer's farm. It stood at the head of a narrow, rut-filled lane that stretched about a mile to the old man's white, two-story farmhouse.
He stopped before turning into the lane. It looked muddy as hell. "It don't look good," Charlie observed.
Caril looked down the lane and replied, "Yeah, maybe we better forget it. It don't look good, Charlie." Because of a light snow several days earlier, the warm, afternoon sun had melted everything just enough to turn the lane into a mire of mud and slush.
A look of determination came over Charlie's face as he threw the car in gear and started up the lane.
The Ford immediately slipped to one side and then lurched heavily to the other as he fought for control. They didn't get twenty yards before the car was stuck in mud up to its axles.
"Son of a bitch!" Charlie cursed, as he slammed his fist on the steering wheel. "We're stuck!"
"No shit," Caril huffed. "I told you we should have never tried to make it. Didn't I tell you so?"
Charlie lit up a cigarette and cracked the window.
"We ought to go and blast the crap out of the old man," Caril offered.
"How come?"
"Cause he didn't clean up his driveway, that's how come!"
"You want to kill him just for that?"
"Yeah, why not?"

Caril grabbed Charlie's hunting knife and said, "I'd give this to him if I had a chance."

"Yeah, right," Charlie replied sarcastically.

Charlie got out and looked down at the tires. They were stuck pretty bad, and he didn't figure on getting out without some kind of help. The wind was raw and cold. He hunched his shoulders against the biting cold and motioned for Caril to get out.

"Let's walk up to Meyer's. We'll get the old man to help us."

The couple walked about fifty feet when they came to the remains of the old District #79 Schoolhouse.

"I'll bet you don't know what this place is?" Charlie quizzed Caril. He liked to ask her questions he figured she couldn't answer. It was a game he played with her all the time.

"Here we go again. I'll make it easy for you this time. I don't have any idea; and besides that, I don't really care." Caril replied. She blew on her hands, trying to warm them up. "God, I'm cold."

"This is what's left of some old school. I've been here plenty of times. We used to set up cans on the roof over there and blast them with our guns."

Caril looked at the ground Charlie was pointing to and saw the old ruins. All that was left was the foundation, some debris, and a storm cellar. They walked closer to the cellar and stopped. Most country schools in Nebraska had storm cellars; too many tornadoes in the spring to not have some protection for the kids.

The cellar was no different from many others in the area: the opening, shaped like a large coffin, was close to the ground and surrounded by weeds and a light covering of snow. The heavy wooden door, unhinged but still in place over the entrance, opened to a steep and narrow cement staircase which went down twelve steps to a circular room eight feet in diameter. The room was cluttered with trash and almost a dozen old wooden school desks.

Charlie and Caril clumped down the steps in order to warm up from the cold. They sat for about ten minutes, barely talking to one another. Caril was still mad that Charlie had gotten stuck. After ten minutes or so, they got up and trudged on their way to see August Meyer.

9

It had been one of those long, winter days for August Meyer. A kindly old bachelor, he minded his own business and kept a neat farm. But August didn't much care for winter. No, he didn't like the typical plains winter very much at all. The cold, grey, winter days seemed to last forever, and even before February came he found himself longing for the green warmth of spring.

CHAPTER SIX

He had just finished a bologna sandwich and was sitting in his favorite chair when his dog started barking outside the house. He looked out the window; not seeing anyone out front, he got up and walked through the kitchen to the back door.

Opening the door slightly, he yelled, "Who's out there?"

"It's me, Charlie . . . Charlie Starkweather."

By then, the old man could see the young couple standing out in the yard, covered with mud.

"Charlie, what the samhill are you doing out on a day like this?"

"Me and Caril were out riding around when we got stuck in your driveway. How come you don't get off your ass and clean it out once in a while?"

"Maybe, because I don't get many visitors when it's so damn muddy in the first place," Meyer replied, his voice edged with anger. He didn't have to take shit from Charlie Starkweather.

"All I know is that my car's stuck bigger than hell, and I need you to help me out!" Charlie replied angrily.

"Keep your shirt on, Charlie! I'll help you out, but I sure wish you would have gotten a little closer to the house before getting it high-centered. It's gonna be a mess getting you out."

"Jesus, August, you'd almost think I got stuck on purpose. How 'bout shutting your trap. I don't want to spend all afternoon listening to you lecture me!"

Meyer ignored the insult and studied the teenager. He noticed the sawed-off .410 shotgun Charlie carried.

"How come you got the shotgun?" he asked. "You plan on doing a little huntin', Charlie?"

Charlie was cold and still angry over getting stuck. Caril was on his ass, and he was not in any mood to answer a bunch of stupid questions from some old geezer.

"No, I thought I'd carry it around for something to do," Charlie snapped. "We're riding around 'cause we don't have nothing else to do. I got the gun in case we seen some squirrels. Can we come in and warm up a little?"

"Don't have to talk to me like that, Charlie! I've known you ever since you was a little fellar. Don't play the bigshot with me!" Meyer retorted. "And, no, you can't come in. You're both covered with mud. I don't want that mess tracked in my house."

Charlie thought for a moment before he spoke. "Yeah, that's right. You've know me a long time; so you know when I mean business. If you won't let us in, then at least go get your coat and come outside," Charlie ordered.

"Okay, okay," Meyer replied. "I'll get my coat and be right out." The old man turned around and disappeared back into the house.

Charlie fished a cigarette out of his pocket, and turning his shoulders against the wind, he lit it while he and Caril waited. He took a deep drag and

JANUARY 27, 1958

exhaled. He was still mad. That dirty son of a bitch, he thought. Won't let us in his house, huh? Maybe he and Caril weren't good enough all of a sudden. Or maybe he suspected something. What if they found the bodies in Belmont and put it on the radio or television? Old August might know everything. He checked to make sure the sawed off .410 shotgun was loaded and the safety off. He took another drag on the cigarette and flicked it to the ground.

Meyer then reappeared on the porch holding a rifle. Charlie stiffened when he saw the gun in the old farmer's hands. His hand tightened on the shotgun's stock. "What's the rifle for?" he yelled at Meyer. "No need to bring a gun out here."

Meyer looked startled, "I just figured to take it along, that's all."

Charlie lifted the shotgun and pointed it a few feet from the old farmer's head. "You dirty son of a bitch! You know something!" He squeezed the trigger and the shotgun went off. The full load of the shot caught Meyer in the head at point blank range. The blast knocked him violently back into the port. Charlie walked into the back porch and looked down at the body. Meyer lay on the floor, a pool of dark red blood spreading in an ever-widening circle. There wasn't much left to his head. Shotguns do a hell of a lot of damage at close range.

"Jesus, Charlie!" Caril screamed from outside the house. "What did you do that for? I thought he was your friend."

Charlie stood still for a minute, then ejected the spent shell and chambered another one into the bolt action shotgun.

"He deserved what he got. He was going to shoot me with the rifle. I know it!"

Suddenly, the old man's dog ran around the corner and made straight for Charlie. Charlie snapped off a shot from about thirty feet and hit the dog in the body. The animal howled with pain and ran across the yard down to the creek which ran through the farm.

"Come on, we got work to do."

Charlie dragged Meyer's heavy body fifty feet through the mud out to a nearby frame washhouse. He pushed him into the house and covered the bloody corpse with a dirty, white blanket he found lying in one corner. Taking the man's hat, he threw it down on the floor. "Sorry, old man. It was you or me. You understand, don't you?"

Charlie closed the door and walked back to the house. He spread some throw rugs over the pool of blood on the porch, then they went into the kitchen.

Charlie walked through the kitchen and into the front room. It was typical of the better farms in the area. A two-story farm house with a total of eight rooms. Inside, the green wallpaper had a leaf design and the doors and woodwork were a dark mahogany color.

Charlie walked over to the dining table and picked up a picture in a gilt-

CHAPTER SIX

edged frame. It was a picture of August and some of his relatives. He laughed and threw it on the floor. His eye caught an old Victrola sitting in a corner and a pipe organ against one wall. He went over and played a few notes. Bored, he got up and clumped upstairs.

Caril was sitting alone in the kitchen when Charlie came downstairs a few minutes later. "Hey, Caril. Look what I found."

He carried two heavy shotguns and a smaller .22 caliber rifle. "We got plenty of guns now, but I'm still looking for the money."

"What money?" she asked. "Doesn't look like he'd have any money to me."

"Everyone knows old man Meyer was rich. He saved everything. They say as much as $500, and I'm gonna find it if it kills me."

He disappeared from the room in search of Meyer's money. Caril sat at the kitchen table near an old stove and peered nervously out the kitchen window. What if someone came? They would be caught red-handed. She wished Charlie would forget about the money and they would go.

Charlie walked into the kitchen and leaned dejectedly against the sink. "I found about $100 in an old brown leather pouch. He must have squirreled the rest away pretty good 'cause I sure as hell can't find it." As he talked, his attention was drawn to a bowl of red Jell-O and a plate of oatmeal cookies sitting on the kitchen counter.

"Hey, how about a cookie and some Jell-O?" he asked Caril. "Do ya good."

She shook her head. "I don't want anything to eat. I just want to go. I don't like it here. This place gives me the creeps."

Charlie laughed. He shook his head and stuck his hand in the Jell-O, pulled it out and popped a piece of banana in his mouth. "Not bad," he murmured. "Maybe you're right. No sense getting caught out here. We got more—a lot more—to do before they catch us. I do think we better find the dog before we go. He could make it to the neighbor's, and someone might come snooping."

Caril nodded her head in agreement. She didn't care what they did as long as they got out of the house.

Charlie hustled outside and found a trail of blood left by the dog. Motioning for Caril to follow, he tracked it down to the creek. They walked along the small, narrow creek for a short distance until they found the dog lying motionless on the bank. Charlie knelt down and looked at the dog. He felt bad. Seeing its body lying there reminded him of a time when he killed a rabbit. He remembered holding the limp rabbit in his hands and asking if it was hurt. No sense in making an animal suffer. It was his job as the hunter to make sure of the kill. A good hunter always aimed for the head.

Satisfied, he abruptly turned, and together they trudged back to the Meyer farm house. He would need to find a spade or shovel to dig the car out of the mud. They needed the car for their getaway. They had no choice.

CHAPTER SEVEN

Monday, January 27
4:30 p.m.

1

Bob Von Busch sat silently in his car and peered out the window at the Bartlett house. He couldn't figure out what was happening. How could the family go somewhere without their only car? There it was, sitting in the driveway just as it had been for over a week. He didn't care what the cops thought; something was wrong and he was worried. He looked over at Rodney Starkweather and asked, "What do you think?"

Rodney shook his head, "I don't know what to think. I kind of wonder if Charlie went off the deep end. Too many weird things going on the way I figure it. I ain't never seen Caril look like she did today, that scared and all. I don't know what to make of it."

Bob sighed, "I'd feel a lot better if we went ahead and checked the house real good. I don't think the cops went out back and looked around. They got that old outhouse and chicken coop back by the alley, you know."

"I suppose we'd better," Rodney reluctantly agreed.

The two men got out of the car and walked across the yard and up to the front door. The yellow card Caril stuck in the door warning everyone about the flu fluttered weakly in the wind. Bob knocked on the door but nobody answered. He tried the handle but it was locked.

"Shit, let's go around and see if we can get a window open," Bob growled.

They tried each window but found they were all locked up nice and tight.

"Rodney, go get the car and drive it around back, down the alley. I'll check the back door and meet you at the outhouse," Bob instructed.

Bob went around the house and tried the back door but found it was also locked. His attention then turned toward the two rundown wooden buildings sitting back near the alley. He had almost reached them when Rodney drove down the alley and stopped. He got out and waited for Bob.

Rodney sniffed the air and asked, "Do you smell something?"

Bob took a deep breath.

"Yeah, I smell an outhouse, what the hell do you think I should smell?"

"Naw, it don't smell like shit. It smells sweet, kind of good."

"Shut up, will you!" Bob ordered as he opened the outhouse door, "I'm kind of spooked the way it is."

"Sorry," Rodney replied as he lit up a cigarette.

CHAPTER SEVEN

"Oh, my god!" Bob shouted as he slammed the door shut with a loud bang.
"Jesus, Bob, what's the matter?" Rodney shouted, dropping his cigarette.
"It's Velda and Betty Jean! They're dead! She's stuck halfway down the toilet and Betty's on the seat!"
"You're sure?"
"Sure as hell! Let's get out of here and call the cops! This is bad, real bad and I think Charlie's up to his neck in it."
The two men jumped into the car and drove downtown to the Lincoln Police Station. This time, Captain Harbaugh listened to what they had to say.

5:00 p.m.

2

"Goddamn it! Look out, Caril!" Charlie yelled. He fought the steering wheel as the Ford fishtailed across the muddy lane and plunged out of control into the ditch. Slamming the car door, he got out and walked around to the front of the car, his cowboy boots slipping and sliding in the half-melted snow and mud.
"Take it easy for God's sake, Charlie!" Caril yelled from her rolled-down window.
"Son of a bitch!" Charlie muttered under his breath as he looked at the stuck car. This was all he needed. Things were not going well. He was mad and wished Caril would shut her trap.
Bending over, he looked under the car. It wasn't good. The Ford was stuck up to its axles in thick, clay-like mud. Charlie struggled back around the fender and crawled into the driver's seat. He had worked steadily for an hour, almost freezing his ass off trying to dig out the car, and now that they were almost back to the road, this happens!
Ramming the gearshift first into forward then quickly back into reverse, Charlie tried to "rock" the car, hoping it would pop free. The engine's roar echoed loudly across the flat, wide open cornfields, but Charlie didn't care . . . he wanted the car out, and he wanted it out now!
Just as he shoved the gearshift into reverse for the fourth time, a tremendous grinding sound echoed across the silent countryside. He had completely stripped out the reverse gear.
It was deathly quiet. The last remnants of the car's exhaust dissipated in the night air.
Charlie, dejected by his bad luck, reached up and grabbed the pack of Winstons lying on the dash. He took the last cigarette, crumpled up the package, and threw it out the window. Smoothing the crooked fag with his forefinger

and thumb, he stuck it between his teeth, lit up, and looked over at Caril who stared straight ahead through the mud-splattered windshield.

"Jesus, Caril, what the hell's the problem now?" he growled, blowing a lungful of smoke out his open window.

Before Caril could open her mouth to reply, two round, yellowish lights appeared fifty yards away on the road.

5:15 p.m.

3

"How's the coffee today, Les? If that isn't the same pot since this morning, go ahead and pour me a cup. It's cold out there."

The young farmer dressed in faded overalls, sat down heavily at the long wooden bar. He took off his old, greasy work gloves and set them on the empty stool next to him.

It had been a typical winter for Howard Genuchi. After a full morning of chores, he ran up to Lincoln after spare parts for the combine he was repairing. Returning to Bennet about three o'clock in the afternoon, he stopped and spent the remaining hours before suppertime relaxing at the old Star Tavern. Even the local farmers who fed cattle during the long winter months found time to stop at the Star for a glass of Budweiser or a hot cup of coffee and some good conversation. It wouldn't take long before somebody asked for a deck of cards or took the well-used cribbage board down from the wall. Before you knew it, small groups of friends sat around tables shuffling cards and sipping their drinks.

Conversations ranged from how much corn their farms had yielded that fall or how cold it was to how this "rock and roll" music was ruining the nation's young folks. They ought to ban all that Elvis Presley music, one farmer would say to another. The others would grunt their approval and light up another Lucky Strike.

Howard had lived on the family farm a mile north and a mile east of Bennet since 1942. Thirty-five years old and unmarried, he spent his days working the farm and the rest of the time taking care of his mother. It was a good life, the only one he had ever known. The pace was slow, and one had time to appreciate the things around him.

Howard spent most of the afternoon in the tavern when he decided it was time to go. Gulping down his last swallow of coffee, Genuchi said goodbye to his friends. Throwing a quarter onto the bar, he stuck his dirty gloves back on and shoved his DeKalb cap down over his ears.

Walking out into the brisk January air, he jumped into his 1937 Ford and

CHAPTER SEVEN

started to drive home. Passing old District #79, he happened to look down the lane and saw what appeared to be a car stuck in the ditch. Putting on his brakes, he stopped, thinking someone might be in trouble.

5:20 p.m.

4

When Charlie saw the headlights glaring down the darkened lane, he knew his luck had changed. Getting out of the car, he walked several yards in the direction of the lights and waited. Caril remained glued to her seat—she was still mad at him for getting stuck in the first place.

Genuchi rolled down his window and asked, "Is there any trouble? Can I help?"

Charlie, shoulders hunched over in a losing effort to block the bitter north wind, walked up to the car. A Winston hung loosely from his mouth while he studied the farmer for a minute. Finally, he replied, "I'm stuck, and my reverse gear's tore out."

Genuchi looked past Charlie and saw a young girl sitting in the front seat of the stuck car. She couldn't be more than 16, he thought. He figured they were a pair of kids out parking and had slipped accidentally into the ditch. No big deal.

"If you have a chain, a cable, a rope or something, I'll try pulling you up in the road."

Charlie nodded his head and walked around to the back of his car.

"Dammit!"

He remembered he didn't have a key to the trunk, but that didn't stop him from getting it open. He pulled out a sharp, pointed hunting knife, and after a few minutes of fiddling with the lock, the trunk popped open. He found a quarter-inch light steel cable and walked back to where Genuchi was waiting.

"This ought to do the trick," Charlie said, showing him the cable.

Genuchi took the wire, walked over to his car, and attached one end to the bumper. Stretching it over the muddy ground, he attached the other end to the bumper of Charlie's car.

After connecting both cars, Genuchi got into his Ford and slowly pulled Charlie's car out of the ditch and onto the road. Caril guided the steering wheel while Charlie watched to make sure the cable between the two cars remained hooked.

Charlie grinned and walked over to where Genuchi sat parked.

"What do I owe you?" he asked pulling out his wallet.

"You don't owe me a thing."

Charlie got a funny look on his face. He wasn't used to someone doing him a favor. He didn't even know what to say.

Embarrassed he replied, "Sure I do," insisting he should pay for Genuchi's service.

Genuchi shrugged his shoulders while Charlie handed him two one-dollar bills. "Suit yourself," he replied. Taking the money, he drove off, leaving the boy and girl alone on the road.

Looking back in his rear view mirror, he muttered, "They should go home. It's too cold to be out tonight."

5:43 p.m.

5

After verifying the license information, the Lincoln Police Department issued a pick-up alert for the Starkweather car. At 5:43 p.m. a radio message was sent out as follows, "Pick-up for investigation, murder, Charles R. Starkweather. May live at 3024 N Street, 19 years old. Also pick up Caril A. Fugate, 924 Belmont. Starkweather will be driving a 1949 Ford, black color, license 2-15628. This is a sedan, no grill, and is painted red where the grill was, and has no hub caps."

The search was on to find the murderers but the killing had only just begun. The authorities would consistently find bodies behind Charlie and Caril for the next eight days.

6

"What are we going to do now?" Caril asked. She was tired, and up to then the whole day had been a disaster.

Charlie peered over the steering wheel out the windshield and answered, "I figure we might as well go back to Meyer's. I need to check something out."

Caril sat silently as Charlie turned into another entrance that he knew led to the Meyer place. He maneuvered down the narrow lane and braked in front of the darkened house. They both got out.

Charlie opened the back door and took out one of the shotguns. He broke it open and slipped in a shell, then snapped it shut. He gave it to Caril. "Here, take this."

"What for?"

"Just take it and shut up. You never know what you might run into."

Charlie walked up to the washhouse where he had put the old man's body.

CHAPTER SEVEN

He looked in the window and came running to where Caril stood.
"Jesus Christ!" he yelled. "Let's get out of here!"
Caril started to run. "What's wrong?"
"Somebody's been here. You know that white blanket I put over Meyer? Well, it ain't there no more!"
They jumped into the car and drove off. He came to a dead end and stopped. "Shit!"
"Just reverse and turn around."
"I can't! This car don't have any reverse!"
Charlie rammed into first and started out across a cornfield. Corn flew in every direction as Charlie gunned the Ford across the field. Finally he reached the dirt road and started back to Highway 77.

7

It was past 5:30 in the afternoon, and Marvin Krueger was dead tired. The traffic between Beatrice and Lincoln had picked up in mid-afternoon, and he had been run ragged servicing cars that stopped for gas. It would not be much longer before he would go home and relax.

He was stocking shelves when out of the corner of one eye he saw that same black '49 Ford pull in from the north and park next to the north island. He stopped, and after putting on his jacket, walked out and over to the car.

Charlie rolled down his window and said, "Why don't you fill it up. By the way, do you carry road maps?"

Krueger nodded his head.

"Okay, that's good. I need a Kansas road map and some more shells. I figure two boxes of .22 longs ought to do it."

Marv turned to walk away. He reached the front door when Charlie stuck his head out the window and yelled, "Make those shells hollow-heads!" It was too late. The attendant had already disappeared into the building. Moments later, he came back with the map and boxes of shells. "Here they are," he said, as he handed them through the window to Charlie.

Charlie looked up and said, "I wanted hollow-heads, but I guess this will do."

Krueger shrugged his shoulders and looked across the driver's side and saw the same young girl sitting on the passenger side. She looked nervous. His eyes immediately dropped to a shotgun and rifle laying across her lap.

"Gotta go," Charlie said. He gunned the engine and they pulled back out onto Highway 77.

That's funny, Krueger thought to himself as he watched the black Ford pull away. Since it was kind of late in the day to be buying shells, he pulled out a notepad from his breast pocket and jotted down the car's license plate—2-15628.

Picking up the phone, he dialed the Lincoln Police Department. Would they be interested in knowing that a young couple had been there twice today acting suspiciously? It seemed the teenage male bought shells twice, and something about that couple made him suspect they were up to something. The voice on the other end thanked him for the information, and that was the end of the conversation. Marvin Krueger never heard back from the Lincoln Police Department; and, although there was a pick-up order for Charles Starkweather and Caril Ann Fugate, the lead was never followed up.

8

As Charlie drove away from Tate's for the second time, he kept thinking about old man Meyer. He felt foolish about running away. He sure as hell wasn't a chicken! The fact that the blanket was missing from the old man's body didn't necessarily mean anything, he reasoned. The wind could have blown it off. Even though the door and window of the building were shut, the north wind was blowing hard enough to maybe cause a draft under the door. Besides, they needed a place to spend the night. He turned off Highway 77 and headed back toward the Meyer farm once again.

9

Bennet, Nebraska, was like many other small, rural towns in the midwest during the late 1950s. Struggling to hang on as a community, its population of 400 included dogs, cats, and some people probably counted twice. It existed solely because of the farming community that surrounded it.

Bennet's main street was short compared to some other Nebraska towns, but it did have the basic ingredients of most small towns—a tavern, cafe, grocery store, and filling station. If you had those, you had a town.

Everyone loved the OK Cafe. It was the type of place you counted on to fill your belly with chicken fried steak or pork chops and mashed potatoes, not to mention the cafe's famous Fried Chicken Night. Usually scheduled for Thursday nights, it was a delight to stop in and eat your fill of home-cooked fried chicken. You got a thigh, leg and back plus french fries for only $1.75; drink was extra.

If you needed to find someone, the best place to start looking was the Star Tavern, and if they weren't there they probably would be later. Although the locals trooped in and out during the week, Saturday nights were the most popular to stop in. It was a nice cozy place—a great place to have a few beers

CHAPTER SEVEN

or a highball and relax. Dad talked farm with his buddies, mom gossiped with the other wives, and the kids liked to, well, just be kids.

Jensen's General Store was another popular place in Bennet. Someone always seemed to be there shopping. Housewives stopped to buy a couple loaves of Rainbow bread or a pound of thickly-sliced minced ham. The store pretty much had whatever they needed, although some still drove into Lincoln to do their grocery shopping.

Kids stopped in before and after school to buy multi-colored Pixie Sticks and small wax pop bottles—the kind you could chew after sucking out the sweet, colored liquid. If you really had money, you could buy a creamy Three Musketeers bar.

10

Robert Jensen, Sr., stood behind the meat counter talking to each customer in a relaxed down-home manner, proud of his little store and how it withstood the challenge of the huge grocery store chains in Lincoln ten miles to the northwest.

To people like the Jensens, Bennet was their home and they meant to live there forever. It was a good life.

Mr. Jensen glanced up at the clock on the south wall, then over at his son who was stocking Cheerios boxes.

"It's almost six o'clock, Bob. Why don't you go ahead and leave. I'll close the store tonight. Besides, you need to drop off a half gallon of milk at the Boldt's. Make sure it's Meadow Gold; last time we took the wrong brand."

The husky seventeen-year-old untied the white apron he wore around his waist, wadded it up into a tight ball, and, pretending it was a basketball, tossed it into a nearby shopping cart.

"Sounds good, Dad. I'll drop off the milk and meet you home in a little bit."

With that, he grabbed a carton of milk, threw on his high school letter jacket, and ran outside. Jumping into his cherry 1950 Ford parked out in front, he backed into the street and was on his way.

Robert Sr. smiled. As he watched his son drive away, he felt a sense of pride. Bob was a good kid. What more could a parent ask for?

Robert Sr. closed the store and got into his car. Driving home, he could not help but reflect upon his life.

He and his wife, Pauline, had lived in Bennet their whole adult lives. Robert had owned the store since 1950, adding a dry-goods line and appliances only recently. He took a big chance leaving the local cold storage plant where he butchered meat ten hours a day to go into business for himself. But then it wasn't really a big chance as far as Robert saw it. He was a hard worker, and he knew things would work out okay.

Robert was blessed with a wonderful family. In fact, just the other day he'd noticed how fast the boys were growing up. Robert Jr., or Bob, was seventeen now, and younger brother Dewey was fifteen. Proud of them both, Robert made a point to let everyone know how they were doing in school and other related activities.

Bob, a junior in high school, stood over six feet tall and weighed 240 pounds. Even though he was big, there was a certain gentleness about Bob people recognized right away. He loved to play football, but the after-effects from a case of polio he contracted when he was eleven made him reluctantly give up the sport.

An excellent student, Bob was president of the junior class and popular with his classmates. In a town where everyone knew each other, Bob's cheerful nature and leadership qualities were appreciated. He sang in the church choir, attended church fellowship meetings on Sunday nights, and went to Bible school during the summer. Best of all, he was happy. He was happy because he had a girlfriend.

11

While Mrs. Jensen cleared away the dirty supper dishes, Robert Sr. silently disappeared downstairs. He enjoyed going downstairs to his newly remodeled den. It was great to sit in his recliner and read the newspaper—if he stayed awake long enough, that is. It was warm and cozy downstairs, especially in the winter months. The cold northern wind blew and swirled outside as it hammered its way down across the plains, but he was just fine downstairs.

Dozing back in his chair, he woke up as Bob bounded downstairs.

"Dad, is it okay to buy those tire recaps I talked to you about last week?"

"I can't remember; did Ernie have them at the station?" Robert replied.

"I don't know for sure, but I was going to pick up Carol and stop at Hunt's tonight and see."

Robert yawned. "That sounds fine. By the way, can you do me a favor?"

"Sure, Dad; what do ya need?"

"Can you two stop at John Galway's house and pick up some Legion cards for me? They're membership cards . . . he said he'd have them ready."

"No problem, Dad. Do you want them right away?"

"No, that's all right. Just as long as you get them tonight. Are you going to be out late?"

Running up the stairs two at a time, Bob yelled over his shoulder, "Not too late, Dad."

CHAPTER SEVEN

12

Carol King lived a half block east and on the opposite side of the street from the Jensen home. The tall, slender brunette had been going steady with the Jensen boy for over six months now. They were considered a "couple" in school and in fact had talked seriously about getting married when they graduated from high school.

Carol was assistant cheerleader, played volleyball, was in the school band and sang in the church choir. Her dad had passed away three weeks earlier, and she was having a rough time getting over the tragedy. Bob came over almost every night to keep her company, but it was still hard. She loved her dad very much. She and her mother had moved in with her brother Warren and his wife after Mr. King's death.

The family was quietly eating supper when Warren spoke up.

"I hear report cards came out today. Is that right?"

Slightly embarrassed by the attention, Carol fidgeted at the dinner table and looked down at her plate.

"Warren, you know I don't like to talk about my grades."

"I'll bet you got straight A's again. Your brains must have come from me," Warren persisted.

"Sure, Warren," Carol retorted.

"Now, Warren, leave your sister alone." Turning to Carol, her mother asked, "Do you have any plans tonight?"

"I don't think so, Mom. I've had this dumb head cold all day, so I thought I'd just lay around tonight. Maybe even go to bed early."

"That's probably a good idea, honey. If Bob calls, do you want me to tell him you're not feeling well?"

"That's okay; if he calls, I'll talk to him. Can we do the dishes now, Mom?"

13

Carol lay on the living room divan when the phone rang, interrupting her catnap. She reached over and grabbed the phone sitting on a nearby lamp table.

"Hello, King residence. This is Carol."

"Hi, how ya feeling?" Bob asked, concerned about her cold.

"Not too bad; what are you doing?"

"I just called to see if you wanted to ride around a little tonight. I've got to do some errands and thought you might like to come."

JANUARY 27, 1958

Carol placed her hand over the receiver and asked her mother if it was all right to go out. She promised they'd be back before ten o'clock.

"It's okay, Bob. When can you pick me up?"

"I'll be over in ten minutes. See ya then."

Ten minutes later the doorbell rang. Carol opened up the front door. It was Bob. He was wearing his letter jacket and a pair of blue jeans. Carol was dressed in a pair of old, faded blue jeans, white sweatshirt, and wore a pair of low-cut oxfords.

She opened the hall closet door and grabbed a small narrow scarf and her heavy winter coat. Throwing them on, she turned toward where her mother sat at the kitchen table. "See you in a little while, Mom."

With that, she grabbed Bob's arm, and they walked out to his car.

14

Bob and Carol stopped and picked up Mr. Jensen's Legion enrollment cards, then drove out to Hunt's Filling Station located at the intersection of U.S. Highway 34 and Bennet's main street. Pulling up in front of the station, Bob saw Dennis Nelson was working that night. He knew Dennis and thought he was a good guy.

Twenty-year-old Dennis Nelson enjoyed working nights at Hunt's Filling Station, mainly because he liked to keep busy. Since it was Bennet's only filling station, the traffic in and out was usually pretty good, and the time went fast.

Nelson was hard at work when he saw Ernest Hunt's pickup pull up next to the station at about the same time Bob arrived. Nelson liked working for the middle-aged Hunt. Hunt, a life-long Bennet resident, had owned the filling station for the last six years. It was a good business, and he seemed to be able to keep things afloat.

"Working tonight, huh, boss?" Dennis asked, wiping his greasy hands on a rag.

"I guess so. Has it been very busy?"

"Not too bad . . . nothing I couldn't handle anyway."

By then, Bob Jensen had pulled up in front of the station. Mr. Hunt looked out the window and waved at the teenager.

Bob entered the station and walked up to where Hunt stood.

"Mr. Hunt, do you have any recaps I could put on the car? I need some real bad," Bob asked.

Noticing Nelson standing near the bay, Bob continued, "Say, Dennis, can you give me $3.00 worth of gas while I talk to your boss?"

Dennis nodded, "Sure thing, Bob."

Mr. Hunt checked the supply room and then came back out to see Bob.

CHAPTER SEVEN

"I'm sorry, but we don't have any ready to go right now, Bob. How soon do you want them?"

"As soon as I can get 'em, but I guess I can wait," Bob answered dejectedly.

Hunt scratched his head, then said, "You know, Bob, I think I've got a pair of whitewalls in the back we could recap. What about that?"

"Sounds great, Mr. Hunt!" Bob eagerly replied. "Go ahead and get started. I'll stop in next week to see if they're ready."

Bob walked out to where Carol was waiting. He felt a lot better about the tires. They left the station and drove out of town.

It was a little after seven in the evening, and Bob was happy. There was plenty of time before Carol had to be home and he knew just where to take her—lover's lane near old District #79.

CHAPTER EIGHT

Monday, January 27
8:30 p.m.

1

Charlie and Caril trudged up the muddy, frozen road leading from the Meyer farm. How many goddamn times was he going to get stuck for Christ's sake! He should have never listened to Caril's whining about going back to the house. She was scared and that really pissed him off. How could a body sit up on its own accord? That's what Caril was worried about, that the old man would somehow come back to life. He couldn't believe her! Trying to keep her happy, he turned around in Meyer's lane and got stuck for the third time.

A bitterly cold wind whipped their faces with stinging flecks of snow as they trudged up the lane. Charlie periodically changed the position of the two weapons he carried, first on one shoulder then the other. Meyer's .22 was light, but Bartlett's sawed-off .410 was getting heavier all the time.

Charlie stopped and peered down the lane. He thought he had heard the sound of a car engine coming their way; sure enough, he could see the two headlights as a car lurched down the half-frozen, half-muddy lane.

The car careened to a stop and Bob Jensen rolled down his window.

"Having some trouble?" he asked.

"Yeah," Charlie said. "Our car's stuck, and we've got a gear out."

Bob looked the teenager over, trying to place him. He thought he had seen him somewhere before.

"You own a Ford, don't you?"

"Yeah."

"Black? 1949?"

"Yeah."

"Come on and get in. It's too cold to be walking around out there," Bob offered.

Charlie opened the door and let Caril crawl into the back seat. He followed her, when Bob suddenly grabbed the barrel of Charlie's .22 pump. "I'll take this, okay?"

"What for?" Charlie snapped. "Neither one is loaded."

"We don't walk around with loaded guns," Caril added impatiently.

Bob looked over at Carol and shrugged, "I guess it's all right. I just don't want anyone to get hurt, that's all."

Bob backed the car up, turned around, and headed back to Bennet.

CHAPTER EIGHT

Charlie stared out the window while they drove toward town. The more he thought about it, the more suspicious he became. How come this guy knew what kind of car he was driving? How come he asked for the guns? He wondered if he knew more about what was going on than he let on.

Several miles passed before Charlie made his decision. Now that the couple had seen him close to the Meyer farm, they would have to be eliminated. It was as simple as that.

As they neared Bennet, Charlie leaned forward and asked quietly, "Can you get us to a pay phone?"

Bob nodded and pulled into the closed and deserted gas station. "There's the phone booth, but it's all locked up. We can go to my house and call."

Charlie slowly raised the rifle and stuck it firmly against the back of Bob's head.

"Oh, no, you ain't," Charlie croaked, his voice tight with emotion. "You better do what I tell you, or somebody will get hurt!"

Bob felt the cold rifle barrel against his skin. He swallowed and asked, "What do you want?"

"Drive us to Lincoln, now!" Charlie ordered.

Bob pulled onto Highway 2 and headed northwest toward Lincoln. Several minutes later, Charlie changed his mind.

"I changed my mind. Head for that old abandoned school. You know the one I'm talking about."

"I think so," Bob replied. "But what for?"

"Just do what I tell ya."

"What are you going to do with us?"

"Nothing. We're just gonna leave you there," Charlie replied.

"Are you gonna take my car?"

"Yeah."

"Well, try not to burn it up. And be careful about the drive shaft when you go over any bumps," Jensen instructed.

It was quiet in the car; the silence was broken only by an occasional bump when the car hit some frozen gravel. Then Caril said, "Have you asked him for his money yet, Charlie?"

"Not yet," Charlie barked. He thought Caril was getting too damn bossy. He was silent for a few minutes, then broke the silence by saying, "Bob, pass your billfold back here and be quick about it."

The Jensen boy hesitated then reached in his back pocket and pulled out the billfold. He handed it back to Caril who took out four one-dollar bills and put the money in Charlie's wallet.

"Here, you take it," she instructed Carol King as she offered her the empty wallet.

JANUARY 27, 1958

Carol took the billfold and, in a voice quivering with fear, said, "I want to thank you for not being mean to us."

Caril snapped, "Shut up!"

Bob asked, "You won't shoot us, will you?"

"I will if you don't do what I say," Charlie retorted.

"You've got to be kidding. Is this some kind of joke?"

Caril snarled, "If you don't watch it, I'll shoot her and show you if we're kidding or not!"

Bob turned slowly down the road that led to old District #79.

2

The school at District #79 had been torn down several years earlier, leaving only the foundation and the storm cellar. The cellar was made of brick, plaster and concrete and was about eight feet in diameter. Its low domed roof was covered with dirt, leaving only a small ventilator peeking up to the outside world. Eleven concrete steps, each one three feet wide, led down to the bottom of the cellar that was filled with leaves and other debris.

Charlie got out of the car and motioned for Bob Jensen to follow. "Get out, goddamn it!" he snarled. "That goes for you, too," he growled at Carol King. Caril waited until they stepped out, then she crawled over to the front seat. She turned the radio on and waited as the trio walked slowly over to the storm cellar.

Charlie looked around to make sure no one was coming, then ordered, "Get down those goddamn steps!" He jabbed the rifle barrel in Bob Jensen's back. The terrified youth hesitantly started down the steps, when suddenly he turned and grabbed for Charlie's rifle. The sharp, staccato report of the rifle echoed loudly in the confines of the small storm cellar. A spray of warm blood shot upwards and smeared against the ceiling. Jensen collapsed halfway down the steps, his body scraping along the brick wall as he fell. Charlie crowded past Carol and jumped down next to where Jensen sprawled on the steps. He placed the rifle behind Bob's right ear and pulled the trigger two times, stuck the barrel in his ear and fired twice more. Then he aimed in front of the ear and fired for the last time. Jensen groaned and was still. Dark red blood formed a pool on the dirty cement.

Charlie, a crazed animal look on his face, turned his attention to Carol.

"Take your pants down," he ordered the terrified teenager.

"No, don't do this!" she cried hysterically.

"Shut up and do it!" he yelled.

Carol slowly unzipped her slacks and, trembling, pulled them down around her ankles.

CHAPTER EIGHT

"Now, do the panties." Carol did what he ordered.

Charlie pulled his own pants down to his knees. He tried to get hard, but nothing happened. It was too cold. He cursed.

"Turn around, goddamn it!"

The trembling teenager turned slowly until she faced away from Charlie. He quickly picked up the rifle, ejected a shell and pointed it just behind her right ear. He squeezed the trigger, and it went off. Carol's head jerked from the impact of the .22 caliber bullet and she collapsed in a heap on top of the Jensen boy, halfway down the stairs.

Charlie came down the steps, pulled a long, narrow knife from his belt and knelt over her twitching body. He stabbed her again and again in the groin. Then he spread her legs and stabbed her deep in the cervix, twisting the blade before taking it back out.

Caril twisted uncomfortably in her seat when she heard the sharp staccato reports of the rifle. She knew what was happening. How could she not? She got out of the car and walked slowly over to the cellar entrance. A sudden burst of moonlight illuminated a bizarre scene. She saw Charlie standing halfway down the cellar with his pants pulled down.

"You dirty bastard! You screwed her!" she screamed.

Charlie pulled up his pants and ran up the cellar steps. "I didn't either. Shut up and help me!"

"Help yourself, you bastard!" she yelled angrily.

Charlie gave her a dirty look and began searching for something he could place over the cellar entrance. Finally, he took the old broken door and laid it over the cellar and covered it with some rubbish. Perspiring heavily despite the cold weather, Charlie shoved several boards under the car tires, jacked up the car and finally got the vehicle free. Caril jumped in the front seat and they roared down the lane onto the farm road. He turned onto Highway 2 and headed for Lincoln, tires throwing up mud and gravel in all directions.

3

It had been a long day, dairy farmer Everett Broening thought, as he milked the last of his 24 cows. He heard the cold, gusting wind rattling against the barn walls; he was happy to be inside where it was warm and cozy. He watched with amusement as several scrawny farm cats scampered from under the holes in the hay. They sat down in a line next to the milking stool and stared intently at him.

"You want some of this, don't you?" he asked out loud. Ever since he was a kid, he got a kick out of squirting milk at the cats. Taking one of the teats he squirted a stream of milk into each one's face, sending the furry creatures into

JANUARY 27, 1958

ecstasy rubbing their faces and whiskers. He chuckled and gave them one last squirt before finishing for the night.

Everett had been farming this ground about a mile east and a half mile north of Bennet for over ten years. He raised a little corn and a little milo, but for the most part, it was the milk that sustained them. He liked farm life, being your own man and all that. He had good neighbors, and he lived close enough to Lincoln that they could drive in whenever he needed something.

Everett was tired. He shuffled back to the house, went into the back porch and pulled off his galoshes. Grabbing a cup of steaming coffee in the kitchen, he went into the living room and plopped down in his easy chair. He had no more than sat down when the family dog began barking outside.

"What's the matter with that dog?" Everett's teenage son asked.

Everett listened for a couple of minutes. "I don't know; maybe the cows are fighting again," he replied.

"You'd better check it out," Mrs. Broening remarked from where she sat at the dining room table.

Everett grumbled under his breath and went out to the back porch. He yanked on his galoshes and put on a coat. He went outside and walked over to where the dog stood tugging on his chain.

"What's the matter, boy? What's bothering you?"

The dog barked for a few more seconds, then settled down and just whined.

Everett petted him, then walked over to the barn. He opened the door to check on the cattle and found they were quiet. He turned and looked around the barnyard, but nothing seemed strange or out of place.

Stomping back into the house, he paused in the kitchen long enough to check the time. It was 9:30. He went back and sat down in his chair. Everett woke up when his wife gently shook his arm. "Aren't you going the watch the news?" she asked.

"Thanks. I think I'll watch Joe Kinney and see what the weather's gonna do before I come to bed." He liked to watch Joe because everyone said he didn't have part of his tongue. Rumor had it the Japs cut it out on the Bataan death march. He still gave a good report, regardless of whether or not he had all of his tongue.

After the weather report, Everett was getting ready for bed when the dog started barking again.

"I can't believe it!" he snapped. "What's the matter with him?" He rolled over and checked the time. It was 10:30. He got up and was trying to decide what to do when a car roared past the house. He ran over to the window and looked down the road. He thought it was the same car that had turned around earlier in his driveway, and it was heading north.

He walked out of the bedroom and went down the hallway until he met his son, who was also wide awake.

CHAPTER EIGHT

"There goes Bob Jensen," he said while he looked out the window.

"How do you know?"

"Gee, Dad, it's easy to tell whose car is whose. No two sets of pipes make the same sound. I know that was Bob Jensen's car."

Everett went back to the bedroom and crawled into bed. He pulled the covers up around his head and closed his eyes. The Jensen boy should be home by now, especially on a school night. Oh, well, if Bob was out catting around, his dad would take care of it when he got home. He rolled over and was soon fast asleep.

4

Warren King glanced nervously at the clock on the living room wall. It was well past ten o'clock, and he was worried. Carol should have been home by then, especially since she was not feeling well. It wasn't like Bob to keep her out this late on a school night without calling. Maybe they had stopped off at a friend's house. But why hadn't she called?

Mrs. King walked into the living room and saw the worried look etched on Warren's face.

"Are you thinking the same thing I'm thinking?" she asked.

"I don't know what to think. She should have been home by now. I guess I shouldn't be worried, but all the same, I'm concerned." He looked at the clock. "I'll give them another fifteen minutes or so. If they don't show up by then, I think I'll run over to Jensen's and see if he knows anything."

The woman nodded and went back into the kitchen.

5

It was close to midnight when Warren King knocked on the Jensen front door. Robert Jensen, Sr., opened it and the two men talked. He had stayed up waiting for his son to come home, but it was so late now, he was really worried. Jensen saw the look on Warren King's face and knew the kids weren't over at his house.

"You mean to say they haven't come back to your house either?" Jensen asked.

"No, they haven't. I don't know what to think. You haven't heard from them?"

"No. I asked Bob to pick up some Legion cards from a friend of mine. After that, I think he was going to stop over at the filling station and check on some tire recaps."

JANUARY 27, 1958

"I'm going to drive around for a little while and see what I can find out. You want to go with me?" King asked.

"Let me get my coat," Jensen replied.

The two worried men drove out of the Bennet city limits and started checking up and down the dirt roads that led into the small town.

It was cold, and Warren had the heater-defroster working on full power as they quietly searched the deserted country roads.

Bob Jensen Sr. could not help but think the worst. Where could they be? It didn't make sense. Both Bob and Carol were responsible young adults. They had never given him any reason to doubt them in the past, so their disappearance began to take on a more sinister form. But what could have happened? Who would want to harm them? This was small-town Nebraska, not the big city. He could see it if they were in Omaha or Kansas City. There was more opportunity to run into some crazy people in the big city, but in Bennet, Nebraska? Surely not.

He stared out the window as the headlights illuminated the bleak winter countryside. No sign of the kids. Finally, he broke the silence.

"You know, Warren, we've been searching for the last two hours and haven't seen a thing. I think we'd better go home and call the Nebraska Highway Patrol." His heart sank at the thought of giving up.

"I suppose you're right. I'll take you home, and then I'll give the highway patrol a call."

He drove back to Bennet, and after letting Mr. Jensen off, drove home and parked the car in the driveway. He went inside, picked up the phone and dialed.

A female voice answered, "Nebraska Highway Patrol, may I help you?"

"Yes, my name's Warren King and I think there may be a problem. My sister and her boyfriend left the house earlier tonight, and we haven't seen them since. I'm worried something has happened to them."

"Has this type of thing ever happened before?" the voice asked.

"No, never."

"Thank you for calling. I'll make sure an officer gets the message as soon as possible. I'm sure someone will call you in the morning."

"Okay," Warren King replied and slowly hung up the phone. He knew something terrible had happened to his sister; there was no other explanation. It was two o'clock in the morning and he was scared.

6

All Charlie cared about was getting the hell away from the storm cellar. He wasn't real happy about killing the teenage boy and his girlfriend. It had been sloppy and too damn bloody, not the clean kill he strived for when he was

CHAPTER EIGHT

hunting. On top of that, he wished Caril had never looked down into the cellar and seen what was going on.

"You really piss me off, you know that!" Caril squawked.

"How come? I did what I had to do. He came at me, and if I wouldn't have shot, he would have killed me. So what's your problem?"

"That's not what I'm talking about and you know it," she snapped.

Charlie knew what she was pissed off about, and he didn't want to talk about it. She saw him with his pants down and now she was mad.

"Tell me one thing and don't lie, okay?" Caril asked.

"What?"

"Did you screw her? I want to know"

"Jesus Christ, Caril, let it be! I don't want to talk about it!"

Caril just sat and stared at Charlie.

"All I can say is that you better not have!"

"Yeah, right. You really scare me," Charlie mocked.

Charlie pushed in the car lighter and waited until it popped out. The lighter's red glow illuminated his face for a moment as he lit a Winston. He cracked his window and blew out a lungful of smoke.

"Caril, I've been thinking—maybe we should give ourselves up. You know, just stop this whole thing right now. We got rid of your folks and all."

Caril could not believe what she was hearing. "What the hell are you talking about? Why should we do that?"

"I don't know, maybe I'm getting nervous about the killing. What difference does it make why I'm thinking it? I'm just thinking that's what we should do."

Caril took the .410 shotgun she held on her lap and nudged the barrel a little closer toward Charlie.

"No way we're giving up. We done what we had to do and nothing's going to stand in our way."

Charlie glanced down at the shotgun pointed at his groin and took another drag on his cigarette. He wasn't the smartest guy in the world, but he knew what she was trying to say.

"Okay, okay. We'll do it your way. I was just thinking, that's all."

"Well, don't."

The inside of the car fell silent while Caril busied herself checking out the glove compartment. "Nothing in there," she said and turned around to look at the back seat.

"Look what I found," she offered.

"What?"

"Some school books; must be Jensen's."

"Get rid of them."

"How?"

"Throw 'em out the goddamned window. What's the matter with you?"

"Okay, okay, you don't have to be such an asshole."

Caril rolled down her window and threw the books out onto the highway, "That takes care of that."

"Good. Let's go back to your house and see what's going on."

Charlie started humming "Great Balls of Fire" by Jerry Lee Lewis as it played on the radio. Once again he felt ready for whatever happened next.

7

Charlie entered Lincoln's city limits, driving directly past the Lincoln Police Station. He laughed and almost honked the horn as he went past the squad building. Why not? He had Jensen's car and no one would be looking for them in it. Hell, maybe they hadn't even found the Bartlett bodies yet. Anxious to see what was going on, he drove to Belmont and stopped at the end of the block leading to the Bartlett house. Several police cars were parked in front of the house, so Charlie turned the car around and drove away.

He headed west on Highway 6. Miles passed quickly as they drove through Friend, Fairmont and Sutton, all sleepy little farm towns in south central Nebraska. They were headed toward his brother Leonard's place out in Washington state.

When they reached the eastern outskirts of Hastings, Charlie pulled into the Showboat Gas Station and filled up with gas. He was tired and angry that the car was running rough; he didn't think it would last all the way to Washington. He got in the car and told Caril they were going back. Charlie thought it would be easier to steal another car back in Lincoln; besides, the cops would never suspect he would be coming in from the west. They were too stupid. He turned around and headed east, anxious to get back to Lincoln and find a place where they could rest.

CHAPTER NINE

Tuesday, January 28
8:00 p.m.

1

Charlie and Caril spent a long night sleeping in Jensen's car parked near the corner of 24th and Van Dorn. It was cold, and their jackets offered little protection. Although the corner was usually busy with traffic, no one who passed the parked car that night suspected it held two people wanted for a triple murder.

Charlie's luck was still holding true. By arriving early in the morning, they happened to hit the time the Lincoln Police Department had the lowest number of units on the road. They had one car with two detectives in the downtown area, one patrol car with two officers in south Lincoln, and one car with two officers in the northern part of Lincoln. The sheriff's office was just as thin, having only one car with two deputies for the entire county. It's not surprising the two fugitives slept undisturbed along a busy street.

Charlie and Caril woke up a little past dawn and immediately began making plans for the day. Obtaining money was a priority. They needed a lot more than what Charlie had taken at the Meyer farm to get to Washington. A measly hundred dollars wouldn't cut it.

As they drove around the wealthy Country Club section of Lincoln, Charlie and Caril scrutinized each house for one that might be good to break in and rob. Not only did they need money, but more importantly, they needed another car. Charlie knew that sooner or later someone would find the bodies in Belmont and Bennet and the cops would be looking for Jensen's car. If they were to have any chance of escaping, they needed to dump the car and get another one.

Charlie knew this affluent area of Lincoln since many of the houses were on his garbage route or his brother-in-law's. In fact, not more than a month before, Charlie had scooped snow from the sidewalks and driveways in the area in order to make a little money. He was well aware that some of the wealthiest people in Lincoln lived nearby.

As they drove past an attractive two-story on South 24th, Charlie looked over at Caril and she nodded. This was the one.

The two-story mansion belonged to C. Lauer Ward, a 47-year-old Lincoln businessman. Ward had lived in Lincoln for some time and was president of two large companies: the Capital Bridge Company and the Capital Steel

CHAPTER NINE

Company. A graduate of the University of Nebraska, he had attended Harvard and the University of Chicago. He was on the Board of Trustees of Bankers Life of Nebraska and was a director of Provident Savings and Loan Association, Norden Laboratories, and National Bank of Commerce. He was a member of the Lincoln Rotary Club, the Lincoln Country Club and University Club, as well as a personal friend to Governor Victor Anderson. Charlie picked the right house all right. He was sure the Wards would be able to provide the things they needed before leaving town for good.

Clara, Ward's 46-year-old wife, was also a graduate of the University of Nebraska, and was vice-president of the Nebraska Alumni Association. The Wards had only one child, 14-year-old Michael, who was attending a private school in Connecticut. Only one other person lived in the house—51-year-old Lillian Fencl. She had been the Wards' maid for over twenty-six years.

"What do you think, Charlie?" Caril asked as she stared at the Ward house out the passenger window. Any house would do as far as she was concerned, but she knew Charlie would have the final say.

"Looks good to me. Let's do it," he said cheerfully.

Charlie stopped the car along the curb and stared past Caril at the house. "I picked this one because I know the place. It's old man Ward's house and he's rich as hell."

"Are you sure?"

"Sure, I'm sure. Look at the house for Christ's sake! You don't see many like this in Belmont, do ya?" he snorted.

"I guess not."

"Not only that, but I've been in it before."

"Ooo . . . some big shot!" Caril chided. "How did you ever get into a house like that? I'll bet you're lying."

Charlie shot her a dirty look, "Like hell, I am! I been in it, and I know the maid, too! A couple of times she let me in to warm up when I was helping Bob on the route. Guess she felt sorry for me or something. I think she's kind of deaf but she seemed friendly enough."

Charlie spent a few more minutes studying the front of the house. It was a nice set-up. He remembered that the driveway circled around the back of the house to a double-car garage. Any car parked in the driveway was invisible to the street in front of the house.

"This is perfect," Charlie chuckled. "You can go right through the garage into the kitchen. You can't see it from the street and there's no way to tell if anyone's coming or going from back there. If we park in the back, no one will ever know."

"So what do we do now?" Caril asked. "I really need some coffee."

Charlie stretched and smiled, "Why don't we invite ourselves in for breakfast? Sure, that's it. We'll go and have breakfast with the Wards. They won't mind the company, and if they do," he patted the rifle sitting next to him on the front seat, "then I guess we'll handle that when the time comes."

He put the car in gear, drove around to the alley, turned down its gravel surface and pulled into the secluded driveway. One of the garage doors was closed, but the other one was open and the spot unoccupied. He parked the car about halfway into the garage.

Charlie turned off the engine, looked over at Caril, "The old man must have gone to work already. Wait here and I'll go in and check it out."

She nodded and watched Charlie stick her mother's kitchen knife down his boot, then grab the rifle from the back seat. He checked to make sure it was loaded, then stepped out of the car. Hiding the rifle behind his back, Charlie walked through the garage and over to the kitchen door. He banged on the door with the rifle barrel and waited a few minutes.

Lillian Fencl, the housekeeper, had noticed the strange car pull into the driveway through the kitchen window minutes earlier. She watched as the teenager got out of the car and disappeared into the garage. She thought she recognized him as one of the boys who had worked the garbage route before but wasn't sure. When she heard the tapping on the door, she opened it only to see a rifle pointed at her midsection. Charlie grinned and shoved the door open, forcing Lillian further back into the kitchen.

Charlie had just kicked the door shut behind him when the Wards' 60-pound Chesapeake retriever, Queenie, ran into the kitchen and began barking furiously. Charlie lowered the rifle and was ready to shoot the animal when Mrs. Fencl noticed his intentions and grabbed the dog by the collar. The dog strained against her grip but the maid was able to restrain the animal.

"Put that damn dog in the basement before I blow it to hell!" Charlie shouted.

Misunderstanding Charlie's command, Mrs. Fencl dragged the dog into a hallway bathroom, shutting the door behind it. Charlie watched as the maid walked back into the kitchen.

He glanced over at the table and noticed the *Lincoln Star* newspaper sitting open to the front page. The headline read "Belmont Family Slain," and beneath it in smaller headlines: "Daughter, boyfriend sought for questioning."

So everyone in Lincoln and probably the whole damn state knew, he thought to himself. Good, he was glad they all knew. He didn't give a shit. Someone was going to find out sooner or later, and besides, the cops didn't have any idea where they were.

"Is anyone else here?" Charlie asked Mrs. Fencl, slowly mouthing each word, "Where do they keep the money?"

CHAPTER NINE

The frightened woman stared at him, unable to comprehend what he was asking. She pointed to her ears and then shook her head from side to side.

Keeping the rifle trained on her, Charlie looked around the kitchen until he saw a pencil and some paper lying on a counter next to the telephone. He grabbed the pencil and scribbled, SIT DOWN AND SHUT UP! and handed it to her. She read it and sat down in one of the kitchen chairs, her hands trembling with fear. He wrote another note and set it on the table in front of the woman, IS THERE ANYONE ELSE IN THE HOUSE? ANYONE UPSTAIRS?

The maid took the pencil and wrote, MRS. WARD IS UPSTAIRS AND WILL BE COMING DOWN SOON TO EAT. I AM MAKING BREAKFAST ON THE STOVE.

Charlie wrote, GO ON AND FINISH FIXING IT, and sat down at the table to wait.

A few minutes later, Mrs. Ward came down into the kitchen wearing a robe and nightgown. Her face registered a combination of fear and puzzlement when she saw Charlie sitting at the table, a rifle laying across his lap.

"What's going on here?" she demanded. "Who are you?"

"Shut the hell up and sit down!" Charlie barked.

She glanced at the paper on the table and back at Charlie but said nothing.

Charlie noticed the puzzled look on her face and said, "You don't have to worry. Nothing's going to happen. We're going to stay here till night, then we're going to tie you up and leave."

Mrs. Ward replied, "All right. That will be okay, you can trust us. You don't have to hold the gun on us or anything like that."

Charlie asked, "Do you have any guns in the house?"

Mrs. Ward thought for a minute.

"Well, I'm waiting." Charlie snorted.

"I don't think so. The only one I know about is a BB gun upstairs. I think Mr. Ward uses it to shoot gophers and squirrels in the back yard."

"Good, I'd hate to have someone get hurt playing with guns," Charlie grinned.

Satisfied everything was under control, Charlie opened the kitchen door and waved at Caril to come inside.

"Make sure you bring the other gun and my jacket," he shouted. The jacket pockets were full of shells, and Charlie thought he might need them before the day was out.

Caril waved back to Charlie and came inside.

JANUARY 28, 1958

10:15 a.m.

2

Fifty-year-old Leo Schwenke concentrated on keeping the dump truck full of oily blacktop away from the center line and more in the right hand lane of the highway. He was careful not to get too close to the edge and risk losing control of the vehicle on the soft road shoulder. The last thing he wanted to do was dump a load of blacktop all over the road.

Schwenke had been employed as a truck driver for the Nebraska State Highway Department for over fourteen years. He lived in Lincoln and worked out of the state shops on 6th and South, across from Gooch's Mills. He liked driving a truck and was good at it.

For the past week he'd been driving sixteen miles or so from Lincoln to the junction of Highway 2 and Highway 43, a half mile or so east of Bennet. Once there, he would pick up a load of blacktop and drive back to the shops and dump the load.

It was a typical winter morning on the plains—cold and clear with a bright blue sky overhead. Leo looked out the front windshield at the surrounding countryside. Harvested cornfields strewn with twisted, yellowing stalks stretched for miles on either side of the highway. Not until early spring would the farmers be able to get into the fields and disc for miles on either side of the highway. That was okay with Leo, because the fields would provide great cover all winter long for pheasants and quail, helping them weather the blizzards which blew down from the Dakotas. He wished he was allowed to have a shotgun in the cab so he could take a shot at the birds scratching for grit near the side of the road.

Schwenke was almost eleven miles west of Bennet when a flash of color lying near the highway caught his eye. He down-shifted and slowed the truck in order to get a better look. As the truck drew closer, he saw two or three books scattered along the edge of the ditch, just off the highway shoulder. He braked and pulled off the road. There were three of them—an English book, a math text, and a history book. Curious, the state employee opened the math book and looked inside the front cover. A label stuck inside the cover read PROPERTY OF THE BENNET PUBLIC SCHOOLS. Further back in the book, stuck neatly between several pages, was a folded paper. It was a test that a boy named Robert Jensen had taken. There were red markings and a grade written at the top.

That's funny, he thought to himself. Why would some high school kid dump his school books along the highway? He knew kids weren't overly fond of school, but how many would just throw away their books like that? He looked up and down the weed-choked ditch but didn't see anything that might

CHAPTER NINE

help explain it. Shrugging his shoulders, he took the books, climbed back in the truck and set them on the seat.

He sat in the cab for a few minutes, then lit up a Camel. The more he thought about the books, the more it bothered him. He just could not shake the feeling that something was wrong. He decided to stop at the Nebraska Highway Patrol headquarters on his way back to Lincoln and show them what he found. Surely they would know what to do with them. He took several more drags on the cigarette, then stubbed it out against his rear view mirror. He needed to get going.

When he arrived twenty minutes later at State Patrol headquarters, Schwenke was told to wait and a trooper would be with him shortly. Not more than ten minutes later, ten-year veteran trooper John O'Neal came in to see what he wanted.

Leo showed him the books and told him how and where he found them. O'Neal agreed that it was a bit unusual for the books to be found along a highway like that. He assured Mr. Schwenke that he would drive to Bennet that morning and check it out. He would visit with the Jensen family and make sure everything was okay. Schwenke thanked him for his time and left; he needed to get back to work.

11:45 a.m.

3

Merle Boldt, owner of the Bennet Champlain Station, had been busy all morning searching for the missing teenagers. Robert Jensen Sr. called him at about seven o'clock and told him his son and the King girl had been missing since early the previous evening. He was worried that something had happened to them and wondered if Boldt could help with the search.

Merle told him he could and immediately called a friend, Dennis Nelson, to keep him company. He and Nelson searched the countryside south and east of Bennet all morning, but came up with nothing.

It was now well past eleven o'clock, and Merle decided to go back into Bennet and get his four-wheel-drive pickup. The late morning sun had melted the morning frost, and the dirt roads were getting awfully muddy. He stopped at home, changed vehicles and then dropped Nelson off at the Bennet Standard Station where he worked. Determined to find the missing kids, he drove east out of Bennet on a narrow country road.

About a mile and a half east of Bennet, he turned up a lane leading to the August Meyer farm. He drove down the potted road until he saw a car sitting in an open cornfield about a hundred yards away. It was a black 1949 Ford stuck up to its axles in mud. Although it was not the Jensen car, it sure looked out of place stuck out in the open like that. Whose car could it be?

Since he didn't know Meyer well enough to start driving around his land, Boldt turned around and drove to one of Meyer's neighbors. He stopped at the Hubert Beecham farm and found the older man working on a farm truck next to the barn. Boldt told him what was going on and asked if he wouldn't mind going with him to see Meyer. Beecham agreed and together they drove over to the Meyer farm.

Boldt drove up Meyer's lane and stopped about fifty feet from the stuck automobile. He got out and inspected the unoccupied vehicle. Since there wasn't a license plate on the front of the car, he went around to the back to see if one was there. To his satisfaction, there was a Nebraska license plate with the number 2-15628.

"Jesus, Hubert!" he gasped, "It ain't the Jensen boy's car, but I think it's the one all the cops are looking for from Lincoln! You know, the Starkweather car!"

"God Almighty!" Beecham exclaimed, "What should we do?"

"We better get back to Bennet and call the Highway Patrol right away! They've been looking for this car all night and it looks like we found it!"

They hopped back into the pickup and drove as fast as they dared on the muddy roads toward Bennet. Every once in a while Boldt caught himself looking back in his rear view mirror to make sure nobody was following.

12:05 p.m.

4

Driving east on Highway 2 toward Bennet, State Trooper O'Neal couldn't help but be concerned with Schwenke's discovery. Could there be a connection between the dead bodies found in Belmont the night before, the missing teenagers, and the school books? Early that morning, the dispatcher at headquarters told him about Mr. King's urgent call and he was worried.

Arriving at Bennet, he stopped at the Bennet Standard Station long enough to get directions to the Jensen and King homes. Robert Jensen Sr. was standing on his front steps talking to a neighbor when Trooper O'Neal pulled into his driveway.

Jensen sadly confirmed the books were his son's and was bringing O'Neal up to date on the search when the two-way radio in the trooper's patrol car squawked with a call. It was headquarters indicating they had just received a call from a man named Boldt in Bennet. Boldt requested an officer stop by the Bennet Champlain Station; it seemed he had information regarding the car currently being sought in connection with the triple murder discovered in

CHAPTER NINE

Lincoln the previous day. O'Neal acknowledged the call, and after apologizing to Mr. Jensen for having to leave, drove quickly over to the station.

O'Neal pulled up near one of the gas pumps where a man dressed in overalls stood waving at him. It was Merle Boldt.

"I think I found the car you've been looking for," Boldt offered.

"You mean the Jensen car?" O'Neal asked.

"No, I mean the Starkweather car. We found it high-centered in August Meyer's cornfield not more than fifteen minutes ago. It's got the same license plate the radio said. I checked."

"How far is it from here, do you think?" O'Neal asked.

"Not far, just a couple of miles to the east, then a little north. Follow me and I'll get you there."

O'Neal nodded and jumped back into his cruiser. He followed Boldt's pickup until they reached the lane leading toward the Meyer farm. He drove down the narrow path and stopped about twenty yards from the abandoned car. He pulled his service revolver and slowly stepped out of the cruiser, his heart pounding. It was a black 1949 Ford, all right. There was no license plate on the front bumper so he walked cautiously around to the rear of the car. He saw the license plate number 2-15628.

He opened the driver's side door and noticed the car keys were still in the ignition. He quickly searched the front seat and floorboard area. Several road maps sat on the front seat, along with a half-eaten hamburger wrapped in tissue paper. He leaned over and picked up an envelope addressed to Charles R. Starkweather, 305 North 10th Street, Lincoln, Nebraska. It was a 1040A form from the Internal Revenue Service. There were three spare tires and wheels in the back seat and loaded .22 caliber shells scattered all over the floor.

He shut the door and walked around to the rear of the car. He tried the trunk handle but it was broken and would not open. Holstering his weapon, O'Neal went back to the cruiser and radioed in the information. He finished the call and turned to observe the surrounding fields. He prayed to God the two teenagers hadn't stumbled upon Starkweather.

CHAPTER TEN

Tuesday, January 28
12:30 p.m.

1

By noon the atmosphere in the Ward kitchen was strained. Caril stayed away from the kitchen, content to nap on the couch in the living room while Charlie kept watch over the two captives. It was painfully evident to Mrs. Ward and her housekeeper that the teenage boy sitting in their kitchen was dangerous. The story in the *Lincoln Star* made it quite plain that Charlie and Caril were wanted for questioning regarding a mass murder and not to be trusted.

Mrs. Ward stood up, went over and washed her hands in the kitchen sink. She dried them with a tea towel and turned to face Charlie, "You don't care if we do some housework, do you? We can't just sit here doing nothing all day."

Charlie glared at the woman. "I guess it's okay, but don't try any funny stuff. We already killed once and we can do it again. No going outside, no using the phone, got it?"

Mrs. Ward nodded her head, "That's fine with us. At least we'll have something to do."

Charlie watched Mrs. Ward jot a note to Mrs. Fencl, who then went down to the basement and brought up an ironing board. She took an iron out of the pantry closet, plugged it in and began ironing a basketful of clothes. At the same time, Mrs. Ward busied herself waxing the dining room table.

Charlie kept an eye on both women for a while, then found his attention wandering to other things. He grabbed a radio from the kitchen counter, went into the living room and tuned in a local rock and roll station. He smiled when the news came on and it was announced he and Caril were wanted for questioning in connection with a series of murders. But he grew bored once again and began ransacking each room in the two-story house. The elegance of the furniture and other furnishings confirmed in his mind that the Wards were people of great wealth.

About eleven o'clock Charlie walked back into the kitchen and ordered Mrs. Fencl to make him breakfast. He asked for pancakes, then changed his order to waffles. He ate six and drank several cups of coffee.

Mrs. Ward came and told Charlie she had a coffee to attend at a friend's house and asked what she should do about it. He thought for a minute, then ordered her to call and tell the friend she was ill and would not be able to

CHAPTER TEN

come. Mrs. Ward made the phone call with Charlie standing next to her so he could make sure she said the right thing.

After he ate, Charlie went into the living room and woke Caril up from her nap. He told her to watch the two women so he could get some sleep. He laid down on the couch; eventually he fell into a fitful sleep and began to dream.

He was a small child, only five years old and was sitting in his old kindergarten room. It was the first day of school and Mrs. Mott had just asked all the kids to share their summer experiences with the class. Charlie was excited; he couldn't wait to tell his. One by one, starting with the last names beginning with A, each youngster marched up in front of the class and told what they had done during the summer.

Charlie sat in anticipation as his classmates talked about going swimming, fishing, to the movies, or camping. Some of the kids even went to other states to see their relatives. They all had such grand stories to tell—he was impressed.

Charlie became more and more anxious. He squirmed in his seat, waiting his turn. He did not have any hobbies to tell about, but he could talk about the adventures he had with his older brothers. Not only that, but he could tell about helping his mom put up fruit in jars. Even though he had never been swimming, he did go the movies with his mom a couple of times.

Finally, she reached the S's and it was his turn. Mrs. Mott looked up over her glasses and called, "Charles Starkweather." He jumped up from behind his desk and hurried to the front of the room. As he walked past the other kids, they began to giggle. His heart pounded hard inside his chest. Why were they laughing? He hadn't done anything funny.

He stopped at the front of the room and looked out over his classmates. They were laughing and pointing at his bow-legs. They were making fun of his red hair. He tried to talk but his mouth was dry and he couldn't say anything. He just stood there and stared at his laughing classmates. He was able to choke out a few words about going to the movies with his mom.

"Speak up, Charles," Mrs. Mott said sternly. "We can't hear you."

Charlie started again, his voice a little louder. He tried to tell what happened, but his words kept getting mixed up. The harder he tried, the worse he mixed them around. They were still laughing at him. "Bow-legged, red-headed woodpecker! Bow-legged, red-headed woodpecker!" Finally, his eyes blurred and he began to cry.

He looked over at Mrs. Mott through tear-filled eyes, hoping she would tell the kids to be quiet, but she said nothing. She just sat there. It was like she didn't care.

Deeply humiliated, Charles stumbled back to his desk while the kids laughed and mocked him. He cursed them all and Mrs. Mott for their cruelty. He wished they were all dead and that he was home with his mom. He was ready to run out of the room, but before he could leave Mrs. Mott shoved her chair back and ran over to his desk. "What's the matter? What's the matter?" she squealed. "Quit your crying! What's the matter with you?"

He tried to answer, but he couldn't talk. He couldn't do anything but sit there and stare up into her hideous face. She reached down and grabbed his shirt collar . . . suddenly he rolled off the couch and hit his head on the floor. He woke up with a start and looked around. Where was he? He was confused for a second or two. Then it came to him, he was in the Ward house on 24th Street.

He stood up, went into the kitchen and washed his face with cool tap water. Wiping his face with a towel, he stood there for a few minutes alone until Mrs. Ward came in and said, "Since I'm doing this housework, I was wondering if it would be okay to change my shoes. These aren't very comfortable. I really need to change them."

Charlie studied her face. "I suppose it's okay, but don't take forever and don't make me come upstairs to get you," he warned.

She nodded and left the room.

Charlie picked up the paper and sat down at the table. He took off his glasses and rubbed his eyes. He was getting another headache and that always pissed him off. He looked the paper over while he waited for Mrs. Ward to return. After a few minutes he noticed a stack of stationery sitting on the counter and got an idea. Picking up a pencil, he wrote:

> This is for the cops or law-men who fines us. Caril and i are writing this so that you and ever body will know what has happem. On tue day 7 days befor you have seen the bodys of my non, dad and baby sister, there dead because of me and Chuck, Chuck came down that tue day happy and full of jokes but when he came in nom said for him to get out and never come back, Chuck look at her" and said why" at that my dad got mad and begin to hit him and was pushing him all over the room, then Chuck got mad and there was no stopping him, he had his gun whit him cause him and my dad was going hunting, well Chuck pill it and the [drawing of a bullet] come out and my dad drop to the foor, at this my mon was so mad the she had a [drawing of a knife] and was going to cut him she Knot the gun from Chucks hands, Chuck just stood there saying he was sorry he didn't want to do it. i got Chucks gun and stop my mon fron killing Chuck. Betty Jean was about 10 steps fron her, he let it go it stop some where would not stop Chuck had the [drawing of a knife] so he was about ten steps from her, he let it go it stop some where by her head. me and Chuck just look at them for about 4 hrs. then we wrapped them and pull them out in the house in back. my sisters and everone eles we not belived this but it's the true and i say it by god then me and Chuck live with each other and monday the day the bodys were found, we were going to kill ourselves, but Bob VonBruck and every body would not stay a way and hate my older sister and bob for what they are they all

CHAPTER TEN

ways wanted be to stop going with Chuck show that some kid bob Kwen could go with me. Chuck and i are sorry for what we did, but now were going to the end. i feel sorry for Bar. to have a ask like bob, i and Caril feel sorry for what has happen. cause i have hurt every body cause of it and so has caril, but i'm saying one thing every body that came out here there was lukie there not dead even Caril's sister. so far we have kill 7 persons
           Chuck S.
           Caril F.

Charlie smiled and carefully folded the papers down the middle. Then he stuck them in his jacket pocket.

He suddenly remembered Mrs. Ward—she should have been back by now. What was taking her so damn long? All she had to do was change some stupid shoes.

"Goddamnit!" he muttered as he grabbed the rifle and clumped upstairs.

He had reached the top of the stairs when suddenly Mrs. Ward stepped out into the narrow hallway and pointed a rifle at him. Charlie just stood there, a look of surprise and shock across his face. Before he could react, Mrs. Ward pulled the trigger and the gun's report echoed through the upstairs. Charlie cringed as the bullet drilled a hole in the wall inches above his head.

Mrs. Ward frantically attempted to fire again, but she did not know how to work the ejection mechanism. Desperate, she threw the heavy gun at Charlie, pushed past him and ran down the hallway toward the stairs. Charlie quickly turned and pulled a long, narrow knife from his boot. He straightened up and threw it at the fleeing woman as hard as he could. She screamed as the knife buried itself between her shoulder blades. She fell heavily to the floor, clawing at the knife stuck halfway in her back.

Charlie walked over to the bleeding woman and, after admiring his aim, yanked the knife out of her body. She gasped with pain as he pulled her up off the floor. He dragged the bleeding woman into the nearest bedroom and threw her roughly on the bed.

"Please don't kill me!" she moaned over and over.

"Shut up! Shut the hell up!" Charlie screamed in her face. "You shouldn't have tried to kill me! I didn't have no choice, you brought it on yourself!" He reached up under her nightgown and pulled her panties around her ankles.

Mrs. Ward groaned and closed her eyes. He closed his eyes and concentrated. He tried to get hard, but couldn't. What was the matter with him? He opened his eyes and watched Mrs. Ward struggle for breath, her lifeblood soaking the bedspread. Satisfied the woman was dying, he walked out of the room and went downstairs where he met Caril just outside the kitchen.

"What's going on? I thought I heard some stuff from upstairs," she asked, searching Charlie's face.

Charlie ignored the question and pulled her away from the kitchen door. He shoved one of the rifles into Caril's hands and growled, "Take this and watch the maid! I gotta go back up stairs and take care of something."

Caril noticed the fresh blood on Charlie's shirt and the crazed look in his eyes.

"You went and killed her, didn't you!" she accused.

"Shut up and do what the hell I tell you!" Charlie snapped.

Caril shut her mouth. She knew it was not a good time to argue with him. She took the rifle and went into the kitchen just like Charlie told her to do while he scrambled back upstairs.

Charlie stepped back into the bedroom just in time to see Mrs. Ward reach over to pick up the telephone from a nearby nightstand.

Charlie leaped across the room and knocked the receiver out of her hand while at the same time pushing the older woman roughly to the floor.

"That's not a good idea," he snarled. "Just when I thought you weren't a problem, look what happens."

Charlie raised his hand to strike the poor woman, but stopped when Mrs. Ward's black poodle, Lucy, ran into the room. The dog stood next to the bed, its lips pulled back revealing a row of sharp teeth while a low growling came from its throat. Before the dog could attack, Charlie took the .22 rifle by the barrel and swung it at the poodle as hard as he could. The rifle butt caught it full across the side of the head. There was a sickening crunch as the animal flew three feet across the room and hit the opposite wall. Charlie held the rifle ready to strike another blow, but relaxed when it appeared the dog's neck was broken.

Satisfied the dog was no longer a threat, Charlie turned his attention back to Mrs. Ward. He yanked a sheet from the bed and ripped it down the middle, then tore one of the halves in two pieces. He tied the woman's hands and feet as tight as he could.

"Don't do this, please don't do this," she begged. "Why are you doing this?" Charlie ignored her pathetic pleas. What did he care about her? She was nothing to him. In fact, she was just like all the rest. She was in his way and when that happened, there was only one thing to do.

He took the long-handled knife and stood over the terrified woman. Her eyes grew big when she saw the knife. He grinned and brutally stabbed her in the neck and chest. Her cries for mercy echoed throughout the upstairs, but soon it was quiet. Charlie stabbed her one last time, and it was over. He sat down on the bed, exhausted and breathing heavily. He felt a little better. It was good to eliminate problems, to tie up loose ends. He knew she would not call the police. He dropped the bloody knife on the floor and bounded downstairs, taking two steps at a time.

When he reached the kitchen, he stopped outside the door and called to Caril.

CHAPTER TEN

"Come here, I've got to talk to you but I don't want her to know what's going on," Charlie said pointing in the direction of the maid.

"Jesus, Charlie, she's deaf."

"Maybe so, but come out here all the same," he insisted.

Caril came out of the kitchen. "Now what's going on?"

"Mrs. Ward tried to kill me so I stuck her with a knife."

Caril stared at him.

"Did you kill her?" she asked.

"Naw, she ain't dead, not yet anyway."

"Where is she now?" Caril asked.

"I tied her up and left her in a bedroom," he replied. "We gotta keep the maid from finding out what's going on. If she does, she'll go ape."

Caril nodded her head.

"You watch her while I go out and move the cars around," Charlie instructed.

Caril stood by the kitchen window and kept watch while Charlie went outside and backed the Ward's Packard out of the garage, put Jensen's Ford in its place and parked the Packard back behind it. He was satisfied. There was no way their car could be seen.

1:30 p.m.

2

Once Starkweather's car had been found, it wasn't long before officers from the Lancaster County Sheriff's Department, the Lincoln Police Department and the Nebraska State Patrol converged on the August Meyer farm. In addition, at least thirty farmers from the Bennet area, armed with high-powered deer rifles, surrounded the Meyer house.

Newsmen from Lincoln soon arrived, and it became evident that everyone present was convinced Starkweather and Fugate were holed up inside the Meyer farm house.

Assistant Police Chief Eugene Masters hid behind a tall elm tree and called to the house through a loudspeaker: "We know you're in there. We'll give you five minutes to come out with your hands up."

There was no answer.

Finally, Sheriff Karnopp and eight officers crept closer to the house and each fired a teargas canister through the nearest window. Everyone waited, hoping the teargas would flush out the fugitives, but no one emerged from the house. It was obvious the fugitive couple had left. While the officers waited for the tear gas to dissipate, a state trooper named Gerald Tesch kicked open the small white washhouse door and found August Meyer's bloody corpse. The body count was up to four, and they still hadn't found the missing teenagers from Bennet.

3:00 p.m.

4

Everett Broening left the Meyer farm after Meyer's body was found and went home. He didn't feel very well. It was a shock to know someone that close to home had been murdered. Meyer never hurt anyone in his life, yet he was dead. It made no sense. Not only that, but the early feeling of optimism that the missing teenagers would be found safely had turned to one of pessimism. Broening overheard the authorities quietly agree the longer they were missing, the lower the odds the two teenagers would be found alive.

He went home and puttered around the workshop in his garage for a half hour or so. He just could not get his mind off the Meyer murder. The more he thought about it, the more he wanted to help find those missing kids. Finally, he went inside the house and found his wife folding clothes in the kitchen.

She saw the look on his face.

"You're worried about those kids, aren't you?" she observed.

"Yeah. I gotta go look for them. I just can't sit here and do nothing. They could be out there anywhere, lost or hurt. See you in a little bit."

"Do you have to go?" she asked worriedly. "I don't think it's a good idea for you to go by yourself. What if you run into Starkweather?"

Everett squeezed her arm and said, "Now don't you worry about me. I can take care of myself. I've got the rifle, and I figure Starkweather's long gone by now. He wouldn't be stupid enough to hang around here, not with all the police and highway patrol out here."

He opened the hallway closet door and grabbed his .30-30 Winchester lever action rifle. He stuck a box of shells in his coat pocket and walked out the front door.

Mrs. Broening watched from the front window as her husband got into his car and drove away. He turned onto the country road that ran in front of the house and headed south. She shuddered and wondered what he would find.

After a quarter mile or so, Broening got out and searched through several shelter belts for signs of the missing teenagers, but found nothing. He got back into his car and drove further down the road.

Several minutes later, Broening came upon the deserted and broken-down remains of District #79. He drove slowly, his eyes searching for anything that seemed out of order. He stopped and stared at the ruins—something wasn't

CHAPTER TEN

right. He sat and studied the twisted ruins a little longer. Then it hit him! He was sure the cellar door had been sitting off to one side the last time he went past, but there it was lying on top of the cellar. The more he thought about it, the more he felt someone had moved the door.

Broening opened the car door and grabbed his rifle. He closed the door, careful not to let it slam. He checked the Winchester's chamber to make sure it was loaded, then he checked it again. He looked up and down the road and then out across the surrounding cornfield. It was dark, but he wanted to be very careful.

Satisfied he was alone, Broening walked cautiously toward the cellar. Suddenly, he froze in his tracks. On the ground about a foot from the cellar opening was a large pool of what appeared to be congealed blood. The hair on the nape of his neck stood up, and he was unsure what to do next. He looked around the ruins once again. He wasn't sure if he wanted to see what was down in the cellar, but he knew it had to be checked out.

Broening's heart beat faster and faster and he was having a hard time breathing. He pushed back the green and yellow DeKalb cap and wiped the sweat from his forehead. Gathering all the courage he could muster, he took the rifle and placed its barrel under the old door. With a quick flip, he pushed it away from the opening. Broening gasped! His stomach churned as he saw the partially nude body of a girl lying on the bottom steps. He did not recognize the girl, but it had to be Carol King!

His eyes quickly took in the grisly sight. There was blood everywhere, on the steps, the floor, and splashed against the ceiling. The dead girl was half naked, her slacks and panties pulled around her ankles. It was obvious she had been stabbed several times; her buttocks were smeared with blood.

Broening hesitated, then took several steps down the cellar, wondering if the Jensen boy was down there also. He looked around the cluttered cellar and then he saw them, a pair of oxfords sticking out from under the girl's body. It was Robert Jensen. His stomach churned and he choked on an upsurge of bile as he struggled up the steps. When he reached the top, a rush of cold air hit him in the face and kept him from puking. He took several deep breaths, then stumbled back to the car. He tried to think. What should he do? His head pounded and he was sweating in spite of the cold. He waited a few minutes, and after regaining some composure decided to drive over to the Meyer farm. There would be plenty of lawmen still there and he needed to tell someone right away what he had found.

JANUARY 28, 1958

4:00 p.m.

5

Once the media reported the discovery of August Meyer, Robert Jensen and Carol King, law enforcement officials from all over eastern Nebraska were called to Bennet. Troopers from Omaha, Lincoln, Fremont, Columbus and as far west as Grand Island were called in to search in and around the small town southeast of Lincoln.

Lancaster County Sheriff Karnopp organized the men into a grid pattern and assigned check points on highways and county roads. Small parties of law enforcement personnel began to comb the fields around Bennet. In addition, a large contingent of local farmers armed themselves with shotguns, deer rifles, and pistols and joined the search.

As the media reported the murders, a slow spreading panic began that would eventually reach epidemic proportions. People wondered why the murders were being done and the fact bodies had been found in Lincoln and near Bennet. Lincoln residents were shocked, and when the news media reported the Jensen and King bodies being found, their uneasiness turned into fear and terror.

After seeing the condition of the King body, several law enforcement officials speculated they were dealing with a sex killer and that Charlie had probably already killed and disposed of Caril Fugate. Although this seemed feasible, Deputy County Attorney Elmer Scheele filed charges of first-degree murder against *both* Caril and Charlie. Descriptions of them were released to the news media as follows:

> **Starkweather**—Five feet five inches tall. 150 pounds. Scar over right eye. Green eyes. Dark red hair cut short on top, long on sides and back. Bow-legged and pigeon-toed, swaggers when he walks. Believed to be wearing blue jeans and black leather motorcycle jacket, black boots or cowboy boots. Sometimes has a speech impediment, trouble pronouncing W's and R's.
>
> **Caril Fugate**—Five feet one inch tall. 105 pounds. Looks about 18. Blue eyes. Dark brown hair usually worn in a pony tail. Sometimes wears glasses, possibly wearing ring with red setting. Dressed in jeans and blouse or sweater, may be wearing a medium blue parka. Might have on white baton boots or grey suede loafers.

4:15 p.m.

6

At the same time Everett Broening found the Jensen and King bodies, something else was taking place in Lincoln involving Caril's brother-in-law, Bob

CHAPTER TEN

Von Busch. Charlie's brother Rodney told him that Charlie had called his dad and said he and Caril had left town but were coming back to Lincoln to kill Bob. He would come in from the west on Highway 6 and Bob had better clear out if he knew what was good for him.

This angered Bob, and together with Rodney he drove out to the old 'O' Street viaduct and waited for Charlie's arrival. Their plan was to talk to him, then jump him and tie him up. They would then take him down to the police station.

The two young men waited in the frigid winter air for several hours, but Charlie never showed. They finally decided he wasn't coming and went home.

5:15 p.m.

7

Charlie spent the better part of that afternoon continuing to ransack the Ward house. He began by searching for guns, but knowing how wealthy the Wards were, it became a treasure hunt. He found a pair of binoculars and some gloves, but no cash. Frustrated, Charlie told Caril to go into Mrs. Ward's closet and find a coat for herself. She picked out a nice jacket and packed a suitcase full of the older woman's clothes.

Around 5:30, Charlie was sitting downstairs in the living room when he heard the thump of a paper hitting the front of the house. He opened up the door and quickly picked up the *Lincoln Journal*. He smiled. On the front page there was a picture of him and Caril smiling at the camera. By God, he was making a name for himself! He'd show everyone that he was a somebody!

"Hey, Caril get a load of this! We're stars! Made the front page of the *Journal*," he cried.

Caril entered the room and walked over to where Charlie was sitting. She looked over his shoulder as he studied the pictures.

"Mrs. Hawley took that one. Don't you remember?" he pointed out.

She nodded and read the headline, "Farmer Found—Youths Sought." Her eyes widened as she noticed several pictures of her parents and stepsister in the paper. There were smaller articles, including one about Carol King and Robert Jensen, two teenagers missing from Bennet. There was even one that began, "Colvert Case Recalled."

"Go get some scissors and we'll cut 'em out," Charlie instructed. "I think I saw some in the kitchen, maybe on the counter."

Caril disappeared, then returned seconds later with the scissors. She handed them to Charlie who methodically cut out each article and picture until he got

JANUARY 28, 1958

to the one with him and Caril smiling at the camera. He set the paper down on the table.

"This is fun," he said, smiling as he neatly stacked the articles and pictures on the living room coffee table. Caril took the scissors and cut out the picture of her and Charlie standing together.

"I need you to go upstairs and get my knife. Take it in the bathroom and get the blood off it. It's on the floor by the bed. And sprinkle some perfume around in that bedroom upstairs."

"Get it yourself!" Caril retorted. "Why should I do all your dirty work?"

Charlie glared at her and snapped, "Quit your goddamned bitching and go get it!"

Caril reluctantly left the room and shuffled upstairs. She walked down the hallway, drawn by a peculiar smell. She stuck her head in the room that smelled the worst and saw Mrs. Ward lying on the bed. She wrinkled her nose at the blood smell. Walking over to the commode, she found a bottle of perfume and sprinkled the perfume all over the room. There was no movement, no sign of life from the woman. Caril set the perfume bottle back on the commode, picked up the knife and hurried downstairs. She went into the downstairs bathroom, washed off the knife and dried it on a towel, then walked into the living room.

"It really stinks up there," she complained.

"So what?" Charlie replied indifferently.

"So, I did what you told me to, that's what."

"Fine. Did you clean up the knife?"

She handed him the clean knife and watched as he stuck it in his boot. Charlie went into the kitchen, followed by Caril, and glanced up at the kitchen clock. It was almost six o'clock and old man Ward should be coming home anytime. Charlie grabbed his .22 rifle and waited by the kitchen door.

"Go watch for Ward through the front window. Let me know when he pulls into the driveway," he instructed.

Caril took a bottle of 7-Up from the refrigerator, found an opener in a drawer and popped the cap off. She took a long swig and replied, "Okay, but what are you going to do in the meantime?"

"Don't worry about me, but if you need to know, I'm gonna make sure we got a car for our getaway. We can't use Jensen's anymore, the whole damn police department will be looking for it. They'd pick us up before we got to Emerald."

Caril hurried into the living room and stood near the front picture window. She peeked out from behind the drapes, keeping watch for Mr. Ward. Ten minutes later, she saw a late-model Chevy pull into the driveway. It had to be Mr. Ward coming home from work.

"Here he comes, he just pulled in!" she shouted. She then ran into the hallway bathroom and shut the door.

CHAPTER TEN

Charlie heard Caril's warning and checked to make sure the Winchester was loaded. A car door slammed and he heard the sound of someone opening the garage. Suddenly the door opened and Mr. Ward stepped inside the brightly-lit kitchen.

The older man's eyes widened with surprise as he saw an unkempt, red-haired teenager standing in the kitchen. But more importantly, he saw the rifle pointed at his gut and realized the man meant business.

"What's going on? How come you're in my house? Where's Mrs. Ward?" he asked, looking around the kitchen.

"Shut the hell up!" Charlie barked. "Sure took you long enough to get home. I'm glad you finally made it because we need your car."

Ward swallowed and stared at the youth. He replied, "Sure, whatever you want. Just don't do anything crazy."

Ward watched while Charlie leaned the rifle up against the kitchen counter and pulled two strips of torn bedsheet from his back pocket. He spun the old man around and began to tie his hands behind his back, when Ward suddenly pushed the teenager away and clutched for Charlie's rifle. Charlie recovered his balance and grabbed the rifle the same time Ward did. They struggled silently, each trying to take the rifle and shoot the other. They moved closer and closer to the doorway leading downstairs to the basement. Charlie grunted as he shoved Ward toward the opening. Finally, Charlie gave Ward a tremendous shove and pushed him down the steps. Ward lost his balance, and although able to wrench the rifle out of Charlie's grip, fell heavily down the steps.

The air rushed out of Ward's stomach as he landed on the concrete basement floor. He fought to regain his breath. Charlie flipped on the light switch at the top of the stairs and spotted Ward lying on his back, blinking up at him.

Ward glanced at the rifle lying on the floor about ten feet away and read Charlie's thoughts. The first one to the rifle would have the advantage in this death struggle. Charlie scrambled down the steps, intent on reaching the rifle before Ward did.

Ward struggled to regain his feet, but it seemed he was moving in slow motion. Seeing how quickly Charlie flew down the steps, he realized there was no chance to get the rifle, so he looked around for some kind of weapon. Anything would do. He struggled to his feet and spotted an iron sitting on a nearby table. He picked it up and raised the heavy appliance over his head. Screaming, he staggered toward the teenager only to stop when Charlie picked up the rifle and pointed it directly in his face.

"Hold it!" he yelled. "Drop it or I'll blow your head off!" Charlie ordered.

Ward hesitated, then lowered the iron to his side, finally letting it drop to the floor.

"Good, that's real good," Charlie hissed. "Now get your ass up those stairs! I should kill you right now but I'm not gonna, not yet anyway."

Ward reluctantly turned his back on Charlie and started up the steps. His mind raced. Was his wife already dead? What about Mrs. Fencl? Should he try to get away? Halfway up the stairs he made a desperate break for freedom. He had almost reached the top step when Charlie pulled the trigger and a single shot rang out. The .22 caliber bullet struck Ward in the lower right side of his back. Staggering from the force of the bullet, he somehow kept on his feet and reached the top of the stairs. He stumbled through the kitchen and into the living room. Charlie followed the wounded man through the living room, ejecting the shell as he went. Ward opened the front door and was halfway outside when Charlie took aim and fired from only five feet away. The high-velocity bullet tore into Ward's left temple, splattering brains and blood against the door frame. Ward crumpled on the doorstep, blood forming a pool on the floor. Charlie leaned over the prostrate man, pulled the knife out of his boot and stabbed him in the neck. Ward groaned and then he was still.

Charlie pulled the body back inside the house and closed the front door. He left the dead man in front of the door and went to look for Caril and the maid.

"Caril! Caril! Where are you?" No answer. He walked back through the kitchen, into the hallway and knocked on the bathroom door. "Are you in there?"

The door opened and Caril came out.

"Where's the maid?" he asked impatiently.

"I don't know!"

"What do you mean, you don't know!" he screamed. "You been in there the whole time when you were supposed to be watching her?"

"Yeah—besides, she's got a gun," Caril whined.

"What do you mean, she's got a gun? How'd she get a gun?"

"I don't know."

"You don't know shit!"

Charlie wanted to slap her stupid face. She was worthless as tits on a boar and it was pissing him off. He tried to think. He hoped the maid hadn't left the house and run over to the neighbors. If she had, they would need to get out of there in a hurry. Maybe she went down in the basement to hide. He did not relish the idea of searching for her down there, especially if she had a gun. He walked into the kitchen and was surprised to see Mrs. Fencl come from the basement and walk into the kitchen. Charlie smiled and grabbed her by the arm.

"Caril, we're going upstairs. Grab a flashlight; it'll be dark up there and I want to see what I'm doing."

He pulled the maid out of the kitchen and half-dragged her upstairs, while Caril followed with the flashlight. Charlie pushed Mrs. Fencl into the first bedroom he found and waited for Caril to follow them through the door. While Caril went over to look out the window, Charlie yanked a sheet off the bed and ripped it into several pieces.

CHAPTER TEN

He threw the terrified maid on the bed and began to tie her hands together.

Caril looked over and asked, "Why don't you lay her down on the bed? She's gonna get tired sitting up all night."

Charlie stopped and glanced up at Caril, then back to Mrs. Fencl, "Good idea," he murmered.

He tied the maid's hands to the bedstead and her feet to the end of the bed. It was dark in the room and Mrs. Fencl whimpered, "Turn on the light. I'm scared of the dark. Please turn on the light."

"Shut up!" Charlie yelled. He took a pillow and put it over her face. Then he reached down and pulled the knife out of his boot and began to stab and slash the poor woman. She screamed, but the pillow muffled the sound of her wretched cries.

Charlie stabbed and slashed at her like a crazed animal, grunting with each thrust. He stabbed her in the stomach, the chest and the neck. Her struggles got weaker and weaker, until finally she didn't move at all.

Finished, Charlie fell exhausted on the bed. "Jesus, I didn't think she was ever going to die. Turn on the flashlight and give me some light."

Caril flicked on the flashlight, its white beam revealing a gruesome sight. Charlie was covered with bright red blood—his face, his arms, and his shirt. He got up and laid a blanket over the corpse.

Turning to Caril, he asked, "Go get me a clean shirt, will you?"

Caril left the room and returned with a white shirt.

"Here," she said and threw it at him.

"Thanks." He looked at Caril and said, "I guess that takes care of that."

Charles Starkweather and Caril Ann Fugate

Nebraska State Historical Society

Cellar where King and Jensen bodies were found

Nebraska State Historical Society

Robert Jensen

Nebraska State Historical Society

Nebraska State Historical Society

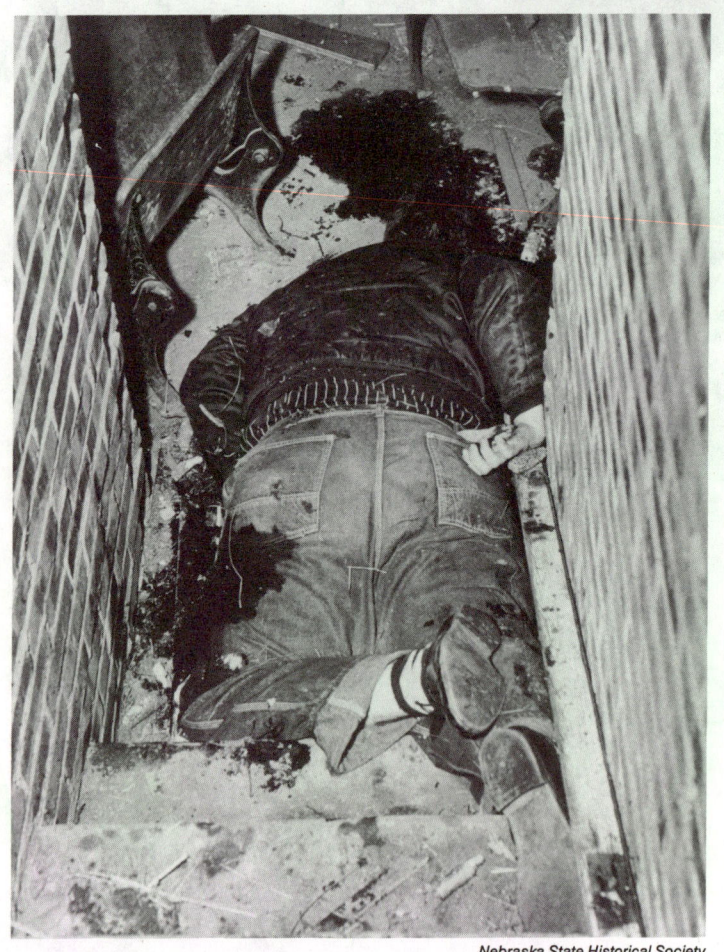

The Ward Residence

Journal-Star Printing Co.

Caril Fugate

Nebraska State Historical Society

Superior Street

Colvert's Body Found
Dec. 1

City Limits

924 Belmont
Bartlett Home
(3 bodies found Monday evening.
Starkweather left Monday morning,
spent night at Meyer farm)

Highway 77   6

Belmont St.

Cornhusker

34

1545 Cornhusker Hwy.
Where Colvert Worked

Salt Creek

No. 10th St.

14th St.

C. B. + Q. R.R.

43

Schoolhouse
(2 bodies found
Tuesday afternoon)

Bennet

425 No. 10th
Starkweather's
Room

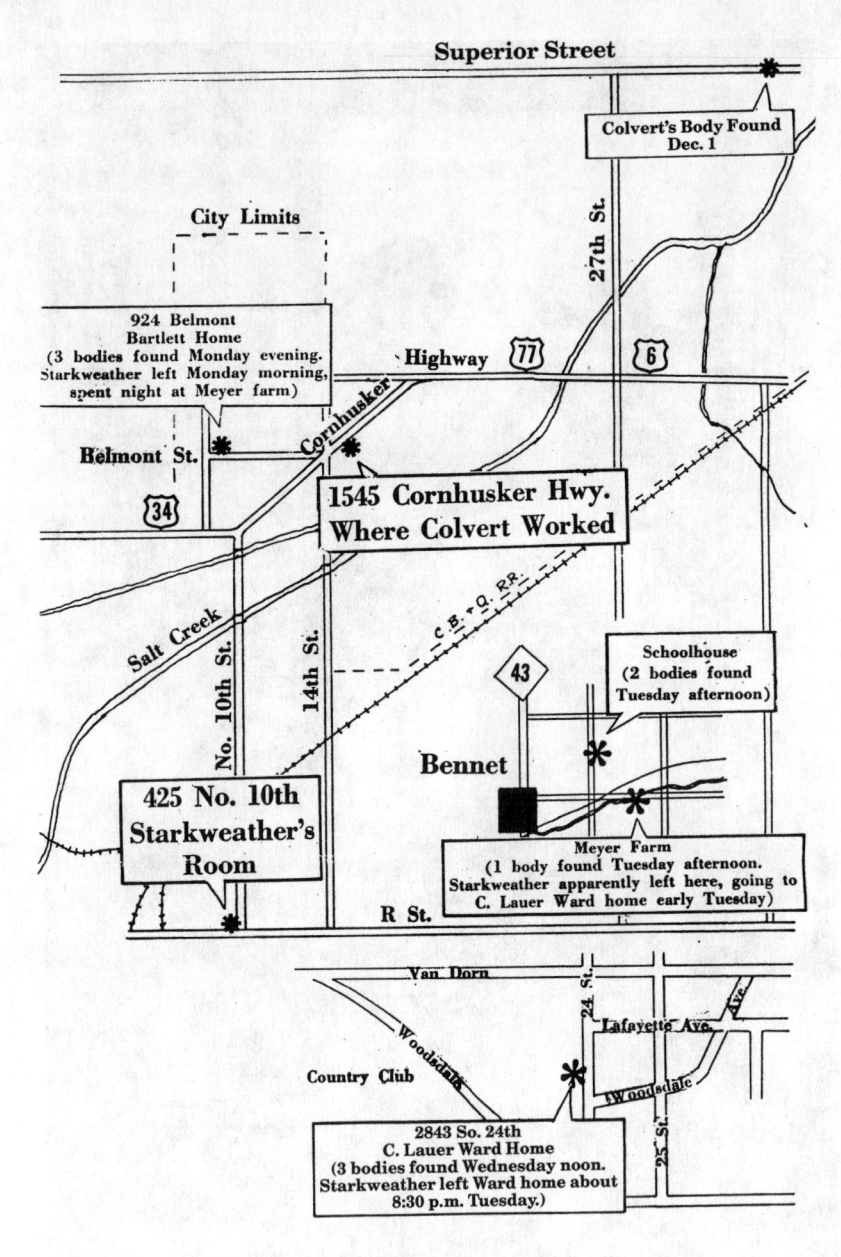

Meyer Farm
(1 body found Tuesday afternoon.
Starkweather apparently left here, going to
C. Lauer Ward home early Tuesday)

R St.

Van Dorn

24 St.

Lafayette Ave.

Woodsdale

Country Club

Woodsdale

25 St.

2843 So. 24th
C. Lauer Ward Home
(3 bodies found Wednesday noon.
Starkweather left Ward home about
8:30 p.m. Tuesday.)

Map of where bodies were found

CHAPTER ELEVEN

Tuesday, January 28
8:00 p.m.

1

Charlie knew they needed to leave the Ward house right away. There were too many bodies lying around and sooner or later someone would stop by or call. The thought of a neighbor hearing the shots and snooping around also worried him. He told Caril to gather up her things and get ready to leave. He went into the bathroom and found a bottle of brown shoe polish under the sink. Caril waited in the kitchen while he poured the dark liquid in his hands and rubbed it in his hair. It looked like hell, but he didn't give a shit.

Caril waited in the kitchen when suddenly the phone rang. She hesitated, then picked up the receiver and answered.

"Hello?"

A voice asked, "Is this the Wards'?"

"Yes, it is."

"Can I talk to Mrs. Ward?"

"No, they're all asleep." Before the person could say another word, Caril slammed down the phone.

Charlie came into the kitchen and asked, "Who was that?"

"Don't know."

He shrugged his shoulders, took one look around and turned out the lights. Locking the kitchen door behind them, the two fugitives went out to the garage and got into Ward's 1956 Packard.

He backed out of the driveway, pulled onto 24th and then drove north to Van Dorn Street. Charlie was unsettled and hesitant as to what to do next. He drove aimlessly around Lincoln for fifteen or twenty minutes, then once again decided to drive back to Belmont.

Charlie and Caril noticed the outside light was on at the Bartlett house and could see a car in the driveway. Charlie didn't stop, but kept going until they were out of Belmont. He pulled onto Highway 34 and headed west toward Washington.

Several miles outside Seward, Caril crawled into the back seat and changed her shirt. As they drove down the two-lane highway, she rolled down the window and threw the shirt and Charlie's knife out the window. It was ten o'clock before they reached the outskirts of Grand Island. While Caril hid

CHAPTER ELEVEN

under a blanket in the front seat, Charlie pulled into the first gas station he saw and waited for an attendant to come out and fill their gas tank.

The operator's wife, Mrs. Walter Cummings, walked over to the car and told him her husband had left for a few minutes and she did not know how to operate the pumps. She went back into the station, but five minutes later she noticed the Packard was still sitting by the pumps. She went back out and asked Charlie if he still wanted some gas.

Charlie told her no but that "he might be back later." He drove north out of Grand Island until they reached Highway 2. He figured to make Washington by using the most isolated highways he could find that ran east and west across Nebraska. Highway 2 would take them through the sparsely populated sandhills and give them the best chance to make it to Washington undetected.

Wednesday, January 29
2:00 a.m.

2

It was one of those nights for Ed Bolen. He operated the Bow Oil Company Service Station in Broken Bow and he was tired. Business was slow so he was splitting time between the gas station and the adjoining cafe. He was in the main office looking through a magazine when he noticed a '56 Packard pull up in front of the gas pumps. He got up and went outside, reaching the car just as a short, bow-legged teenager stepped out and asked him to fill it up. Bolen scrutinized the youth as he stuck the nozzle in the Packard's gas tank. The young man seemed edgy, nervous, and his hair looked funny. It was a strange color, like the kid tried to dye it and didn't know what he was doing. As soon as Bolen finished filling the tank, he and Charlie went back into the office.

Charlie leaned wearily against the counter and asked, "Do you have any maps? You know state maps?"

"Yeah, I know what you're talking about," Bolen replied. He rummaged around a desk behind the counter until he found a couple of maps. "Here they are. I got Nebraska and it looks like Wyoming. How's that?"

"What about Utah or Washington? I really need Washington."

"No, don't have them. Them states are too far away. Why don't I give you the Nebraska and a Wyoming one?"

Charlie nodded, "Okay."

Bolen laid the maps on the counter.

"Where you heading? Maybe I can help with some directions."

Charlie stood there staring out into space, then slowly picked up the maps.

He searched for the right answer, but no words came to him. Finally, he shook his head and said, "I guess it really don't matter."

Bolen stared at the youth, "Suit yourself."

Charlie stuck the maps in his coat pocket, paid for the gas and shuffled slowly back to the car, his shoulders bent against a chilly north wind. He wondered if he would get far enough to use the Washington map.

4:00 a.m.

3

"Holy shit!" Charlie shouted as the Packard careened off the blacktop and down into the ditch. He whipped the steering wheel hard to the right and fought for control of the car. Weeds and brush flew as he tried desperately to keep the Packard from overturning. Finally, he slowed down enough so he could wrestle the car back onto the highway. He pulled over to the shoulder and stopped. Trembling, he grabbed the pack of Winstons on the dash, pulled one out and lit up.

Caril sat next to her door, clutching the door handle, her face white as chalk. "What the hell happened? I was dozing and all of a sudden you're driving down in the ditch!" she shouted.

"I fell asleep, goddamn it! That's what happened!"

"Oh, that's just great! We're lucky you didn't kill us both!"

Charlie glared at her.

"Well?" Caril asked, expecting a better answer.

"Well, what? I told you I'm damn tired, and besides I couldn't help it. I need to get some sleep. How about we stay here for awhile?"

"Right here on the side of the road?" Caril whined.

"Yeah, right here."

"We can't stop now. We got to keep going."

Charlie slumped against the seat and stared out the front windshield. He rolled down the window and flicked the cigarette outside onto the highway. "I know how to stay awake a little longer," he said.

Caril asked suspiciously, "How?"

"If we make love, I'll drive for another hour."

Caril looked out the window.

"You want to do it right here on the highway?" she finally asked.

"Sure, why not? Nobody's around."

"Is that the only way you'll keep driving?"

"Yeah, the only way."

Caril sighed and crawled into the back seat while at the same time undoing

CHAPTER ELEVEN

the buttons on her blouse. Charlie smiled—maybe it was going to be a good day after all.

4:45 a.m.

4

Maynard Behrends liked truck driving. He enjoyed hauling loads through the sandhills of western Nebraska back and forth from Broken Bow, Alliance, Chadron, Scottsbluff and Cheyenne. He headquartered out of Broken Bow and always had plenty of work.

It was dark when Maynard left Broken Bow on his way to Alliance. He was heading west on Highway 2 when he came upon what appeared to be an unoccupied car sitting on the side of the highway. It seemed odd to see a car with Lincoln plates sitting in the middle of nowhere.

Slowing down, Behrends studied the car to see if it was occupied. From what he could see, the car seemed empty and deserted. Awful nice-looking car to just leave on the side of the road, he thought to himself. He took the time to jot down the license plate number on a notepad: 2-17415. Oh well, maybe somebody had car trouble and had left for help. He shifted gears and gave the rig some gas, half thinking he would probably see someone walking down the highway within the next mile or two.

8:30 a.m.

5

Fred Ward was worried. He couldn't figure out why Lauer was late to work that morning. It wasn't like his cousin and business associate not to call if he was going to be late. He was usually very punctual and seldom late for anything. It bothered the executive. Fred reached across the desk and picked up the phone. He dialed Lauer's home number and let the phone ring, but no one answered. Thinking he had the wrong number, Ward hung up and redialed. Still no answer. That's funny, he thought to himself. Even if Lauer and his wife were gone, Mrs. Fencl, the housekeeper, should have answered the phone. He buzzed his secretary on the intercom and asked if she knew whether Mr. Ward had an appointment out of the office that morning. She checked Lauer's calendar and told him no, there wasn't anything on the schedule.

Fred Ward sat back in his chair. There probably wasn't anything wrong, but he was concerned. He decided to keep calling; sooner or later someone would pick up the phone.

JANUARY 28, 1958

8:45 a.m.

6

County Attorney Elmer Scheele sat in his office and read the article in the *Omaha World Herald:*

Fear Rouses Countryside With Multiple Killer Abroad

Bennet, Neb.—Terror stalked the countryside Tuesday night. Farm houses became armed camps and grim-lipped men and women here, 16 miles southeast of Lincoln, burned lights far past the usual bedtime.

There was only one conversation topic, a gun-crazy teenage murder suspect and his 14-year-old girlfriend.

Where would Charles R. Starkweather, 19, strike next?

Was his girlfriend, Carol [sic] Fugate, a willing accessory, dead herself or accompanying the youth out of terror?

Authorities working around the clock said there is no doubt the stubby, green-eyed youth with a shock of red hair worn in a popular teenage style is responsible for the six killings.

"All our deductions add up to the same answer," said Lincoln Police Chief Joe Caroll.

"Starkweather's our man. I just hope he doesn't kill anyone else."

"Never in my 27 years on the force have I seen anything to compare with these wanton murders," Mr. Caroll declared.

"That goes for me, too," said Assistant Chief Eugene Masters. "There can't be any other answer."

Horror mounted in Lincoln and throughout eastern Nebraska as dusk fell and the word got around that three more killings had been added to the triple murder discovered in Lincoln Monday.

Volunteer posses were formed.

Off-duty policemen and other law enforcement officers called control points with offers to work around the clock on their own time.

In farm houses shotguns, rifles, and pistols were taken from closets and racks and placed in strategic, easy-to-reach places.

Mrs. Conrad Leader, who with her husband operates a filling station here, paused while sounding the 6 o'clock whistle.

"Three-quarters of the men in this town were on the hunt for Carol and Robert (Carol King, 16, and Robert Jensen, 17) all day," she said.

"My husband was among them. No one carried a gun. I'll guarantee you, they will all be carrying guns when they go out again."

Herbert Randall, hardware store operator, appeared haggard after his all day search. He looked at his powerful hands with hard eyes, started to say something and stopped. He walked out of the station.

On the porch of a modest home on a muddy street here, Warren King, twenty-six-year-old brother of Carol stood with jutted jaw, fighting back tears.

CHAPTER ELEVEN

"When she left Monday night she told me she would have Bob bring her home at about ten thirty," he said.

He said that Carol had been living with him and his wife because their father died of a heart attack three weeks ago.

"And then came this . . . and then came this!"

Those who knew seventy-year-old August Meyer, who was slain on the back porch of his well-kept white, two-story farm house, were outraged as well as grieved.

"He cared for his mother until she died not too long ago. And then along comes this kill-crazy punk and shoots him."

As the night wore on the lights in the small town and farm houses continued to glow.

No women and children walked the streets.

Terror stalked the countryside.

Scheele set the paper down and rubbed his eyes. He was tired and it was late. He stared at two papers laid out in a row on his desk. The headlines read: "Belmont Family Slain—Tot and Parents Found Dead in Apparent Murder."

The second paper read: "3 More Bodies Found—Bennet Victims Bring Toll to 6."

This guy's leaving dead bodies all over the place and we don't have any idea where the hell he is! He had already seen reports saying the fugitives had been sighted in Blue Rapids, Kansas; Mt. Vernon, Iowa; Kansas City, Missouri; and Milford, Nebraska.

He knew the citizens of Lincoln as well as the whole state were scared, and they had the right to be. You couldn't figure a guy like Starkweather. It seemed he was killing at random, with no established pattern, which made it much more frightening. No one knew where Starkweather would strike next. Although the chances of meeting him face to face were slight, people were terrified. School officials tried to decide whether or not to send kids home. Nebraskans began locking their doors for the first time in their lives.

Scheele knew all too well what the two fugitives were capable of doing. He was at St. Elizabeth's hospital about 10:30 the night before when Dr. Zeman conducted an autopsy on the Jensen boy. It wasn't a pretty sight. Charlie shot the boy six times in the head, any one of the shots being fatal. After seeing the poor boy's body laid out on the autopsy table, Scheele vowed he would prosecute Charlie to the fullest extent of the law when he was caught.

Assistant Deputy Attorney Charles Farnbruch entered Scheele's office and plopped down wearily in a chair across from his boss.

"This is getting bad, Elmer. I've never seen people so scared. Do you know Governor Anderson called out two hundred members of the National Guard? They've already started patroling downtown in jeeps. Johnson called me and said the hardware stores have damn near sold out all their guns. People figure Charlie might show up on their doorstep and they want to be ready if he does.

Not only that, but we just got rid of about a hundred vigilantes wanting to know why Charlie hasn't been caught yet."

Scheele sighed wearily, "Yeah, I saw them outside from my window. Fear's a strong emotion, and right now people are scared out of their wits." He turned and faced Farnbruch, "I guess I can't blame them, can you?" He continued, "What's Karnopp and Carroll doing? Can you give me an update?"

"From what I understand, they've completely sealed off the city and are conducting a block-by-block search. The FBI's opened an investigation and Mayor Martin just offered a $500 reward for any information leading to Starkweather's arrest. John Carter, head of the Garbageman's Union, called and offered another $100 reward money."

Scheele turned and stared out the window. "If they're still in Lincoln, we'll find them."

9:00 to 12:05 p.m.

7

Charlie and Caril slept for several hours after they made love, then once again set off for Washington. Charlie drove through Ellsworth but decided to turn around and get gas. The gas station attendant, Roy Graham, thought Charlie was acting strange, so he notified the Nebraska State Highway Patrol after they left.

The couple continued west on Highway 2 through Alliance, rested there for half an hour, then stopped again for gas at Crawford near the junction of Highways 2 and 20. They bought some candy bars and nine bottles of Pepsi-Cola.

Maynard Behrends was returning from Alliance when he saw the same Packard he saw earlier, traveling west. The driver appeared to be a young man, and he felt it odd that someone so young would be driving a car that nice. When he got back home he called the State Highway Patrol, but they didn't broadcast the report until several hours later.

About nine o'clock, Charlie turned onto Highway 20 and slipped across the Wyoming state line. Charlie seemed to be relieved once he left Nebraska. He quit hurrying and stopped more often to rest and eat. It took three hours for them to make the one-hour drive from the state line to Douglas.

Charlie had just reached the small Wyoming town of Douglas when a news bulletin came over the radio. "More bodies have been found in Lincoln, Nebraska. Murder suspects Charlie Starkweather and Caril Fugate may be traveling in a 1956 Packard."

"Jesus," Charlie growled as he snapped off the radio. "We need to dump the

CHAPTER ELEVEN

car and get a different one right away! Every cop in the country's gonna be looking for this goddamn Packard!"

They were about ten miles west of Douglas when Charlie passed a sign that read AYERS PARK AND NATURAL BRIDGE CUTOFF. Continuing down the highway, he noticed a newer model Buick parked just off the road. It sat all by itself on a little road next to a borrow pit, where the land had been excavated and used elsewhere as fill. Charlie pulled up about a hundred feet behind the car and stopped. How lucky could you get! Just when he needed to change cars, there sat one all by itself. This would be easy.

Minutes passed, then Charlie got out and walked over to the Buick. He peered through the window and saw a man sound asleep on the front at seat. Charlie reached down and tried to open the driver's side door, but it was locked.

"Shit," he said under his breath.

Thirty-seven-year-old Mere Collison, a traveling shoe salesman from Montana, was sound asleep. Charlie tapped on the window until Collison woke up.

"Unlock your door," Charlie ordered.

The startled man looked up and asked, "What for?"

"Because we're gonna trade cars. Hurry it up!"

"I'm not interested, leave me alone," Collison snapped.

Charlie turned and walked back to the Packard. Leaning over, he reached through the open driver's side window and grabbed one of the .22 caliber rifles sitting on the back seat. Checking to make sure it was loaded, he walked slowly toward Collison's car.

Without a moment's hesitation, he pointed the rifle at the terrified salesman and pulled the trigger, then ejected the shell and fired once more. The shoe salesman slumped in the seat as the bullets smashed through the window and ripped into his neck and chest. Charlie reached in through the shattered window and unlocked the door from inside. Collison moaned and tried to move away from his assailant, but found he couldn't. Bleeding heavily from the bullet wounds, he was getting weak from the loss of blood. Looking up at Charlie with fear-stricken eyes, Collison begged, "Don't shoot, don't shoot anymore! I got a wife and kids! Jesus, please don't shoot anymore!"

Charlie grinned down at the badly wounded man and replied, "That's too damn bad."

He raised the .22 Winchester and attempted to eject the spent shell but it was jammed tightly in the breech and he couldn't get it out. He tried to remove the shell with his finger but no matter how hard he tried, it wouldn't budge. Cursing under his breath, he trudged back to the Packard and took out the other .22 rifle. Returning to the Buick, he aimed the rifle at Collison and fired seven shots, each time methodically pumping the spent cartridges onto the gravel. Collison

JANUARY 29, 1958

jerked with each impact until his lifeless body slipped down onto the floorboard beneath the front seat, blood staining the floor mat.

Charlie returned to the Packard and began unloading the car. Caril got out and waited until he had everything sitting on the side of the road.

"Well, we got us another car," he said as he grabbed the bag and the guns. "Let's get the hell out of here!"

Caril followed Charlie across the highway until they reached the Buick. She peeked in the passenger side window and saw a man's body sprawled on the floor. She purposely got into the back seat and waited for Charlie to get in the front.

"What's the matter with you? You scared?" Charlie snapped.

"I'm not riding up front with that body," she warned.

Charlie ignored Caril while he fiddled with the emergency hand brake. He tried and tried, but couldn't get it to release.

"Son of a bitch! I can't get the damn brake off," Charlie cursed as he tried unsuccessfully to release the hand brake. Caril sat in the back seat and stared out the window.

8

Twenty-nine-year-old Joe Sprinkle, a geologist from Casper, hummed to himself as he drove down Highway 20 on the way to Douglas. As he came over a slight rise in the road, he noticed two vehicles parked one behind the other. Both vehicles, a Packard and a Buick, were fairly new—maybe only a couple years old.

Passing the parked cars, he glanced up in the rear view mirror and saw a man get out of the Packard. No sense passing someone who might need help, he thought to himself. He turned around in the highway and drove back to where the two cars were parked. Pulling in behind the Buick, he got out and walked up to the car.

He could see a teenager stooped over inside the front door having some trouble with the hand brake.

Sprinkle stopped and asked, "Can I help you?"

Charlie straightened up and spun around to face the geologist. Sprinkle's eyes immediately locked on the rifle the teenager clutched in his hands. Charlie pointed the .22 at Sprinkle and ordered, "Help me release the brake or I'll kill you."

Sprinkle glanced through the open car door and into the front seat. His eyes widened with fright when he saw the dead body sprawled across the floorboard. Before Charlie could react, Sprinkle grabbed for the rifle. His fingers locked onto the barrel, and the two men began a deadly tug of war. Sprinkle

CHAPTER ELEVEN

knew if the teenager was able to rip the rifle out of his hands, his life was over. He didn't want to die and the thought of never seeing his family again gave him added strength.

Charlie attempted to wrench the rifle out of Sprinkle's hands but try as he might, he couldn't get it away from the muscular six-footer. Sprinkle weighed over a hundred and eighty pounds and he used the weight to his advantage. Charlie pulled and pushed, but it was no use, Sprinkle wasn't about to let go.

1:05 p.m.

9

It was midweek and Deputy Sheriff Bill Romer was on his way to Douglas to handle a rent receipt inspection. He left Casper about 12:30 and was traveling with a friend named Sidney Baldry, who offered to ride along to keep him company. Romer had been Deputy Sheriff of Natrona County the past five years and lived in Casper.

"What do you think about this Starkweather thing?" Romer asked trying to make conversation.

"Is that the guy who killed those people in Nebraska?" Baldry replied.

"Yeah, the paper had something about it this morning. There was a picture, but not much of a story."

"I thought I saw something on it. What happened? How many did he kill?"

"They've found six bodies so far, but haven't been able to find him or the girl who's riding with him."

"I imagine he's long gone by now. I doubt if he's stupid enough to hang around Nebraska after doing all that."

"Yeah, he's probably fifteen hundred miles away by now."

They were almost fifteen miles west of Douglas when Romer came up behind a milk truck. He slowed down to about ten miles per hour while the bigger truck struggled up a hill. Once they reached the crest, Romer was forced to put on his brakes as the truck suddenly screeched to a halt in the middle of the highway.

"What the samhill's going on? You just can't stop a vehicle like that!" he huffed.

Romer tried to pull out around the truck, but a car was stopped in the oncoming lane, blocking the road. A man and a woman stood next to the car watching something with great interest.

Romer got out and walked over to the side of the road until he could see what everyone was looking at. There appeared to be two men wrestling with some kind of object in the middle of the highway. He squinted and looked closer. He wasn't sure, but he thought they were fighting over a rifle or shotgun!

Before Romer could pull his revolver and approach the scene, a teenage girl burst from the Buick and zig-zagged up the highway toward him. She ran screaming, "He's going to kill me! He's going to kill me! He's already killed one man!"

Romer tried to calm the girl but she was hysterical.

He asked, "Where did he kill this man?"

Pointing back toward the Buick, she sobbed, "Right there!"

Romer glanced at the Buick and had just pulled his revolver when Caril screamed, "Take me to the police!"

"Take it easy, I'm a deputy sheriff," Romer replied. "What's your name?"

She choked, "Caril Fugate."

"Who's trying to kill you, Caril?"

In between huge sobs, she replied, "Charles Starkweather's going to kill me!"

Romer stiffened when he heard the name Starkweather. One of those men fighting had to be Starkweather!

He grabbed Caril by the arm and shouted, "Come on! Get in the car!" He dragged the girl over to the car, "Get in."

Caril got in and slid over next to Baldry. Romer turned his attention back to the struggle and watched as one of the men ran across the highway and jumped into the Packard. The other man ran over to the side of the road and jumped into the borrow pit. Romer turned his attention back to the one who got into the car. He watched as the man put the car in gear, and screeched down the highway, rubber burning up the pavement.

Romer reached down, grabbed the two-way and radioed Bill Morton, dispatcher for the Wyoming Highway Patrol in Casper.

"Bill, this is Deputy Romer. We got Charles Starkweather out here fifteen miles west of Douglas on Highway 20. He just killed someone and is heading east. I need a roadblock west of Douglas on 20 in a hurry! Do you read me, I mean we need that roadblock now!"

The radio crackled, "We read you, Bill. I'll call Douglas and let them know right away."

"Good, I will pursue. Over and out!"

Romer swung his car out from behind the milk truck and down one side of the ditch. As soon as he cleared the truck, he pulled up onto the concrete and took off after the fleeing murderer. He pursued the Packard for several miles to make sure Charlie didn't double back. Satisfied, he turned his car around and went back to the murder scene.

"This is Romer! Suspect is heading like a bat out of hell for Douglas! I made sure he didn't double back on me but I gotta go back to the scene. We got a dead man out here."

Caril sniffled, "I seen him kill ten people. He killed my mother, stepfather,

CHAPTER ELEVEN

stepsister, a boy and a girl, a farmhand and three other people. I was there and seen it all."

Romer glanced over at Baldry, "What happened?"

"My mom and Charlie were having an argument and she slapped him. Charlie hit her back and my stepfather saw him. Charlie killed him, my mom and stepsister. The baby was crying so Charlie took the barrel of his gun and pushed it in her throat."

Romer would remember what Caril said, and those words would become important in the month to come.

1:30 p.m.

10

Douglas Police Chief Robert Ainslie drove as fast as he could over to the sheriff's office and waited impatiently for Sheriff Earl Heflin to come out and get in his cruiser. Seconds later, Heflin emerged carrying a .30-.30 rifle. He finished inserting a cartridge in the Winchester as he hurried out to the car.

He got in the passenger side and asked, "What the hell's going on, Bob?"

Ainslie took a deep breath, "Bill Romer radioed the dispatcher in Casper and requested a roadblock west of Douglas. I guess he ran into a situation about fifteen miles west of here. I don't know what happened for sure, but he needs help. I tried to listen to the radio coming to pick you up, but there's too damn much yakking. All hell's breaking loose and I don't know why."

Ainslie sped out of Douglas and headed west on Highway 20. Heflin's heart pounded with excitement as he wondered what they would run into down the highway. About three miles out of town, he leaned over, grabbed the two way radio and tried to call Romer.

"Calling Deputy Romer, come in. Calling Deputy Romer, come in."

He waited a few minutes, then repeated the call.

Finally, a voice came on the radio. "This is Deputy Sheriff Romer from Natrona County. Is that you, Sheriff Heflin?"

"Yeah, what the blazes is going on? Who are we suppose to be after?"

Romer replied in a high pitched voice. "It's Starkweather, the murderer from Nebraska, and he's headed your way!"

Heflin shot a quick glance at Ainslie. "Okay, Bill, we'll take it from here. Good job."

Both officers scanned the highway for oncoming cars when Ainslie spotted a black Packard approaching rapidly from the west.

"That could be our man!" he shouted.

"I think you're right," Heflin confirmed as he watched the Packard roar down the highway. He squinted and tried to pick up the license plate but could only make out it was a Nebraska plate and the number 2.

"It's a Nebraska plate all right! That's got to be him! Let's go!"

When Charlie saw the cruiser turned around in the highway, he floored the gas pedal. By God, they would have to work hard if they were going to catch him!

Ainslie turned on the siren and flashing red light, whipped the car around and took off after the fleeing fugitive.

Both cars approached speeds in excess of 100 mph as they neared the Douglas city limits. Charlie had a lead but Ainslie gained ground when the fugitive was forced to slow down for traffic.

Charlie cursed when he was forced to stop behind a truck and two cars waiting for a red light at one of Douglas' main intersections. He glanced nervously at his rear view mirror, not sure what to do when the police car caught up to him. He tried to pull around the truck when Ainslie's fast-closing cruiser rammed the Packard from the side. There was a crunching sound as metal hit metal and the two vehicles locked bumpers.

"Shit!" Charlie yelled. He was in for it now! He thought about jumping out and blasting away but remembered that the .32 revolver sitting on the seat was empty and he had left the rifles back in the Buick. Heflin pulled his .38 caliber revolver and fired three quick shots at Charlie's car, one of the shots blasting a hole in Charlie's front windshield.

"You dirty, rotten sons of bitches!" Charlie screamed as he gunned the Packard. A terrible grinding sound rent the air as the bumper pulled away from the car's body. A moment later, Charlie was back on the open highway headed for Nebraska.

"Don't lose him!" Heflin yelled at Ainslie.

"I won't!" Ainslie shouted back at the sheriff.

He pushed the cruiser up to almost 120 mph, not wanting to get too far behind the fleeing fugitive. When they hit open country, Heflin leaned out his window and aimed the .30-.30 at Charlie's car. He fired and missed, ejected the shell and fired again, another miss. Steadying his arm as best he could, he squeezed off another round. The high velocity slug drilled a hole in the Packard's back window, sending a shower of sharp-edged glass into the front seat.

"Hell of a shot!" Ainslie yelled.

Charlie's car disappeared over a rise in the road, and seconds later both lawmen were surprised to see the Packard sitting in the middle of the highway, its brake lights on. They parked about a hundred yards away and watched anxiously as the driver's side door opened and a small figure emerged.

Instantly, Ainslie and Heflin climbed out of the cruiser, their guns drawn and ready. The lone figure straightened up and stood unmoving about ten yards from his car. Then, slowly and deliberately, Charlie moved back toward the Packard. It appeared to the lawmen that he was trying to get back into the car.

CHAPTER ELEVEN

Ainslie raised his revolver and squeezed off a round. Charlie stopped in his tracks as the slug whistled between him and the car.

"Raise your hands and get over here!" Ainslie shouted.

Charlie never moved.

Ainslie pointed his revolver at the ground in front of Charlie's feet and fired again. The bullet dug into the blacktop, yet Charlie still did not move a muscle.

"Lie down!" Ainslie yelled.

His finger tightened on the trigger when Charlie reached behind his back.

"What the hell's he doing, Earl?"

"I'm not sure, but don't shoot. I think he's tucking in his shirt. Jesus, this guy's something else!" Heflin replied.

Ainslie let up on the trigger but kept the revolver trained on the teenager's chest.

"How 'bout I put one right between his legs, Earl?"

Instead he lowered the revolver and fired once again into the blacktop. This time Charlie laid face down on the highway and stretched his arms out on the pavement.

Ainslie and Heflin cautiously approached the fugitive from two different angles. Heflin walked in behind the prone fugitive and checked him for weapons. Finding none, he handcuffed Charlie's hands behind his back.

Heflin helped Charlie to his feet and walked him over to Ainslie's cruiser. Charlie felt something warm running down the side of his neck, "I'm shot! You shot me!" he shouted.

Heflin quickly examined the whining teenager. "You're gonna be all right. It's just a cut for Christ's sake! And not a very big one at that. Probably happened when I shot the window. Don't worry about it!"

Charlie meekly nodded his head. Heflin helped him climb into the back seat.

While Ainslie turned around and started back toward Douglas, Heflin turned around and asked, "How come you stopped in the middle of the road?"

Charlie shrugged, "It didn't matter. I would have hit head on with somebody anyway."

It was silent for several minutes, then Charlie looked out the window and said quietly, "Don't be rough on the girl. She didn't have anything to do with it."

The eight-day murder spree was over.

CHAPTER TWELVE

Wednesday, January 29

1

Charlie sat back in his chair and looked around the small Wyoming county jail cell. Heflin and Ainslie had taken him directly to the Converse County jail, which was also the home of Sheriff Earle Heflin. He smelled bad, his shirt was torn and splattered with blood from the cut on his ear. It had not been a good day.

Charlie was glad he told the mass of reporters hanging around the jail to kiss off. He wasn't in the mood to talk to anyone but the two lawmen who captured him. He chuckled to himself when he remembered telling them they would not have caught him if he had not stopped. Not only that, but if he had had a gun he would have shot them both. It was his bad luck that all he had was a knife and an empty .32 revolver when they ran him down.

He turned his attention to the blank piece of paper on the table in front of him. He thought for several minutes, then scribbled:

> Dear Mom and Dad. i'm a way i hat to write This or maybe will not read it, but if you will i would like to have you read it, it would help me a lot.
> i'm sorry for what i did in a lot of ways caus i know i hurt everybody, and you and mom did all you could to rise me up right and you all ways help me when i got in bad with something But this time i would like you not to do any thing to help me out. i hope you will understand . . . it would make me happy if everybody well go on just like anything didn't happen. the cops up here have been more than nice to me but these dam reporters, the next one that comes in here is going to get a glass of water.
> But dad i'm not real sorry for what i did cause for the first time me and Caril have more fun, she help me a lot, but if she come back don't hate her she had not a thing to do with the Killing all we wanted to do is get out of town
>   tell every body to take care. Chuck.
> P.S. tell Bob VonBruck to thing of somebody besids him he help cause this.

Charlie put the pencil down and stared off into space. He was big news. In fact, he was national news. That's what he had wanted, so what the hell. Now he had to pay the piper for all the dancing. Well, that was okay too. He crawled onto the cot and eventually fell asleep. It had been a long nineteen years.

CHAPTER TWELVE

2

By now, residents of Lincoln as well as the entire state of Nebraska had heard about the capture and were greatly relieved. Lancaster County Sheriff Karnopp said, "I hate to think what might have happened after dark Wednesday if they hadn't been captured. People would have been shooting at anything that moved. There were a lot of armed men who had been drinking who were roaming around town."

Floyd Kalber of KMTV in Omaha devoted the majority of his ten o'clock report to Charlie's capture. Teletype machines flashed the following:

> Douglas, Wyo., Jan 29 (AP) Charles Starkweather, 19, runty Nebraska gunman sought in nine slayings was captured today in the Badlands near this Wyoming cowtown.

Another news flash read,

> The two teenagers were run to earth in rugged country where Old West gunmen often holed up.
> The girl was almost hysterical and ran fleeing to Deputy Sheriff Bill Romer crying out her fear Starkweather would kill her. She was in a state of shock shortly afterward.
> Romer said she screamed to him: "He's going to kill me. He's crazy. He just killed a man."

Lincoln Police Lieutenant Robert Henninger arrived in Douglas around 9:30 p.m. that night. He went to the jail and went to work trying to get Charlie's confession. An experienced interrogator, he was able to get a full statement within a short period of time. Charlie said he killed the Bartletts before Caril came home from school and then admitted killing everyone except Clara Ward and Lilian Fencl. It was a start.

Thursday, January 30

3

Late Thursday night, six Nebraska city and county officials flew to Douglas in an Air National Guard C-47. Among them were the Lancaster County Attorney and Lancaster County Sheriff Merle Karnopp. Charlie knew Sheriff Karnopp, having once lived across from the old Lancaster County jail where the Karnopps had lived for eighteen years. Starkweather knew the family and had gone to school with one of Karnopp's sons. Charlie was anxious to see Sheriff Karnopp, and as soon as he knew they were there, he asked to talk with him.

Charlie was ready to talk. He explained that he had wanted to be an outlaw ever since he was a child, but admitted he got a little out of control. He told the

JANUARY 30, 1958

officials about how the hatred had built up in him so bad that killing all those people was his way of being somebody. Besides that, what else could he do? Those people wanted to kill him, they wanted to stand in his way and not let him have what was his. He had to do something.

Scheele was non-sympathetic to the whining murderer. He bluntly told Charlie that he would do everything in his power to put him in the electric chair. Instead of becoming angry, Charlie took an immediate liking to the county attorney.

Both Charlie and Caril signed their extradition papers, clearing the way for them to be brought back to Lincoln for trial and punishment. Scheele took great pains to make sure both Charlie and Caril understood what they were signing. Caril, later in her trial, claimed she was not aware of what she was signing, but there was no doubt in Scheele's mind the fourteen-year-old was capable of understanding.

Charlie was unaware of Wyoming's Governor Milward Simpson's attitude toward capital punishment. Once news got out of Starkweather's capture, Simpson stated publicly his opposition to the death penalty and that he would commute a death sentence to a life sentence if given the chance. Simpson also understood the magnitude of the pair's crimes and was not opposed to sending them back across the state line for Nebraska justice.

It was reported the reason Charlie signed the extradition papers was because, as he said, "Wyoming uses the gas chamber and I don't like the smell of gas." Whether or not he would have elected to stay in Wyoming for trial knowing the Governor's feelings about capital punishment is something we can only speculate. Given Charlie's later actions and attitudes, I doubt he would have stayed in Wyoming. He welcomed the prospect of a major trial back in Lincoln, and then a rebellious death.

After the extradition papers were signed, Scheele decided they should get on their way back to Lincoln. Neither Charlie nor Caril felt like flying and because it was rumored Charlie would not have signed the papers if they couldn't drive, Scheele agreed.

The caravan consisted of four cars, with Charlie and Caril traveling in the two center ones. Although Caril was not handcuffed, Charlie wore leg shackles, handcuffs, and a leather transportation belt with a chain on it. They made it as far as Gering, Nebraska the first night. When they arrived at the Gering city jail, a mob of reporters and photographers were there waiting. They found out Charlie had admitted to Sheriff Karnopp that he killed Robert Colvert back in December, which created quite a sensation. If the Colvert murder had been solved and Charlie arrested, the whole murder spree would have been avoided and ten people would be alive. This concern about the Colvert case would have long-range repercussions.

CHAPTER TWELVE

Friday, January 31
10:15 a.m.

4

Charlie looked around to make sure no one was coming, then took a pencil stub from his shirt pocket and jumped up on the toilet. Standing on his tiptoes he wrote:

> Caril is the one who said to go to Washington State.
> by the time any body will read this i will be dead for all the killings THEN THEY CANNOT GIVE CARIL THE CHAIR TO.
> from Lincoln Nebraska they got us Jan 29, 1958.

He stopped for a minute. He heard someone coming. Charlie finished the rest of his message as fast as he could go.

> 1958 Kill 11 persons
> Charles kill   9) all men
> Caril kill   2) all girls
>   11
> They have so many cops and people watching us leave i can't add all of them of.

Charlie hurriedly drew a heart on the wall, put an arrow through it and wrote Charles Starkweather and Caril Fugate in the middle of it. He just finished when he heard someone coming into the cell block. It was Sheriff Karnopp.

"Come on, Charlie. It's time to go," the sheriff said as he handcuffed the teenager.

"Okay, okay. Hey, I gotta go to the bathroom," Charlie whined.

Karnopp replied, "Sure, go ahead."

Charlie looked puzzled. "Well, take off the handcuffs. I can't go with them on."

"You know I can't do that, Charlie."

"How come? I'll pee my pants."

"I can't help that,"

"All right then I just won't go."

Karnopp finished putting on the leg shackles and then the restraining belt. He ran a chain through the belt and guided Charlie out of the cell. They needed to get on the road.

Crowds gathered along the route as the caravan made its way back to Lincoln. People strained to get a glimpse of the man who had terrorized an entire state. Charlie didn't pay much attention but Caril appeared to enjoy the attention, waving and smiling at them as they rode through the towns along the way.

JANUARY 31, 1958

Finally, the law enforcement officials decided to get gas at state government facilities. Instead of eating in a public restaurant in Kearney, they decided to have a picnic lunch in an area outside of Kearney.

Once they reached Lincoln, Charlie was taken directly to the Nebraska State Penitentiary rather than to the city or county jail for security reasons. Caril was taken to the state hospital. They arrived at the west gate of the prison around 6:30 p.m. and were greeted by a crowd of newsmen, photographers and movie cameramen. Caril covered her head with a scarf and pretended to ignore everyone. Charlie, on the other hand, played the part of a young rebellious killer. He wore chains, his black motorcycle jacket, tight black denim pants, blue and white cowboy boots and had a cigarette hanging out of his mouth. He looked the part of his favorite movie actor—James Dean—but unlike playing a part in a movie, Charlie was going to be put on trial for his life.

5

Both Charlie and Caril were charged with two counts of first-degree murder for the death of Robert W. Jensen: murder with premeditation and murder while perpetrating a robbery. Nebraska law allowed both of them to be tried as adults and if found guilty, they could be sentenced to the electric chair.

Lancaster County Attorney Elmer Scheele picked the Jensen killing to try them for several reasons. First of all, Jensen's murder seemed the one that had the most shock value; in other words, the one that would jolt the jury's conscience the most. It was obvious Robert Jensen was the complete opposite of Charlie—a good, clean-cut boy who was violently murdered by a gun-crazed "hood" for $4.00 cash. He also felt after reading Charlie's and Caril's statements it was clear Jensen had been robbed prior to his murder. Caril had actively robbed Jensen and even held a gun on him so it seemed to be the most effective murder for the state to try.

Charlie and Caril's court-appointed lawyers entered pleas of not guilty before the trial. Forty-seven-year-old John McArthur represented Caril, and two other local attorneys, T. Clement Gaughan and William F. Matschullat, were picked to defend Charlie.

Gaughan wasn't pleased to be assigned the case because of Charlie's obvious guilt, but accepted in order to make sure Charlie's Constitutional rights were protected. He and Matschullat divided their duties: Matschullat was responsible for research and preparing court briefs, while Gaughan would present the case in court.

Charlie's plea was interesting. He told his attorneys he wanted to plead not guilty because he felt he killed everyone in "self-defense." Somehow in his tortured mind Charlie actually felt he murdered each person, including all the

CHAPTER TWELVE

women and one child, because they threatened him in some manner. On the other hand, Matschullat and Gaughan agreed Charlie's only chance was to plead not guilty by reason of insanity. This met with extreme opposition from Charlie, and his family as well. Just as Charlie had refused to take a lie detector test, he also refused to allow doctors to administer an electroencephalograph in order to test for brain damage.

As a result of the doctors deciding Charlie was suffering from a deranged and diseased mind, both attorneys decided to build his case around an insanity plea "whether Charlie liked it or not." From this point on, they got little support or help from Charlie's family. In fact, Charlie actually began to support the prosecution. It seemed that both the family and Charlie preferred him to die in the electric chair than to be judged insane.

The trial, *The State of Nebraska vs. Charles Raymond Starkweather,* began May 5, 1958. It took four days to select a jury and three days for County Attorney Scheele to present his case. Judge Harry Spencer presided over the trial held in the county office building in downtown Lincoln.

All County Attorney Elmer Scheele had to do in order to gain a first-degree murder conviction was prove (a) the murder had been committed, (b) the accused did it with premeditation or while committing a felony, and (c) he was sane.

Gaughan and Matschullat had a much tougher job. Courts used the McNaghten formula, created in 1843 in England by the House of Lords to determine whether or not an individual was insane. It asked these questions: Did the accused know the nature and quality of the act or acts with which he is charged? Did he know the act with which he is charged was wrong when he did it?

It is interesting to note that knowing the difference between right and wrong does not automatically mean a person can perform accordingly. A person could be insane and still be able to know the difference between the two—he was just out of control to the point he was unable to act on the knowledge. The only chance for the defense was to paint a picture of Charlie that showed he was overwhelmingly and completely insane regardless of the McNaghten formula.

This would prove to be a difficult task.

CHAPTER THIRTEEN

Thursday, May 8
3:45 p.m.

1

Tall and bespectacled, County Prosecutor Elmer Scheele cleared his voice and looked across the packed courtroom. Scheele had attended Lutheran parochial school, Lincoln High School, and the University of Nebraska. Graduating from law school in 1939, Scheele had the reputation of being a hard worker. He grew up working in his father's furnace shop for twenty-five cents an hour. He learned what it was like to work and it carried over to his adult life.

Two years after receiving his law degree, he joined the FBI and supervised a squad of as many as thirty agents who investigated criminal violations of federal law. He left the FBI and became Lancaster County Prosecutor, a post he had held for the last four years. This was the biggest case of his life, and he was ready. He stepped out into the middle of the courtroom and began his opening statement:

Scheele: The state intends to pursue a conviction of first-degree murder in this case. In order to do that, we will prove that a murder was committed, that Charles Starkweather did it, that he killed with premeditation, which, let me remind you, can be a matter of only a few minutes, and that the murder was done while committing a felony, in this case, robbery.

I will present evidence in this order: the place, the time, the cause of death, the autopsy report, and the introduction of photographs at the scene of the murder.

The state will prove that Robert Jensen was shot from behind six times with a .22 caliber rifle. That Charles Starkweather and Caril Fugate left Lincoln in mid-morning on January 27th, taking with them a .32 caliber revolver and a .410 gauge sawed-off shotgun. They stopped at Tate's Service Station south of Lincoln where they bought ammunition.

From Tate's, they drove to the August Meyer farm near Bennet but got stuck in a lane leading to his house. Both Charles Starkweather and Caril Fugate went to the house where they "acquired" a .22 caliber rifle and then walked to a nearby storm cellar.

Eventually, they went back to their car whereupon a passing farmer pulled them out. They drove back to Tate's station in order to obtain state road maps and more ammunition. They left once again for the Meyer farm where they hoped to spend the night. But their car got stuck once again so they began

CHAPTER THIRTEEN

walking down the road. Robert Jensen and Carol King came upon the killers and asked if they needed help.

Starkweather ordered Jensen to drive to Lincoln, then changed his mind and told him to return to the abandoned school cellar near the August Meyer farm.

Starkweather and Caril Ann Fugate sat in the back seat with Charlie holding the .22 rifle and Caril the .410 shotgun on the frightened couple. While riding in the car, Jensen took his billfold as requested and handed it to Caril Fugate who removed $4.00 and put it into Charlie's wallet.

At the school ruins, Starkweather ordered Jensen to go down into the storm cellar, shooting him at this time. Then he shot the King girl. The case is as simple as that.

During this proceeding, I will read the statement Charles Starkweather made in which he admits the killing.

In closing, members of the jury, let me remind you that Charles Starkweather is presumed sane, but if evidence of insanity is made by the defense, it will be the duty of the state to prove that Starkweather is indeed sane, and liable for these despicable acts of extreme violence. I can assure you that we will do exactly that if needed.

Gaughan: We do not deny that Starkweather killed Jensen, but the defense is insanity, and we will try to show why he killed. Starkweather is an odd young man whose I.Q. has always been sub-normal. At one time a test showed him to be only a grade or two above an idiot. He didn't have things other boys had and was forced to scrounge for whatever he could. Charlie was held back in the third grade and did worse the second year than the first. Finally, he was promoted only because he was getting too big for the other boys in the class.

Charlie was never able to adjust for his deficiencies; instead, things got worse. He suffered several severe blows on the head over the years that affected him tremendously. He has had severe headaches which have made a significant impact on his behavior.

Charlie has not cooperated with us, and even in life and death circumstances, he did not have reasonable responses. He has experienced delusions and will testify that he killed everyone in "self-defense."

But that is Charles Starkweather's story. The defense is insanity.

Friday, May 9
9:00 a.m.

2

Scheele used the first day of testimony to show the jury the crime and its effect on the families. He started by calling the father of the murdered

Robert W. Jensen. With tears in his eyes, Robert Jensen Sr. testified about the evening of January 27 when he last saw his seventeen-year-old son alive. He answered questions regarding his residence, his business, and the members of his family. He talked about his son's slow recovery from a 1951 attack of polio and how it affected his life. He told how his son was a kind, considerate boy who was six feet in height and weighed about 240 pounds. Several times during his 25 minutes on the witness stand he paused to wipe tears from his eyes.

Scheele asked Jensen about the day of January 27. He told about Robert's working after school, the discussion about needing new tires for his car, and Robert leaving to run an errand for his father. And how he planned to see Carol King.

Scheele: Now what happened later that night, so far as Robert is concerned? Did he return home?

Jensen: No, he did not.

Scheele: Just tell the jury in your own words generally what happened that night at your home insofar as Robert was concerned.

Jensen: When they didn't return by 9:30, why, it was a school night and we began to wonder if they weren't watching the movie on TV or something of that nature. You can see the King home from our house. We looked that way, but you can't tell if there is a car parked in the driveway or not, and they usually parked right alongside of the house. We looked at the TV schedule a time or two and wondered about it, but we didn't go over there or anything until approximately midnight. I walked out to the street and tried to find a place where I could have a better view, and a car backed from the King family driveway, and I thought it was probably him coming home; but it was Warren King.

Scheele: Who is Warren King, Mr. Jensen?

Jensen: That is Carol's brother.

Scheele: All right, go ahead.

Jensen: They had become worried, and he was coming over to my place to see if the car was parked in my driveway. I stopped him and we discussed it, and we started looking for the car around there. We could not understand why they hadn't returned home. We looked at all homes and places where they might be and drove the roads around there, and one thing and another, until approximately two o'clock. Then we called the Highway Safety Patrol.

Scheele: And reported the couple missing?

Jensen: Yes, we did.

Scheele: Now, when was Robert's funeral held, Mr. Jensen?

Jensen: The following Friday afternoon.

Scheele: There in Bennet?

Jensen: Yes, sir.

Scheele: At the family church.

Jensen: Yes, sir.

CHAPTER THIRTEEN

Scheele: And you viewed the body?
Jensen: Yes, sir.

Jensen identified a photo of his son, his son's watch, school jacket, billfold, car seat cushion, photos of his son's car, and a blanket kept in the car. Scheele turned all these items in as state's evidence, then he began to call a long list of prosecution witnesses.

Warren King followed Mr. Jensen on the witness stand. King spent most of the time talking about his sister—how she was a member of the church, a member of the school band and assistant cheerleader. He confirmed that Carol left with the Jensen boy about 7:45 p.m. for what was to be a short ride. He also told about his and Mr. Jensen's unsuccessful search for the couple.

L. W. Weaver, Lancaster County Engineer, testified as to the location of the Jensen-King murders near Bennet. Using diagrams of the murder site, he described the area surrounding the August Meyer farm.

State Trooper Winston Flower, who took the pictures of the Jensen-King bodies, also testified about the photographs he took at the murder scene. After Flower finished, Scheele introduced the first photograph. Exhibit 13 was a photograph of the entrance to the storm cellar, seen from a distance. Exhibit 14 was closer and Exhibit 15 was closer yet. Blood stains were visible on the interior brick walls and the rounded concrete at the top.

The eight women and four men jurors examined the pictures silently and swiftly, showing little emotion until they saw Exhibit 16. This was a picture of the brutally murdered Carol King. Her face could not be seen but her bare breasts and abdomen were clearly visible. Her blue jeans were pulled down to her ankles and her bare buttocks were blood-stained. The jurors gasped with horror as the picture was passed around.

Exhibit 17 was a picture of Robert Jensen's body after King's body had been removed. His body was fully clothed and he lay face down. A large pool of blood stretched more than two feet from his head, and there was a large stain of blood on his left leg which had been left by King's bleeding body.

Ernest Hunt, owner of a Bennet gas station, and Dennis Nelson, his employee, testified that Jensen came into the station about 7:00 p.m. to discuss getting some recapped tires and left about 7:30 p.m.

Merle Boldt testified how he and Ivan Baker, while searching for the missing teenagers, came upon the Starkweather car stuck in a lane leading to the Meyer farm and then notified the Highway Patrol.

Homer Tate, operator of Tate's Service Station, testified how Charlie and Caril Fugate came into his station shortly after noon on January 27. According to Tate, they bought gas and several boxes of ammunition. He said Starkweather asked about purchasing some .32 caliber shells for a pistol, but was told they had none. After having a tire fixed, which took about 20 minutes, Charlie and Caril left. Tate didn't feel they acted "suspiciously."

Marvin Krueger of Roca, attendant at Tate's, told how at 5:30 p.m. that same day Charlie and Caril returned to the station to buy more gas and another box of shells. Krueger testified that he saw a rifle and shotgun lying across Caril's lap, and becoming suspicious, took down their license number which he called in to the sheriff's office.

Howard Genuchi of rural Bennet told of pulling Starkweather's car out of the mud about 4:00 p.m. and refusing to accept the two dollars Starkweather offered him for payment. He said a girl with Starkweather steered the car, while Charlie pushed.

Highway maintenance worker Leo Schwenke testified that he found three of Jensen's school books along Highway 2 about two miles west of Cheney on January 28.

State Patrolman Vernon O'Neale told of Schwenke bringing him the books and also of being notified that Starkweather's car might be stuck on the Meyer farm near Bennet. He checked and found it was Charlie's car and called for assistance. O'Neale also testified he found several .22 rifle shells and a blanket identified as belonging to Jensen in the vicinity of the storm cellar.

Bennet farmer Everett Broening told the court how he decided to go to the site of the razed school house January 28 after hearing a car drive by at a high rate of speed around 10:30 p.m. the night before. He removed the rubbish-covered wooden door from the cave, looked in and saw Miss King's body and Robert Jensen's feet. He immediately summoned the authorities who were investigating the murder of August Meyer at Meyer's farm.

Lincoln pathologist Dr. Erwin Zeman was the last witness to testify that afternoon. A veteran of over two thousand autopsies, he said County Attorney Elmer Scheele asked him January 28 to do an autopsy at St. Elizabeth Hospital on a young gunshot victim named Robert Jensen. It was about 10:30 p.m. He performed the autopsy with Scheele, Deputy County Attorney Dale Farnbruch, Paul Douglas and William Johnson of the sheriff's office present.

Zeman testified the cause of Jensen's death was multiple gunshot wounds to the head producing tears and lacerations to the brain and the large vessels from a massive explosive type of force. The wounds were on the right side of the head: three behind the ear, two in the center of the ear and one in front of the ear.

He also said there were minor bruises on his hand and thigh, apparently from falling down the cellar steps after being shot in the head.

CHAPTER THIRTEEN

Monday, May 12

3

Scheele began linking the murders to Charlie by introducing witness after witness who gave testimony dealing with the murder weapons. Robert Zimmer, a ballistics expert from Washington, D.C., testified the .22 rifle sent him for examination was the weapon from which several shots had been fired. The rifle had been recovered in Wyoming, and the bullets were ones recovered from Robert Jensen's body.

Harold Smith, formerly of the Nebraska Highway Patrol, told of searching for and finding several .22 shell casings similar to the ones found in the Meyer rifle near the storm cellar.

Deputy Sheriff Robert Anderson said he found no money in Robert Jensen's wallet the night the autopsy was performed, but at a later time he found a $1.00 bill in what appeared to be a secret compartment. Defense Attorney Gaughan asked if it wasn't a matter of opinion that the compartment was secret. Anderson replied that he had not found it in his earlier search and it appeared to be hidden in the wallet. Earlier testimony had shown Jensen left home with $5.00 and that he was robbed in his car when he picked Charlie and Caril up in the Bennet area.

Louis Meyer, brother of the murdered August Meyer, identified the pump .22 rifle recovered by Deputy Sheriff Bill Romer in Wyoming as having belonged to his deceased brother.

Deputy Sheriff William Johnson testified he found the license plate belonging to the Starkweather vehicle near the abandoned storm cellar where the bodies of Jensen and King were found.

Elmer Shamburg, a free-lance court reporter from Lincoln who took down Charlie's statements, said that they were given freely and voluntarily and without the use of any threats or promises from Charlie at the Nebraska State Penitentiary.

Lancaster County Sheriff Merle Karnopp related how he found Jensen's broken wrist watch in the storm cellar east of Bennet where he was fatally shot. The time on the watch stopped because it was smashed and not because it had run down.

Then the two Wyoming lawmen, William Romer and Earl Heflin, testified. Heflin told how he and Douglas Police Chief Robert Ainslie chased Starkweather at speeds up to 120 mph and finally took him into custody about 3½ miles east of Douglas on January 29. Heflin said Starkweather suddenly stopped in the middle of the road and got out after Heflin had been firing at him with a .38 pistol and a .30-.30 rifle.

May 12, 1958

Gaughan asked Heflin if at any time Starkweather seemed to realize the enormity of the acts he was alleged to have committed. Heflin answered no, he did not, but reversed himself upon further questioning by Scheele. He said Starkweather did seem to realize what he had done. Heflin said Starkweather showed no remorse, but he did not think that unusual for a killer.

While Scheele had Lincoln Assistant Police Chief Eugene Masters on the stand, defense attorney Gaughan pulled the surprise of the trial by introducing two letters into evidence which purported to link Caril Fugate to the murders of her family.

One of the letters was found on Charlie after his capture January 29 near Douglas. Supposedly written by both Charlie and Caril, it stated that after Charlie shot Marion Bartlett, Mrs. Bartlett knocked the rifle out of his hand, but Caril picked up the gun and kept her mother from coming at Charlie. It also said that Caril hit her stepsister with the gun about ten times.

Caril's defense lawyer, John McArthur commented, "I won't believe it until she tells me . . . she's never even suggested such a thing." It was obvious to the press he doubted the truth of the letter.

Charlie also claimed in a statement scrawled on the wall of the Gering jail January 30 that Caril killed all the women who died in the murder spree. His total of nine men victims and two women was faulty, as five of the victims were women.

The afternoon session became even more confused with the introduction of a second letter, this one written by Charlie to his parents while in Wyoming. In it Charlie claimed, "Caril had not a thing to do with the killing" but he did state that she "helped a lot."

By introducing the letters, defense attorneys Gaughan and Matschullat were hoping to show how Starkweather suffered from "delusions" and thus was legally insane. Charlie at first had claimed after his capture that Caril was his hostage, but later changed his story to say she was his accomplice.

Scheele did not object to the letter being introduced, and when Masters stepped down, he called his next witness: Deputy Sheriff William Romer. Romer testified that Caril ran crying to his car saying Starkweather "had just killed a man." He radioed ahead for a road block to halt Starkweather, who had driven off at high speed. He also told of recovering a .22 rifle used to kill Jensen.

Scheele ended the afternoon session by indicating that on Tuesday morning he would offer as evidence those parts of a five-volume statement taken from Starkweather February 1, and also parts of one taken February 27, which dealt with the Robert Jensen murder.

CHAPTER THIRTEEN

Tuesday, May 13

4

County Attorney Elmer Scheele completed the state's case by reading from the two main confessions Charlie had made to Assistant County Attorney Dale Farnbruch and to Scheele. He read slowly, skipping the parts that did not deal with the Jensen murder.

Scheele: Where did you go?

Starkweather: Well, we grabbed the guns and a knife and left.

Scheele: Now who was that man that asked you if he could help you?

Starkweather: It was that kid, I don't know his name.

Scheele: Can you describe him to me?

Starkweather: He was tall and big and wore glasses.

Scheele: Did he go back to the old schoolhouse grounds?

Starkweather: Yes.

Scheele: And what happened there?

Starkweather: Why, I told him to—to walk to the—to that hole there. I was going to put that lid on and then cover it up. I was going to cover it up with that timber of that schoolhouse, you know, that—and we got to the schoolhouse and I told him to go down in there.

Scheele: And what weapon did you have in your possession at that time?

Starkweather: The twenty-two caliber.

Scheele: Did Caril have any weapon?

Starkweather: Yes; she was watching him with a four-ten.

Scheele: Did Caril have the four-ten in her hands at all times that you were in the car with this young boy and young girl?

Starkweather: Yes.

Scheele: So then you got out of the car and Caril got out of the car?

Starkweather: No; Caril stayed in the car.

Scheele: And you and the boy and the girl got out of the car and Caril stayed in the car?

Starkweather: When I came back she was in the front seat.

Scheele: And where did you go when you got out of the car?

Starkweather: We walked up to the hole.

Scheele: What did you do when you got there?

Starkweather: Why, I told him to go down in there.

Scheele: What did he do?

Starkweather: Well, he started down in.

Scheele: And what happened then?

Starkweather: Well, I don't know, but he—

Scheele: Where was the girl with him?
Starkweather: She was just about ready to go down.
Scheele: She was starting down into the cave cellar too?
Starkweather: Yes; he came a-flying up, he said something, I don't know what he said.
Scheele: And what happened then?
Starkweather: Well, he pushed her out of the way and started to come toward me, and I shot him.
Scheele: What happened when you shot him?
Starkweather: He fell, turned around a couple of times, and fell back down in there . . . Then she started screaming, and I shot her . . . I pushed her on down; she was just about—well, she wasn't even at the bottom of the steps when I left her, I just pushed her right down the well out of sight of the top steps and put the door over and left.
Scheele: Where was Caril when this shooting went on?
Starkweather: Well, I don't know whether she was outside or inside the car.

It was almost 3:00 p.m. when Scheele closed the last three-ring spiral notebook, took his glasses off and said, "The State rests."

Wednesday, May 14
1:30 a.m.

5

Wednesday afternoon the defense began presenting their case. Defense witnesses whom Gaughan called to the stand were Dr. Leonard Fitch and Dr. J. E. Burress, optometrists; John Hedge, western Newspaper Union manager; and three of his employees, Francis Grantski, Donald Gillham and Warren Von Essen.

It did not take long for Drs. Fitch and Burress to testify they once fitted Charlie for glasses. This was important to the defense from the aspect of showing how his poor eyesight hindered his early childhood development, which in turn had an adverse affect on Charlie's life. Charlie did not receive his first pair of glasses until he was sixteen years old.

John Hedge said that Charlie was the "dumbest man who ever worked for me," and that he felt sorry for him because he was so slow. Charlie's face turned red and it was obvious he was visibly angered at his ex-boss's testimony.

Gillham and Von Essen stated that Charlie was struck on the head late at work one Friday afternoon, but the youth returned to work the following morning. It seemed that the handle of a paper baler, a length of two-by-four, slipped and hit Charlie in the side of the head.

CHAPTER THIRTEEN

They also said they jokingly asked Charlie what he did "with all that money" following the robbery December 1 at the Crest Service Station. They had no idea at the time that Starkweather was involved in the slaying of Robert Colvert, station attendant.

Others who testified were Mrs. Harvey Griggs, Rodney Starkweather's mother-in-law; and Mrs. Elsie Neal, Charlie's half-aunt. Mrs. Neal testified that Charlie seemed unhappy when he came to her home January 24 and said he had an argument with Mrs. Bartlett. She also admitted that Charlie's father told her not to tell the youth's attorneys that Charles had been having headaches.

Gaughan entered into evidence the confused but graphic confession Charlie made in Wyoming. It was the first account of the Bartlett and Ward killings made in the courtroom and caused quite a stir in the spectators section. In this statement, Starkweather said he stabbed Mrs. Ward with a knife, tied the maid to the bed, and shot Mr. Ward when he came home that evening.

Starkweather also talked about the Bartlett slayings, but differed in one way from a confession he wrote at the Ward home. In that statement, Charlie said he shot both Mr. and Mrs. Bartlett and hit their baby daughter, Betty Jean, following an argument over Caril. In the statement made in Wyoming, he said Caril hit the child about ten times.

Gaughan then read the full text of Charlie's handwritten 7-page statement. Charlie said the following about the Ward killings:

> that night we stay in the car it was cold but we nake I said we was going to have to stay somewhere that day cause of the car we had.
>
> we drove all over thinking what house would be the best place to stay show about 8:30 in the morning & pick out the one on 24th there was two person there they about had a drop dead when i said we was going to spend the day there.
>
> they said they would be nice and nothing would happen like calling the cops. they were until about 2:00 that after noon the one lady was up stairs and was there about 20 nin i went on up to see her she niss ne about ½" with a .22 cal. gun she just look at ne and back up and begen to run all i had was that knife so it go at her it stop right in her back.
>
> the naid was there i tie her up and left her laying on the beb the dog was there so i had to hit hin to keep hin from barking.
>
> About 6:30 or 7:00 that night the nan cane home i told hin not to nove but he did anyway we was by the basement steps we got into a fight he got the gun fron ne show i push hin doun the basenent steps.
>
> the gun landed on the foor and went off he got and start for it but i frist he pick out iron and i said if i had to c'll kill hin show he lay it back doun i said for hin to walk back up the stairs we was to tie hin up and leave toun.
>
> he start to walk up the stairs he got ½ way and begin to run i shot hin in the back one's the he stop i told hin the next time would be it he got to the top of the stairs and ran for the front door he had it ½ open when i shot hin.

he was laying there naking funny noise i told caril to get a blanket and cover hin up.

we got some food from there and left—last night heading for Washington state we got as far as here when we heard about the fine the bodys of the 3 persons, but weh i lef there was only 1 dead person in that house.

After Gaughan read the confession, Judge Spencer recessed the court until after lunch. When they came back, the afternoon session was dominated by more of Charlie's relatives acting as character witnesses. Everyone said Charlie was a nice boy, and no one could understand how a thing like this could happen.

The last person to testify that afternoon was Dr. Julius Humann, director of guidance for the Lincoln Public Schools, who gave information about Charlie's school records and I.Q. tests.

Thursday, May 15
9:00 a.m.

6

Bob Von Busch, Caril Fugate's brother-in-law, was the first witness the next morning. Bob and Charlie had known each other for over five years, spending a lot of their free time together until Bob married Caril's sister. A lot of his testimony dealt with what he knew about Charlie's home life. He told how Charlie gave money to Guy Starkweather (Charlie's dad) to help pay for staying at home. He told how after Charlie started seeing Caril, Guy Starkweather complained that he was spending too much money on her. And how after that happened, Charlie put his fist through a car window.

Bob then brought up the problems Charlie and his dad had over the family car. Bob said that Guy told Charlie if he let Caril drive the car, he didn't need to come back. After that conversation, Charlie moved out of his parents' home and into Bob and Barbara's apartment on North 10th. He stayed there for about a week until an apartment opened up in the same tenement building.

Charlie's mother, Helen Starkweather, was sworn in next. She admitted she was not happy with how Gaughan and Matschullat were handling her son's case. She felt strongly that it was Caril Fugate who caused her son to have his problems.

Gaughan: You don't feel there is anything mentally wrong with Charlie, is that right?

Mrs. Starkweather: Not at the present time.

Gaughan: Mrs. Starkweather, in order to be fair with you and in order to be fair with everybody else, is there anything, while you are sitting on that witness chair, that you can think of that you want to tell the jury?

CHAPTER THIRTEEN

Mrs. Starkweather: Yes, sir . . . it was right after Charles started going with Miss Fugate. Before that, he was the best of friends with his brother. They were together constantly, no arguing or anything. But soon after he started going with Caril, it seemed like his family was pushed behind and his whole life centered around her. That's the way it seemed to me. He wanted to be with her. She seemed to have a hold on him.

Gaughan: You think he was a different boy after that?

Mrs. Starkweather: Yes, sir.

Gaughan: Of course, that was also about the time he got hit on the head with this baler handle, wasn't it, Mrs. Starkweather?

Mrs. Starkweather: I think he started going with her just before that, yes.

Mrs. Starkweather's main concern was that the family did not agree with the insanity plea. She said her son had headaches but she knew of no delusions. At one point she said she raised seven children—six problems and one catastrophe.

Gaughan called Charlie to the stand. His voice was soft and said he didn't need his glasses.

Gaughan: What did you do with the money you earned?

Starkweather: Spend it.

G. What was your first school?

S. Saratoga.

G. Did you have any fights with the other kids?

S. The second day I was there.

G. Did you have any other trouble while you were there?

S. Couldn't see the blackboard half the time.

G. You don't trust people do you Charlie?

S. Myself.

G. You trust me now a little, don't you?

S. No.

G. You're naturally suspicious, aren't you?

S. Yeah.

G. You don't like people, do you Charlie?

S. A little bit.

Gaughan changed the line of questioning and asked Charlie about when he hit his head while working at Western Paper Company.

G. Did your head still hurt the next morning?

S. I got drunk that night and it hurt worse.

G. What did you do that night?

S. I got pretty well pickled, I don't remember what happened.

G. Do you still have headaches?

S. Yeah.

G. How often do you have them?

S. Once in while.
G. How often? Once a day, once a week, once a month?
S. Every other day, sometimes.
G. Are they bad headaches?
S. Some of them.
G. Did you tell your mother and father about them?
S. No.
G. Why?
S. I didn't tell'em.
G. Did you yell at people on the street while driving in the garbage truck?
S. I'd yell at some old guy and tell him how to drive.
G. Why did you kill, Charlie?
S. In self-defense, the ones I killed.
G. Do you feel any remorse for the people you killed?
S. I won't answer that.
G. Why were you mad at Caril Fugate at the cave?
S. For what she did.
G. What did she do?
S. Shot Carol King.
G. Do you feel any remorse for the people you killed?
S. I won't answer that.

The press perked up when Charlie testified Caril shot Carol King. Up to this point, Charlie had hinted Caril was an accomplice, but never had he actually stated she killed anyone.

Charlie smiled and seemed to visibly relax when Elmer Scheele got up to cross-examine him. He regarded the prosecuting attorney as a friend and welcomed his questions.

Scheele: Now, the reason you told me to begin with that you shot Carol King was because you were trying to protect Caril Fugate, is that right?
Starkweather: Yes, sir.
Scheele: That's all.

Charlie smiled while being excused from the stand.

It was late in the morning session when Gaughan stood up and read a letter dated April 9 that Charlie had sent to County Attorney Elmer Scheele. Charlie admitted the letter contradicted several earlier statements he gave the authorities, but said the details were the truth.

Gaughan read:

> i will not claime in this letter to you, on the nurder of Miss King why i'm telling what happened and who shot her. this will tell the truth and the part in what Caril fugate did. but i will be convicted for what i did and thats o.k., but i'll be dan if i want to be sentenced for something i did not do!
>
> this is how is happened when i shot Bob he drop on the steps and landed on

CHAPTER THIRTEEN

the floor, the girl did not run, i said for her to stay where she was, and i gone on in the cave, he was noveing, so i went up out of the cave, the girl was right where i left her. i went to the car caril f was standing in front of the car, but this time she was in the front seat with the 4:10 out the window with the gun pointing to the king girl. i fill the 22 and got a flash light and went back to the cave, while i was down there i got scared and ran back up and told the King girl to go down i think she was shock cause i had to take her by the arn to get her started. id din't wake for her to get in the cave, i ran to the i was so dan scared i drove off the road. it's in the statement what happen then, to when i begin agin."

we walk up to the cave and told her to come on out, she come out slow so caril pull her up alnost off her feet, i gave the 22 to caril f and said to keep a eye on her, i went on back to the car, i was jacking the car body up to get broads under the wheel, i heard a shot and ran back to the cave, the King girl was right where i left her befor when caril was there. Caril said that the King girl was running and shot her. Caril went into the cave. "the rest is in the statement i gave" we go to the car out about a 1½ hr's later we walk back to the cave and i put the door on the opening and a frane of a window, caril put some broads on it. 2 long ones and sone little one's "when King and bob was in the car heading for the cave Caril f. ask me "if, i already ask the boy for his money yet" in then words "i said no, show then i ask him for it. the nan that got killed in Wyoming. he was asleep when i got there, the door was lock so i yell at hin and he got up. we talk about taking his car so i yell at hin and he got up. we talk about taking his car and he said "no" show i shot two times into the window and then said OK. he started the motor, to let the window down, then he unlock the door and open it then somehow he got hole of the gun and were fighting right in the front seat of the car, i believe i shot hin 2 or 3 tines befor the gun stop work "jamb on me" i call caril to get the orther gun when i looked out the window she was standing behind the car already with the orther 22, i put ny gun from the nans and ran round to the front of his car, when i got to the orther side, (after i shot hin he had a hell of lot of fight left in him) cail ran round the back of his car and began shoting him, "he was yelling something to her while she was shoting away there about having a wife and some kids, and caril said that to back" i didn't the rest of what she said to hin, she was calling hin about every nane below gods sun while shoting him. then she got nad about the blood on the sewat and wasn't going to seat there." there's a lot more i could say but i'n running out of paper." i wish now i told this in my first statement. caril fugate was the trigger-happy person i every seen.

That afternoon, Gaughan offered into evidence—in their entirety—Starkweather's confessions as given to Scheele and Farnbruch. Scheele objected since much of the material did not deal with the Jensen murder, but Judge Spencer overruled his motion.

Gaughan began reading and soon everyone's attention began to wander. William Matschullat leaned over and shook Charlie who had fallen asleep. Gaughan was still reading when it came time to adjourn.

Friday, May 16
9:00 a.m.

7

Gaughan began the morning session where he left off the day before, reading Charlie's confessions. After an hour or so, and to everyone's relief, he stopped and called Guy Starkweather to the stand. Charlie's dad was a colorful character, always good for a quote, so they were anxious to hear his testimony.

Gaughan: Do you think your son is crazy, Mr. Starkweather?
Starkweather: He never done nothing to act crazy to me.
G: You think Charles knows the difference between right and wrong, do you, Mr. Starkweather?
S: He knew the difference between right and wrong when he was living with me; yes, sir.
G: Do you think he has the ability or the—do you think he has the ability to exercise the knowledge of the difference between right and wrong?
S: I know Charles is rather good mechanically, yes.
G: You didn't get the question . . . I think the question I asked you was if you thought Charlie exercised the knowledge that he had of differences between right and wrong in these incidents that he is alleged to have committed.
S: No. No, I don't.
G: You don't think he used that knowledge?
S: I don't think he used good judgment, no.
G: I believe that's all, Mr. Starkweather.

Judge Spencer asked if the defense had any more for that day. Gaughan replied the only thing left was the psychiatric testimony, and he did not plan to present anyone until after the weekend. Spencer nodded and adjourned the court until Monday morning.

Monday, May 19
9:00 a.m.

8

Gaughan and Matschullat were forced to go outside of Lincoln in order to find a psychiatrist willing to testify on Charlie's behalf. They found a respected clinical psychiatrist, Dr. Nathan Greenbaum of the Menorah Medical Center in Kansas City who agreed to test Charlie and testify in court as to what he found.

CHAPTER THIRTEEN

Gaughan: Now, have you determined any findings or did you come to any conclusions as a result of your determination as it has to do with the person of Charles Starkweather?

Greenbaum: My conclusions, based on my observations and examinations, leads me to the opinion that Charles Starkweather is suffering from a severe mental disease or illness of such a kind as to influence his acts and has prevented him from using the knowledge of right and wrong at the time of commission of such an act.

Gaughan: Doctor, what if anything did you find concerning the mind of the defendant here, Charles Starkweather, as a result of your examination?

Greenbaum: A number of important facts were found. One of the very important things which I found was that he is suffering from a severe warping of the emotional faculties; that is, he is unable to experience feelings that other people do. People don't mean anything to him. They are no more than a stick or a piece of wood to this boy. And this is one of the symptoms of a very serious disease of the mind. He has grown apart and isolated from other people, as if he has never become a member of society, as if he has never become domesticated by society.

Gaughan: Would you say, Doctor, that is something that has been with him for a long time?

Greenbaum: Yes, sir.

Gaughan: Doctor, have you found or come to any other conclusions concerning the causes, or things you might have found in your diagnosis, which Charles Starkweather is suffering from at this time or which he has at this time?

Greenbaum: Yes. Another important factor which we have found is that he lacks the capacity for control which is part of normal people. In the case of the defendant, there is a short-circuiting of the process that makes us stop before we commit certain acts; the moment the impulse comes upon him he acts immediately. He is unable to stop.

Gaughan: Do you feel, Doctor, that if you had examined this boy six months ago, before he committed any crime, that you could have predicted the very thing that would happen, did happen?

Greenbaum: Without any questions. I could not have predicted specific details. I would have said something like this: "This boy is dangerously sick and is capable of committing dangerous and violent acts."

Gaughan: Doctor, do you have an opinion based upon your findings that the defendant killed Robert Jensen on January 28, 1958 near Bennet, Nebraska—do you have an opinion as to whether this defendant was mentally capable of deliberating and premeditating the act he committed?

Greenbaum: I have an opinion. And I believe he was not. Charles Starkweather was completely detached from people, and he does not have the ability most people have to control anger—that the moment he had an impulse, he acted on it. He is dangerously sick and needs to be put under maximum security because he is dangerous. He tends to perceive things in a somewhat distorted way. He will pick out things which are not important because of his particular way of looking at things. The act of killing meant to him no more than stepping on a bug. You can take a creature out of a jungle and tame him and maybe develop a surface crust of being domesticated . . . but . . . the crust is only on the surface, and it can break through under much less provocation than a creature who is thoroughly domesticated and has always been. It is further true that when such a creature tastes blood it breaks through and a wild rampage occurs in which a primitive impulse comes back.

Prosecuting attorney Scheele stood up and cross-examined the psychiatrist.

Scheele: Doctor, did Charles Starkweather, on January 27, 1958 possess mental capacity to ask the driver of an automobile in which he was riding, while he was armed with a .22 caliber pump rifle and sitting in the back seat of the automobile, "I asked him if he had a billfold, if he had any money?"

Greenbaum: And the question?

Scheele: Did he have sufficient mental capacity to do that?

Greenbaum: I believe so.

Scheele: And understand the nature and purpose of that act?

Greenbaum: Theoretically.

Scheele: Did he possess enough mental capacity on that date to purchase .22 caliber rifle bullets for a .22 rifle?

Greenbaum: Could have.

Scheele: Did he in your opinion?

Greenbaum: It was possible that he did, yes.

Scheele: And to buy gasoline for his vehicle?

Greenbaum: Yes.

Scheele: And to know the use for which road maps are intended and distributed?

Greenbaum: Yes.

Scheele: And to know that if you pull the trigger of a loaded firearm a bullet will come out?

Greenbaum: Yes.

Scheele: And to know if that the bullet strikes a human being in a vital spot, the effect the bullet will have on the person?

Greenbaum: Yes.

Scheele attempted to get Greenbaum to define Charlie's mental illness. Was it paranoia or schizophrenia? But, Greenbaum refused to define his illness. Gaughan redirected in order to clarify this point.

Gaughan: Now, Doctor, you told Mr. Scheele that you would not categorize, that you would not diagnose this case in single terms. Now, Mr. Scheele has made considerable out of that, and I would like to have you explain to the jury

CHAPTER THIRTEEN

why you would not do that.

Greenbaum: We could call it ABC disease or XYZ disease. There is no single word at this time that describes every manifestation of this disease. Giving a name to it would not make it disappear. I would like to use an illustration. Say I have a bookcase that is full of books and you want to organize them or categorize them. Now, you can do it in different ways. You can say you're going to put all the tall books together, or all the short books together, and all the medium-size books together. That would be one way, but it still wouldn't tell you much about what the books are like. Or you could put the blue books together, the black books, the red books, the thin books, the thick books, and history here, language there, and so on. If you're interested in any one book, you still have to look in that one. While it helped you in one way to sort it out, it still doesn't tell you anything about the individual.

After Greenbaum finished testifying, the court recessed for lunch.

Monday, May 19
2:00 p.m.

9

Dr. John O'Hearne, another psychiatrist from Kansas City, testified next.

Gaughan: I wonder if you would tell the jury generally what the result of your findings and conclusions are?

O'Hearne: The result of the physical and neurological examination, a special examination of his nervous system, disclosed a short, stocky young fellow with breasts somewhat large but muscularly developed, with tenderness in the spot where we usually expect it to be if a peptic ulcer is present, with a hole in his left eardrum, which apparently has been there quite a long time, with decreased deep tendon reflexes—the one where the doctor hits you in the knee and the foot flies up. Charles hardly moved on examinations such as these.

O'Hearne testified how easy it was for Charlie to get upset, how easy he was to flush. And the fact he was unable to perform very well under periods of stress.

O'Hearne: If things would come at him one at a time, slowly as in a routine job, he would be able too handle these things, but if things began to flood in on him such as the work not going right, the sprinkler in the ceiling coming on, or somebody yelling and a whistle going all at once, I don't think he could function . . . he would be like a frightened animal.

Gaughan: Now, doctor, from your testimony that you have given, do you have an opinion as to whether the defendant, at the time he killed Robert Jensen, had a sufficient degree of reason to know that he was doing an act he ought not to do? Is there any doubt that Charlie was in this type of state when he committed all the murders?

O'Hearne: Well, if we could have stopped him right in the middle of it and asked him, like a school kid, "Is it wrong to kill or steal?" the answer out of his mouth would have been yes. Perhaps I can give an example of this. Words come easily, and I think they came correctly, to Charlie. But perhaps I could illustrate with an example. On the continuing examination here this morning, when I asked him how he liked what was going on, he said he didn't like it. I said, 'What would you like to do about it?' He said, 'If I had a grenade I would show you.' I said, 'What?' He said, 'A bomb.' I said, 'What would you do with a bomb?' He said, 'I would kill Greenbaum with it.' I said, 'What would you do with the other people in the courtroom?' He said, 'To hell with them.' Anybody that says something he disagrees with, like his ex-boss there, he wants to shoot him. He wants to bomb them. He wants to bomb Greenbaum.

Scheele cross examined and once again attempted to get the witness to admit that Charlie knew what he was doing.

Scheele: Is your opinion that the defendant, Charles Starkweather, was unable to form premeditation prior to the death of Robert Jensen based in part, at least, on the premise that the death of Robert Jensen and the robbery of Robert Jensen took place at the same time?

O'Hearne: Let me see if I understand. You are asking me if I believe that he was able to premeditate under these conditions the death and robbery of Robert Jensen. The answer is no.

Scheele: Now, immediately following the death of Robert Jensen, Starkweather was able to cover up evidence of that crime, wasn't he?

O'Hearne: From what he told me, that wasn't the next thing that happened.

Scheele: But he did, very shortly thereafter, cover up the entrance to the cave where the body of Robert Jensen lay, did he not?

O'Hearne: I am not real clear in my memory whether he said he tried to cover it or not.

Scheele: And he had presence of mind enough to jack up the car and push it over to get it out of the place where it was stuck in the mud in the lane there adjacent to the school yard, didn't he?

O'Hearne: Yes.

Scheele: He had presence of mind when he did get the car unstuck, and mental ability sufficient to enable him to get out of that area completely, didn't he?

O'Hearne: No. By virtue of the fact that, after riding around on the highway for a while, he came back, parked the stolen car on the streets of Lincoln, Nebraska and slept in the car.

Scheele: But he was able to form and carry out these plans, to cover up evidence of the crime, to avoid apprehension and detection, and to plan and to carry out an escape, was he not?

CHAPTER THIRTEEN

O'Hearne: Well, he worked on his escape.
Scheele: He did all these things, didn't he?
O'Hearne: And crossed the state line too.
Scheele: And knew and understood what he was doing at the time he did it?
O'Hearne: I assume that he even knew that crossing the state line would get him in with the federal authorities.
Scheele: When you add up the sum total of his acts he performed after the death of Robert Jensen the following day and up to the date of his capture, then it has significance, the composite sum total of these acts?
O'Hearne: That is the point I am trying to make. No one single thing makes sense.
Scheele: But added together they do make sense?
O'Hearne: Yes.
Scheele: That's all.
Judge Spencer adjourned court until the next day.

Tuesday, May 20
9:00 a.m.

10

Gaughan called his last witness for the defense, Dr. John Steinman, a graduate of Columbia University and a Lincoln psychiatrist.
Gaughan: And from your examinations and observations, based upon your experience and examinations did you come to any conclusions?
Steinman: I did. At the time of my examination, that Charles Starkweather was not of a normally healthy mind. I would say he had a diseased or sick mind.
Gaughan: Now, doctor, based on your examination and findings, is the diseased mind of the defendant, as you have described, such that he is unable to adapt himself to the realities of the society with which he is in contact?
Steinman: Yes, I believe that is true. Perhaps I can best illustrate that with a statement he made to me when I first interviewed him. In talking about his eyesight, his marksmanship, he said, "I'm not as good a shot as they say I am. One thing, though, I am quick on he draw." He said, "That is no good. I get that from watching television." He said, "That is no good even for a lawman because there is no use you can do with it, being quick on the draw, except for a lawman."
Gaughan: Is it or is it not true that the defendant is unable to feel normal emotions like his fellow human beings with his diseased mind?
Steinman: I would say that his range of emotions is limited, that he feels perhaps two that we are familiar with: anger and fear, or anxiety. The other shadings of emotions—pity, sympathy, the feeling of attachment for another

individual—is something that I think he is striving for but actually only has a dim recognition of. When I asked him what happened and how he felt through this when he committed these acts, he has always come back with the same thing: "Self-defense." I said, "Self-defense, how is that?" He said, "Haven't you ever felt what it is like to have a cop chasing you?" He will admit fear but if I were to say he was yellow or a coward he would get angry.

Matschullat: Does the fact that Robert W. Jensen was shot in the right-hand side of the head indicate the self-defense argument is imaginary and a further indication of the defendant's diseased mind?

Steinman: I believe it does. One of Charlie's problems is that he is unable to fully appreciate the value of human life. He thinks he can feel close to certain people—he feels loyal and protective toward them—but he is incapable of feeling closeness with the depth and complexity of a fully developed human being . . . I think he would be a child of five or six with a cap gun in a time of stress or strain, with a gun. "Bang, you're dead." It means just about that much to him.

Gaughan: We have testimony given by family and friends about Chuck's behavior during and after the murders—that he was happy, cheerful, gay, no different than before. What would that indicate?

Steinman: I would say that it would indicate a diseased mind. A person who had committed the act of killing three people including a young child and then returned to friends and family and appeared to be normal and cheerful was not able to feel things the way other people would.

Steinman went on to testify Starkweather showed signs of being paranoid. He said, "An individual should not turn his back on a person suffering from paranoia. A paranoid is distrustful of a person in retreat and feels the individual may return to harm him."

According to Steinman, Starkweather showed much ability in some fields, noting that Dr. Greenbaum testified that one test given Charlie showed his IQ to be 97. But the misspellings and grammatical errors in his notes and letters indicated the status of his mind when he was under great stress.

During cross-examination, in an attempt to prove Starkweather was capable of intent and premeditation, Scheele asked Steinman the following:

Scheele: Doctor Steinman, did he say or do anything prior to Robert Jensen's death that would outwardly disclose the intention to rob Robert Jensen of his automobile?

Steinman: Yes. According to the statement, he said he was going to take his car.

Scheele: Did he at or about that time outwardly display any intention to rob Robert Jensen of his money?

Steinman: I don't believe he outwardly displayed any until some moment—

CHAPTER THIRTEEN

I am not quite sure, from the statement I got the impression, somehow, that Caril Fugate suggested to him that he ask where they had any money, I take it.

Scheele: Could it be, Doctor, that according to the statement he was the one that asked Jensen if he had any money?

Steinman: He asked Jensen, but that was prompted by Caril's reminder, "Better ask them if they have some money," or something of that sort.

Scheele: Doctor, did Charles Starkweather rob Robert Jensen of his money?

Steinman: I am pretty sure.

Scheele: And did he carry out his intention, later on, to rob Robert Jensen of his automobile?

Steinman: Yes. I don't believe that was his original intention.

Scheele: And he knew and appreciated and understood that if he shot Robert Jensen in the head with that .22 caliber six times it would be fatal, didn't he?

Steinman: I think he knew, but perhaps his reaction could be characterized best by what he says his response was after the Bartlett killings. He said, "We were in a hell of a mess."

Scheele: At any rate, he carried out the intention to use the gun, if it became necessary, didn't he?

Steinman: Yes.

Scheele: And it did have fatal results, as far as Robert Jensen was concerned?

Steinman: Yes.

Scheele: So his action on the intention was effectively carried out?

Steinman: Yes.

Scheele: That's all.

Court adjourned.

Wednesday, May 21
9:00 a.m.

11

Charlie flipped absentmindedly through the pages of a psychiatry textbook while three Lincoln psychiatrists testified that although he had a personality disorder, he was legally sane, and thus answerable for his acts.

Dr. Charles Munson, a clinical psychologist at the Nebraska State Hospital, testifies he interviewed Charlie on two occasions—April 2 and April 10—at the State Penitentiary. He administered the Wechsler Intelligence Scale for Adults, the Rorschach, the Thematic Apperception Test, the Draw-A-Person test, the Bender-Gestalt test, The Stress-Bender-Gestalt test, the wide-range Achievement test, and the Minnesota Multiphasic Personality Inventory.

Scheele: Do you have an opinion, as a result of your examination and tests of Charles R. Starkweather, as to whether or not he was legally sane, as defined in McNaghten's Rule, on the dates you saw him?

Munson: If he was—do I have an opinion as to whether he was legally insane at that time?

Scheele: Yes.

Munson: Yes.

Scheele: What is your opinion in that regard?

Munson: My opinion is that Charles R. Starkweather is or was legally sane at the time I saw him.

Scheele: Do you have an opinion as to whether or not he was legally sane on January 27, 1958?

Munson: I do.

Scheele: What is your opinion in that regard?

Munson: My opinion is that Charles R. Starkweather was legally sane as of January 27, 1958.

Defense attorney Gaughan attempted in his cross-examination of Munson to show that he was not a doctor, did not have a master's degree, nor did he have a Ph.D. He made sure the jury understood the fact Munson had been called as a witness for the prosecution and would thus testify the way he did.

Dr. Edwin Coats, a specialist in neuropsychiatry, testified next. Coats was also a doctor at the Nebraska State Hospital, having been employed there since 1938. Scheele was interested in discussing whether or not Charlie was suffering from delusions as claimed by the defense.

Scheele: Now, Doctor, during the course of your examination, did you find any evidence of indications that Charles R. Starkweather was suffering from any delusions?

Coats: No, sir.

Scheele: Or hallucinations?

Coats: No, sir.

Scheele: What were your findings with reference to Charles R. Starkweather?

Coats: I found he was a cooperative, pleasant young man. He readily admitted to the things, the crimes, with which he was charged. He was at all times cooperative. He seemed oriented; he knew where he was and who we were and our relationship with him.

Scheele: Doctor, did you find Charles R. Starkweather to be psychotic?

Coats: No, sir.

Scheele: Did you find him to be suffering from a form of medically recognized form of insanity or mental illness to a degree that he would be a fit subject for commitment to a mental institution?

Coats: No. I found him suffering from a personality disorder, but not to the extent that he would be committable.

Attorney Scheele next called Dr. Robert J. Stein to the stand. Head of the Department of Neurology and Psychiatry at Lincoln General Hospital since 1946, he was now serving chiefly as a consultant to the hospital. Stein had testified as an "expert" witness in other state cases and was considered Scheele's number-one witness.

Scheele: And did you make a diagnosis of the defendant upon the completion of your examination?

Stein: I made the diagnosis that Charles had a personality disorder characterized by emotional instability, considerable emotional insecurity, and impulsiveness; that this would fit into a category under the antisocial type of personality disorder; and that he was legally sane.

Scheele: Now, at the times you saw him, did he appear to you, Doctor, in your opinion, to know the difference between right and wrong?

Stein: He did.

Scheele: In your opinion, did he possess that same mental ability on December 1, 1957, during the month of January, 1958, and specifically on January 27, 1958?

Stein: He did.

Scheele: Is murder itself a normal act?

Stein: No, it is not.

Scheele: But is the act of murder in and by itself a criterion of insanity?

Stein: It is not.

Scheele: Or mental illness?

Stein: It is not.

Scheele: And did Charles R. Starkweather relate to you during the course of your being in his presence his acts in attempting to cover up evidence of the various acts he committed, his attempts to avoid detection and apprehension, and to escape?

Stein: Yes, he did.

Stein further testified that Charlie realized the enormity of the situation he had gotten into during the murder spree. He said Charlie had sufficient mental capacity to form the intention to rob Robert Jensen of his money and automobile, as well as premeditating the death of Robert Jensen.

The defense rested its case at 11:40 a.m. The official part of the trial was over. Judge Spencer told the jury to go home but warned it could be the last time for a while, as they would be put under the charge of an officer of the Court until a verdict was reached. He then adjourned the Court until Thursday morning.

CHAPTER FOURTEEN

Thursday, May 22
9:10 a.m.

1

Assistant County Attorney Dale Farnbruch opened final arguments by repeating the case for the prosecution. He gave the jury of eight women and four men a reminder of the events before and after the death of Robert W. Jensen. It was his intent to show how Charlie was capable of premeditation and knew the difference between right and wrong. He took them through the entire series of events and murders. He also reminded them that they had proven without a doubt that Charlie had robbed Robert Jensen of his car and the money in his billfold and then murdered him.

"Didn't he shoot, purposely, six shots into the side of Jensen's head? He made six decisions when he shot Robert Jensen, a decision every time he pulled the trigger. Every possible fact relative to the Jensen case that is capable of corroboration from physical facts backs up Starkweather's statements. Yet the defense does not want you to believe them. You, the jury, must decide what protection you are going to give this community. Do you want evidence of malice? Remember the picture of Jensen's head. Do you want intent? What about the shotgun sawed off because it would spread more? Self-defense? It would be more accurate to term it self-preservation to avoid detection and apprehension."

Farnbruch reminded the jury that Charlie was being tried for the murder of Robert W. Jensen and that was all. But he said that Judge Spencer would tell them if they could look at the other crimes for Charlie's ability to premeditate and plan. He cited the slayings of Mr. and Mrs. Marion Bartlett, Mr. and Mrs. C. Lauer Ward and August Meyer as evidence Charlie was capable of planning their deaths.

Defense Attorney William Matschullat stood up and began his plea for Charlie's innocence.

"He who sets that boy in the electric chair will have a terrific responsibility; there will be days and months in the future when you will wonder about it. This could happen to your son or daughter. We are not here so much to save Charlie but to see that other boys and girls will have a chance for a fair trial, representation. Think of the men we rehabilitate after a war. If you can do it for millions, you can do it for one other—a brethren of your own community. The state's case has made Charlie out as eligible to be an officer in the U.S. Army. That's

CHAPTER FOURTEEN

ridiculous! Saying he was a "friendly lad." "cheerful," "cooperative," with an IQ of 110, a little better than average—yours and mine!

"Are we going to push this boy down in the electric chair if he has a deranged mind? Why should we kill the boy? Let's kill the devil in him!"

Clement Gaughan was next to plead Charlie's case.

"This boy is a product of our society. Our society that spawned this individual is looking for a scapegoat. Caril Fugate should get the same punishment as this lad, and I can tell you right now that she is never going to get the death penalty. In many ways I think I know this lad as well as anyone alive does. His life, my life, are almost parallels until our nineteenth birthday. I stand here and weep unashamedly. Society treated me exactly as it treated Charles Starkweather. But the Good Lord gave me, possibly, a little better parents.

"I assure you that even an act of Congress will not take him out of the state hospital. The society that spawned this young lad has set up rules for the insane. The Bible commandment which says 'Thou shalt not kill' applies as much to you as to Starkweather. If you return a death verdict I will take you to the death house so you can see him with his trousers cut to the knees, with his arms bare, his head shaved, with electrodes attached. And when the switch is pulled, you will see the electricity snap and the smoke come from his head, his hair stand on end as the electricity goes through his body. You will see him jerk in the straps and see him fall forward. That is your responsibility, not mine. Ladies and gentlemen, I ask you for the life of Charles Starkweather."

Gaughan turned and walked slowly back to the counsel's table. Judge Spencer called for midafternoon recess. When they returned, Attorney Elmer Scheele would have his chance.

3:30 p.m.

2

Prosecuting Attorney Elmer Scheele walked to the center of the courtroom and began his final argument.

"That was one of the most emotional appeals I have ever heard. Such appeals are common when you have a weak case, or no case at all. Then you must distract the jury's attention from the facts. I've got to rely entirely on you twelve ladies and gentlemen to judge this case on facts of evidence. It is unfair and ridiculous to attempt to place blame on society and ask you to do nothing as far as Charles Starkweather, because the blame is on society. Let us get back to earth, get our feet on the ground . . . if justice is to be accomplished and society is to be given the protection it deserves.

"I can be emotional too. I could describe how it felt to go to Robert Colvert's home in December and talk to his widow, the pregnant wife of a dead young man. I could describe the sight I saw in the small abandoned toilet and chicken house behind the Bartlett home . . . the August Meyer farm and what I found there . . . the storm cellar and what I saw there. I could take you to the Ward home to tell you what I saw there, and how the relatives felt when they identified the bodies. But I don't want to put you through that. It took me weeks to get those things out of my mind. Now let's get our feet back on the ground. It is time to face up to our responsibilities."

He declared that evidence by both defense and prosecution psychiatrists showed that Charlie was legally sane and was capable of premeditation when he killed Robert W. Jensen. He said the alleged "short circuit" in Starkweather's mind was pure sham, another attempt to pull the wool over the jury's eyes. He pleaded not to be misled by an age-old trick and sacrifice the interests of society by returning an innocent by reason of insanity verdict.

He told how although Starkweather's confessions seemed to be contradictory, they were remarkably parallel except for the early portions when he was first trying to protect Caril Fugate.

"Charles Starkweather knows the difference between right and wrong and knows the nature and quality of his acts. His own parents will tell you how he acted perfectly normal. The defense tried to hoodwink you into grasping the straw of insanity.

"I have never asked for the death penalty while serving the last four years as County Attorney, but it is one of the duties I have had to face up to since I took my oath of office. This jury has to go all the way to protect this community—our families, yours and mine—from the defendant. I am asking for the death penalty. Can we take a chance and gamble with the safety of persons in this community? It is the only solution, the one answer, for the fate of a confessed slayer."

Judge Spencer instructed the jury that they had six alternatives. They could find Charlie guilt of first-degree murder and sentence him to the electric chair; they could find him guilty but sentence him to life imprisonment; they could find him guilty of second-degree; they could find him guilty of manslaughter; they could find him innocent; or they could find him innocent by reason of insanity. It was 5:25 p.m. when the jury left to deliberate.

CHAPTER FOURTEEN

Friday, May 23
3

At 3:00 p.m., Friday, May 23, 1958, the jury announced its verdict. Charles R. Starkweather was found guilty of first-degree murder and the sentence was death by the electric chair. He would be the first person to be executed in the state of Nebraska since Roland Sundahl was put to death in 1952.

CHAPTER FIFTEEN

October 27, 1958

1

Caril Fugate's trial for the murder of Robert W. Jensen began Monday morning in Judge Harry Spencer's Third District Court, the same place Charlie was tried and convicted. Neither Scheele nor Farnbruch claimed Caril had actually killed the young teenage boy, but that she did help rob him which made her an accomplice and guilty under the eyes of the law.

Caril was the youngest female in United States history to be tried for first-degree murder, and I speculate that if this had happened today, things could have gone quite differently. She was a minor, only fourteen years old and certainly influenced by the actions of a vicious murderer—Charles Starkweather. There seemed to be a question of whether she had been given her rights properly and understood the legal ramifications of being extradited from Wyoming. This alone would have been quite an issue today. Although she probably would have been found guilty, whether or not she would have received a life sentence is open to speculation. This statement in noway excuses her behavior but points out the differences in our society and judicial system over the past thirty-five years.

John McArthur, a successful Lincoln attorney, represented Caril. The trial was almost identical to Charlie's in that many of the same witnesses were called to testify, but it was different in that Caril pleaded innocent but not by reason of insanity. She maintained she had been a hostage throughout the spree, forced to do what Charlie wanted in order to save her family, supposedly being held captive.

After many of the same witnesses who testified at his trial were called, Charlie was brought to the courthouse to give testimony for the state. He began by making it very plain that Caril was in the same room when he killed Marion Bartlett, Velda Bartlett, and Betty Jean. He described how Caril watched television while he cleaned up the murder scene.

He talked about leaving the Bartlett house at night to go to the store. Did he tie up Caril? No. On Wednesday, he went to his aunt's house. Did he tie up Caril? No. On Friday morning he went to the grocery store again. Did he tie up Caril? No.

Charlie went on to testify that Caril held a gun on Robert Jensen and Carol King, and that she took the money from Jensen's billfold. At the Wards' she had stayed out in the car for over twenty minutes while Starkweather was in the

CHAPTER FIFTEEN

house. Weren't there several phones in the house? Yes. Was Charles Starkweather always armed? No.

Starkweather also discussed the trip they made to Wyoming. He showed the jury the Nebraska map and read off the names of the towns circled in pencil. He said Caril was the one who circled each town while they were fleeing. This concluded Charlie's direct testimony.

McArthur spent the next two days cross-examining Charlie very closely. He asked Charlie about his many different confessions and made sure the jury understood that whenever Charlie felt threatened, he did one thing. He killed. He was curious about what Charlie would have done if Caril had tried to escape, but wasn't happy when he answered the questions.

McArthur: What would you have done to Caril if she had tried to warn anyone against you?

Starkweather: I wasn't worried about her talking. I wasn't worried about what she did; she wasn't going to talk.

McArthur: Do you know what you would have done if she had?

Starkweather: Well, I wasn't worried about her doing it, so I didn't think about it.

McArthur: And would that be true of when you went in the different fillings stations?

Starkweather: She wasn't going to talk. She was too worried about being caught.

McArthur read Charlie's statement he made to Elmer Scheele in which he stated that Caril was his hostage.

McArthur: Do you recall that?

Starkweather: That's what I said, but it ain't true. That whole statement is a bunch of hogwash.

After redirect-examination, Scheele asked Charlie why he did not tell the entire truth to him when he asked the questions about those matters.

Starkweather: I told you that once before.

Scheele: Well, will you tell me now?

Starkweather: I was protecting Caril Fugate.

Scheele then swore in witness after witness who testified they had seen them on the trip and said they felt Caril could have escaped if she had wanted to.

Gertrude Karnopp, wife of Lancaster Sheriff Merle Karnopp, took the stand and testified about her conversation with Caril on the trip back from Wyoming.

Karnopp: The first words that were said to me about the events during that time was when Caril asked me, "Are my folks dead?" And I didn't answer immediately. And she said, "Who killed them?" And I believe my answer was, "Don't you know, Caril?" And she told me that the first that she had known about it was when Mrs. Warick, the Scotts Bluff County sheriff's wife, had told her in the jail in Gering. She talked about her family at various times during the day, and she mentioned that she didn't like her stepfather very well, that he was very strict with them . . . And she also told about one time, she started talking about a fight that had taken place at their home when Charles came in and her mother was washing, and they had gotten into a fight, and then Charles said some bad things and her mother said some bad things is the way she put it, and Charles grabbed at her little sister, as I remember her saying it, and then she stopped talking about this fight. She also showed me some pictures that she had of her mother and father and her little sister.

Scheele: What else did she say?

Karnopp: She talked about her sister Barbara . . . She also at one time said that the papers said those three bodies were found where they were shot, but they weren't shot outside, they were shot in the house . . . I asked her which three bodies she meant. She waited a moment and she says, "Mr. Meyer's body was shot in the house and drug out there," and then she refused to talk to me.

There was no doubt Deputy Sheriff William Romer's testimony hurt Caril's case the most. He testified that Caril told him she had seen Charles Starkweather kill ten people. They included the Bartletts, Jensen and King, Meyer, and three other people. This definitely contradicted her story that she had not known about her parents' death until after her capture. In other words, how could she believe her parents were being held hostage when she knew they were dead the whole time?

On Monday, the statement Caril gave Elmer Scheele in Wyoming was admitted as state's evidence over McArthur's strenuous objections. This was important to the defense because McArthur felt that Caril had never understood the legal rights she gave up when the law enforcement people talked to her in Wyoming.

McArthur: And did Mr. Scheele explain to you in Wyoming, did he not, that you could have a lawyer if you wanted one?

Fugate: Yes.

McArthur: And you told him that you did not want a lawyer?

Fugate: No, I never. I didn't know what he meant at that time by that. I thought he meant by the District Attorney.

Then Scheele read the statement Caril gave before she was given the services of an attorney in Wyoming. It began with August Meyer's death and went on until it covered all of the killings. The statement ended with the following:

Scheele: Did you try to warn anyone?

Fugate: Yes, I tried to warn Rodney and Bob . . . I was telling them that it would be best for everyone if they went away for awhile, and for nobody not to come out and I told my grandma that if she didn't want anything to happen to Mom, then she better go . . . I think I told his sister that he was in the house, but I don't think she understood me.

Scheele: Now is there anything else, Caril, that you know of about any of the

CHAPTER FIFTEEN

cases—the Colvert case, the Meyer case, the Jensen, the Carol King case, the Mr. and Mrs. Ward or the maid case—that you haven't told me?

Fugate: Yes. I didn't know he was going to kill any of them.

Scheele rested the State's case.

2

Caril was the first witness McArthur called for the defense when court met once again on Wednesday. She testified that she was tired, scared, and nervous as well as scared to death of Charlie. But how did she happen to be carrying a gun?

Fugate: After he hit the dog with it he told me I was to carry it until he could get it fixed . . . he said it broke something after he had hit Mr. Meyer's dog with it.

McArthur: And what about the Jensen-King murders?

Fugate: He said he was going to flag him down, for me not to say anything, and for me to shut up, and if I said anything it would be too bad.

McArthur asked about her taking Jensen's billfold.

Fugate: I didn't do it at first. I was scared . . . Robert Jensen said, "Do what he says so no one will get hurt," and I was shaking and I didn't want to do it, and he [Starkweather] says, he screamed at me again and told me take it out, and I did.

McArthur asked Caril about going back to her house in Belmont after the Jensen-King murders:

Fugate: I don't know whether he was going to leave me off or not [at her house]; he said he would, and he seen some policemen down there—and he wasn't going to let me off then . . . He said he wouldn't leave me off because I might tell them what he'd done. I asked him to take leave me off and he said no.

McArthur: Why didn't you jump out and run?

Fugate: He had a knife with him.

McArthur: Did you want to get away, Caril?

Fugate: Yes, I did.

McArthur: Was there any time at all that you were with Charles that you did not want to get away?

Fugate: No, sir.

McArthur: You always wanted to get loose, did you?

Fugate: Yes, sir, but he always told me that if I ever got loose my family would be killed, and it would be my fault.

Throughout Caril's testimony, McArthur led her carefully over the entire time she spent with Starkweather. By now, everyone knew what took place in those eight days . . . Caril felt the same way about almost every incident. She had been terrified of Charlie, afraid for her own life and for the lives of her family and everyone he came in contact with. She wanted to get away, but she was afraid. She did not want to do any of the things Charlie made her do—holding the gun on the maid at the Wards', calling out to Charlie when she saw Mr. Ward's car come in the driveway, going in to buy the hamburgers, bringing him the gun when he was shooting Merle Collision by the side of the road in Wyoming. But she had been afraid of what he would do if she disobeyed or defied him. She did not know her parents were dead.

Finally, McArthur finished Caril's direct examination and the court adjourned for lunch. At two o'clock, Caril returned to the stand and watched as Elmer Scheele stood up and began cross-examining her. After clearing up the question regarding her extradition from Wyoming, he moved to the events in January.

Caril became angrier and angrier as Scheele kept asking questions that implied she could have escaped from Charlie if she had wanted to. It went on the rest of the afternoon. No new and enlightening facts came out, but what did sounded worse when Scheele had to ask two or three questions in order to elicit an answer. Caril was being obstinate and very difficult:

Scheele: Did you and Charles Starkweather go to the "old lady's" house after you left the Bartletts' on Monday?

Fugate: I don't exactly remember.

Scheele: You stayed out in the car?

Fugate: He told me to stay there and not to leave.

Scheele: But did you stay in the car?

Fugate: —and he said if I did I'd get shot.

Scheele: But did you stay in the car wile he was in the garage?

Fugate: He told me my family was in the house and if I tried anything they'd get hurt.

Scheele: But do you understand my question—did you remain in the car during the time that he was back in the garage?

Fugate: Yes, sir.

Scheele: And then during that time that you were sitting out there in the car, at that time you thought that's the very place where your family was didn't you?

Fugate: Yes, sir.

Scheele: Did you do anything or make any effort to go to the house while he was out in the garage?

Fugate: I didn't want my family to be hurt, no.

Scheele: But did you make any effort to do that?

Fugate: No, sir.

Scheele finished his cross-examination by asking:

Scheele: And even after you left the Wards' home while you were on your way to Wyoming, did you tell Chuck Starkweather that you loved him?

CHAPTER FIFTEEN

Fugate: Yes, I did; I was afraid he was going to kill me.
Scheele: And did you kiss him?
Fugate: No, sir.
Scheele: You never did that?
Fugate: No, sir; he kissed me.
Scheele: He kissed you?
Fugate: Yes, sir.
Scheele: I believe that's all.

Caril stepped down from the witness stand and strutted defiantly back to the counsel table. She did not look like the poor, defenseless fourteen-year-old McArthur had made her out to be the entire trial. This last bit of testimony regarding kissing Charlie had visibly disgusted the jury. The damage had been done and now it was time for closing arguments.

Wednesday, November 18
9:00 a.m.

3

McArthur opened the closing arguments by refuting the State's contention Caril could have gotten away. When could she have gotten away, he asked? When Charlie left her alone in a gas station, eight feet above the concrete floor? When he sent her in to buy hamburgers, telling her he would be watching her the whole time? How about when her sister came to the door and he was there, out of sight, with a loaded gun? At August Meyer's farm, miles from town, the car stuck in the mud? At the storm cellar with Charlie somewhere out in the darkness? At the Wards' in a neighborhood that was quiet and had very little traffic? From a moving car?

Surely the jury could see that there was virtually no time that Caril could have made a break for freedom without the threat of being killed. He then sat down and let Scheele present his closing remarks.

Elmer Scheele argued that Caril had numerous opportunities to escape, but he would not go over each one in detail, that the jury knew what he was talking about. He just mentioned the most obvious one. This was when the police officers came to the Bartlett house. Two policemen, themselves armed, experienced in dealing with dangerous men, dedicated to helping citizens protect themselves from danger. And Starkweather was asleep. What had Caril Fugate done? Had she welcomed the protection of the officers who could save her from Starkweather? No, she had gone into the bedroom and wakened Charlie, warning him that the police were coming.

She said she was afraid not only for herself but for her parents. If that was true, maybe she would have been afraid to run to the police. But certainly, even after she awakened Starkweather, she could have whispered to the officers. Charlie was, after all, keeping out of sight.

Scheele concluded by saying, "Even fourteen-year-old girls must realize they cannot go on eight-day murder sprees. We have leaned over backward to give this girl a fair trial. Now, ladies and gentlemen, the time has come when she must face the consequences of her conduct. This fourteen-year-old girl is guilty of first-degree murder as charged. We must convince persons of all ages they will be caught, tried, and punished if they break the law. I ask you to bring back the verdict of guilty of first-degree murder for the robbery-slaying of Robert Jensen."

McArthur walked to the middle of the courtroom and gave his final argument. He stated that the reasons Caril was on trial for her life were because:

1) The law enforcement people were looking for a scapegoat because of their poor effort in locating and arresting Starkweather, and Caril was the one on whom they settled. Instead of protecting her rights, they allowed her to sign her legal rights away in Wyoming on Thursday while under a sedative.
2) They had denied Caril due process of law when they denied the assistance of an attorney until after they had gotten a statement that damaged her by telling only of her actions and not the reasons for her behavior.
3) She was a tiny, frightened child. How could anyone expect her to deal with Charlie when bigger, stronger people who tried ended up dead?
4) It was ridiculous that she was being tried for the murder of Robert Jensen. The State's case relied heavily on Charlie's statement, a story that he changed. McArthur was convinced that Charlie was a madman, yet he was the chief witness against Caril. And even he had not said that Caril had anything to do with the actual killing of Robert Jensen.

He concluded by asking the jury to put themselves in Caril's place. "Believing her family to be in danger, she had lived for six days in the company of a wild, angry man who threw a knife against the wall for entertainment. Then, tired, sleepless, and hungry, she was taken by him to a deserted county road and to a farm where, for no reason, he killed a kindly old man who was going to help him. That was followed by the experience of being left alone in a car in the darkness and hearing a series of shots that could only mean Starkweather's insanity was increasing. By the time they reached the Ward house she had no more will to resist than that of a three-year-old child. Who, adult or child, could be sure that he would be able to do otherwise?"

Exhausted, he sat down and let Judge Harry Spencer give the jury their final instructions. The judge reminded them that Caril was being tried on two charges: first-degree murder and murder in the perpetration of a robbery. The jury could find her guilty or innocent of either or both of the charges. They

CHAPTER FIFTEEN

could also, in considering the first charge, find her guilty of second-degree murder, which implied lack of premeditation.

He reminded them that Caril was "not on trial for failing to run away from Starkweather, for failing to report such crimes as he may have committed, or for failing to prevent such crimes."

He also told the jury that if the evidence showed that Caril had accompanied Starkweather under duress, she must be found innocent of both murder counts. He noted that merely being present while a murder is committed does not necessarily make a person an accomplice to it.

He spoke about Charlie, "Extreme care and caution should be used in weighing his testimony. You will scrutinize it closely in the light of all the other evidence in the case and you will give it such weight as you may think it is entitled to have, keeping in mind the credibility of such a witness."

Friday, November 20
11:09 a.m.

4

Caril Ann Fugate was found guilty on the second count, murder while in the perpetration of a robbery and the sentence was life imprisonment. She was taken to the Nebraska Center for Women at York where she stayed until paroled June 20, 1976.

CHAPTER SIXTEEN

June 23, 1959

1

Charlie waited for his execution in an 8'×12' cell in the prison hospital. He was not kept in solitary; however, he was by himself in the cell. He had visiting rights, a TV in the corridor, a daily newspaper. He was able to obtain pencil, paper and art supplies. He spent his days reading, writing, drawing, and looking out the window.

He wrote a letter to his brother Greg:

> Dear Greg:
>
> thank you for letting me read your book there's a lot of pictures in it and its a very nice book. But when you get older read the Bible it tells more about the Lord from the first of life to the end of life. but do not think that there is a end in the life of the Lord. cause there is no end, he is all ways a live. "to hel you." and do this for ne toÑbe nice to mom and dad and do all you can to help your mother. OK.
>
> your brother
> Charles

Charlie worked on an autobiography and sold part of his story to *Parade* magazine for a thousand dollars. It ended:

> Today, after a year of imprisonment, I can count my life in hours. I have had a great deal of time for thought and retrace back over my life. I hold no fear for the electric chair, it is the price I am paying for taking the lives of others. But bringing my life to an end does not answer why certain things took place. Going to the electric chair will bring to an end my search for answers that are hard to find.
>
> Now I feel no rebellion toward anything or anyone, only love and peace. I received this love and peace through the Bible.
>
> And if I could talk to young people today I would tell them to go to school, to go to Sunday school, to go to church and receive the Lord Jesus Christ as your own personal Savior. Our God is a kind God. He'll forgive and accept you as one of His even if your heart is black and heavy with sin.
>
> And I would say to them to obey their parents or guardians, and stay away from bad influences, and never undertake anything that you don't understand, and if in doubt don't do it. And most of all don't ever let your intentions and emotions overpower you.
>
> If I had followed these simple rules, as I was advised to do many times, I would not be where I am today.

CHAPTER SIXTEEN

Wednesday, June 24

2

Charlie was ready to die. He had been ready the previous month when he received a reprieve on May 22 from the U.S. Circuit Court of Appeals just 96 minutes before chair time.

Charlie had made his peace with God and was ready for his execution in May. When the stay came he took the news calmly, but the next morning reality set in and he declared he had died a thousand deaths. Now he faced death once again. He showed very little emotion, expressing his feelings by painting and drawing.

Mr. and Mrs. Starkweather filed petitions at the Lancaster County Courthouse earlier in the day after Charlie signed both documents. They wanted a new trial for the following reasons:

1. Starkweather discovered that Harold G. Robinson, who made an investigation of police handling of the Starkweather case, "intimidated defense witnesses and procured false evidence."

2. Starkweather learned he was prevented by the State of Nebraska from resisting extradition from Wyoming.

3. False testimony was given at his trial.

4. That Charlie was "misled into signing conflicting and contradictory statements."

5. The death penalty verdict was the "result of great pressure."

6. Starkweather discovered that since his son's trial that a witness whose testimony would be highly material was falsely advised by a representative of the state that the witness did not need to testify. This was in reference to Caril Ann Fugate.

All their efforts were in vain, as the courts decided to execute Charlie at or around midnight that night.

3

F. Warner Smith, a Beatrice businessman and member of the Lions Club went to the prison in order to ask Charlie if he would donate his eyes to the Lions Club eye bank.

Smith was stopped at the gate by a guard who said that if his visit concerned the donation of Charlie's eyes, the request had been denied.

Charlie said, "Why should I? No one ever did anything for me, why should I do anything for anyone else?"

JUNE 24, 1959

11:55 p.m.

4

Charlie smiled when the law officers came to his cell. He knew it was time.
"All right, Charlie. It's time to go."
Charlie replied, "What's your hurry?"
They escorted him from the cell and down the hallway until they came to the outside door. It was about a hundred yards from the prison hospital building to the central building where the death chamber waited. Charlie stepped outside and took a deep breath. It was a warm, clear night and a soft, summer breeze rustled the shrubbery. Charlie looked up at a sky full of bright, flickering stars. He felt like standing there forever. He knew he would be in a better place in a very short while. The escorts gently moved him along.

They passed the visitor's room and went into the turnkey's room and then down into the basement by way of some metal stairs. Charlie hoped he looked all right for the newsmen who would be there watching. His red hair had been shaved. He was dressed in denim trousers and a blue shirt with the sleeves rolled up. He reached the small death chamber, lighted only by a bare bulb over the grim, wooden electric chair. Deputy Warden John Greenholtz, Prison Chaplain Robert Klein and several other lawmen stood there waiting for him.

Charlie looked around and managed a half-smile as they hurried him to the chair. It was as if they were embarrassed and wanted to get it over with as soon as possible. They drew a blue curtain around the chair so he could be prepared for the execution.

His arms and legs were secured by leather straps. They rolled up his left trouser leg and dabbed his calf with a solution that would help conduct the electricity through his body. His head was fitted into the headrest on the back of the chair, and the same solution was spread on his shaved head. He took a sharp intake of breath as a partial face mask and headpiece holding the electrode was placed on his head and face. Then the curtain was opened.

Charlie's face was pale. He clenched his fists so hard the knuckles grew white.

"Do you have any last words, Charlie?" Greenholtz asked.
Charlie slowly shook his head.
"No."

Then the executioner, from outstate and unidentified by law, threw the switch three times. Each time, 2200 volts surged through his body. A loud thumping sound was heard and Charlie's legs strained and jerked against the straps as the electricity did its deadly work.

By the third time, Charlie was dead. Charlie was declared officially dead by Dr. P. E. Getscher at 12:04 a.m., June 25, 1959.

CHAPTER SIXTEEN

No members of the Starkweather family nor the Jensen family were present during the execution. Charlie could have named three witnesses but elected not to have anyone there. Charlie's parents heard the final word of the execution at the home of Mrs. Althea Neal, Charlie's grandmother.

Charlie's body was claimed by the family and was removed immediately from the prison grounds. Reverend Robert Klein was asked by the family to conduct a funeral service for Charlie and then he was buried in Lincoln's Wyuka Cemetery.

Charlie's death certificate read, "Age of deceased: 20. Cause of death: Electrocution. Place, Nebraska State Penitentiary 14th and Pioneers."

CHAPTER EIGHTEEN

In this chapter, I've listed three questions that have plagued me since I undertook this project. I suspect they are also questions the public might have asked since Starkweather's murder spree thirty-five years ago.

Was Charlie sane or insane?

In this day and age where murderers joyously plead not guilty by reason of insanity, Charles Starkweather's case was unique. He did not want to plead in this manner and was not happy when his plea was changed. He also was not happy when various defense witnesses gave testimony about his lack of mental facilities. He was visibly angered every time a witness testified as to his mental deficiencies.

I think this question was best answered when the court addressed it during the appeal process prior to carrying out Charlie's death sentence. The court said:

> It's true Charles Starkweather was unable to fit himself normally into human society from the time he started school and he possessed only subnormal mental facilities. His inability to comprehend the reactions of normal people forced him to live apart, even from his own family, and ultimately made it possible for him to look back upon the death of eleven people at his own hands without the slightest real trace of remorse or conscience.
>
> His own delusions and imagination convinced him that it was necessary to kill almost everyone in what he considered to be "self-defense."

In addition to all the evidence which described the defendant's mental shortcomings, hair-trigger reactions, inability to feel any remorse, and abnormal reaction to various situations, there was medical testimony which indicated that Charlie was suffering from a mental illness of long duration; that the fact the defendant had "never become domesticated in society" and his lack of ability to experience basic feelings about other people were symptoms of a very serious disease of the mind. The other symptoms were a lack of normal capacity of self control and the ability to consider the consequences of an act between impulse and the act itself.

While there was evidence that Charlie had subnormal mental equipment, there was also evidence that Charlie was of average intelligence, having an intelligence quotient of 97, an adequate memory and sufficient mental ability to make plans to avoid detection and apprehension. He was able to make plans to acquire firearms, had sufficient mental capacity to ask the victim (Jensen) for his billfold and get the money out of it. He was able to buy shells and cartridges as well as gas for his car. He could and did procure road maps and know their

CHAPTER SIXTEEN

use, to have his tire repaired, to know that if he pulled the trigger of a gun a bullet would fly out and kill a man.

Dr. O'Hearne contradicted Dr. Greenbaum and said that Charlie was mentally capable of forming the intent to rob, and ordinarily was capable of planning and premeditating about matters. He admitted that Charlie appreciated the nature and quality of his acts after they were done and that he gained safety by his murders. He also admitted that Charlie was able to form and carry out plans, to cover up evidence of the crime, to avoid apprehension and to plan and carry out an escape.

Dr. Steinman, testifying for the defense, said Charlie was not, at the time of the killing, mentally capable of forming and entertaining a felonious intent and was not conscious of what he was doing. Yet, on cross-examination, he admitted that there was a delay of some considerable duration between the formulation of the impulse to take the car from Jensen and the act of taking it; that there was a lapse of time between the impulse to kill another of his victims and the act of killing; that he had the mental capacity to form an intent to commit and lay plans for robbery. He also admitted that Charlie took the gun along for the purpose of forcing Jensen into the cave, intending to use it if it became necessary. He knew and appreciated that if he shot Jensen in the head six times with a .22 caliber rifle it would be fatal.

The court felt that Charlie, although classified as having average intelligence, was not psychotic. That he had full knowledge of the nature and consequences of his acts when he killed Jensen, and although he had definite "anti-social sociopathic reactions," this was a personality disorder and not a mental disease. The court ruled on appeal that Charlie had the mental capacity when he killed Jensen to possess deliberate and premeditated malice toward the teenager and to deliberate his robbery and killing.

The court cited the following as to reasons Charlie was sane and deliberate the night he killed Jensen:

> When Charlie met Jensen and the King girl, he was in a bad situation. He was at that moment being sought for the killing of five persons. He had just gotten his automobile stuck in the mud with its reverse gear broken. He and Caril had abandoned it and taken to walking with only their weapons and their wits to aid them in further escape, when Jensen stopped his car to help them.
>
> Charlie was not then ready to give up his efforts to escape and Jensen recognized him too late. A rifle and shotgun were used to persuade Jensen to drive down the highway toward Lincoln some five miles or so, as Charlie began to formulate plans for escape. He robbed Jensen of the money in his billfold, and then informed him he was going to take his car. Charlie ordered Jensen to turn around and go back to the schoolhouse area where he had been first picked up.

According to the court, it was here that Charlie began to show premeditation and deliberation. He did not let the Jensen boy and King girl out of the car and run the risk that they might escape and spread the alarm as a less crafty person would have done. He says he intended to put the boy and girl down in the cave and cover the opening so that they would not get out, but there is no indication that he made any preparation to tie them up, or find anything to cover the cave entrance with so they could not escape.

While he claimed Jensen turned around and came back up the steps at him, he pumped six shots into the right side of Jensen's head all within a small area four inches in diameter. The course of all the bullets indicates anything but frontal attack by Jensen; they indicate deliberate shooting of a defenseless and most probably unmoving victim. Why, if it was not his purpose to kill, did he pump six shots into Jensen, each shot requiring he complete a cycle of operation of a pump action rifle?

And why, if it was not his premeditated and deliberated intent to kill, did he wait there until he was sure Jensen was dead, and even refilled the rifle, and went down in the cave with a flashlight to make sure Jensen was dead?

Even the fact that he came back to the remote area where the cave was located, when to do so meant retracing some five or six miles distance, is indicative of a plan in his mind to repeat what he had done in the other instances of killing—to kill and then to hide the bodies where they were not likely to be easily found. And it worked, too. It was a completely successful plan to gain time and avoid apprehension for another period of time.

Was Caril guilty or innocent? Was she an accomplice or a hostage?

Caril Ann Fugate has maintained her innocence all these years, while appearing on national television and being interviewed in various newspapers. Her story has always been the same.

She says she was an unwilling hostage the whole time. She says she wasn't even going with Charlie at the time, having broken up with him the Sunday before the murders began. She told her attorney, John McArthur, in court, "he came down and he came in the house, and we were doing the washing, and he started spouting off about different things and accusing me of going out with other boys, saying nasty things, and I told him to leave and not to come back and I didn't want to ever see him again. Again my mother was out in the kitchen and so was my little sister. I went out in the kitchen and I told my mother that I told him to go away, and she told him to go away. And his face turned red and he got mad about it, and he was hitting his hand with his fist. And he asked me if I never wanted to see him again, and I said, yes, I never wanted to see him again. And he says, 'all right,' and hung around a few minutes, and he went out the door and slammed it."

In Charlie's first statement (in the beginning, Charlie was disposed to protect his lover), he said Caril was still at school when he went up to the Bartletts'

CHAPTER SIXTEEN

kitchen door and was let in. He murdered the entire family before she got home and then hid the bodies. He then told Caril her family was being held hostage at an old couple's house where he rented a garage for his hot rod. The old couple, the Southworths, were going to rob a bank, and if anything went wrong her parents would be killed. This is the story that helped him keep Caril as a hostage for the full eight days they were on the murder spree.

Caril's attorney, John McArthur, said, "Hers was really a story of a child in fear of her life for eight terrifying days, a child who believed that not only her own life was in danger but the lives of her family. She did not know they were dead. If people knew the truth, they would realize that Caril Fugate was no criminal. She was Starkweather's victim, as were all other victims of Starkweather's madness. Must we condemn Caril for failing to do what no one in Nebraska could do: stop Starkweather? She was no accomplice. She was a captive."

The public should not forget that Caril was convicted of second degree murder (murder while in the perpetration of a robbery) and given a life sentence. There is no doubt Robert Jensen was robbed and murdered. There is also no question that Caril took Jensen's billfold, removed the money and put it in Charlie's wallet. There is no doubt she held a rifle on Jensen, King and Fencl. Did she brandish the loaded rifle because Charlie made her or did she because she wanted to? Only Caril knows the answer to that question.

The question remains, was Caril a hostage? In order to answer this, one might ask whether or not she had any opportunities to escape with at least a relatively good chance of surviving. Did she have opportunities to escape while at the same time be assured she would not be chased down and shot dead? Here are some points to ponder:

- Why didn't Caril make any attempt to tell the two police officers (Soukup and Kahler) that Charlie was holding her hostage when they came to the Bartlett house? She could see the two police officers were armed and at the same time, she knew Charlie was sleeping in a bedroom. Yet, she made no attempt to ask for their help or alert them to Charlie. Why didn't she take a chance and whisper to the police officers there was an armed man in the bedroom who was terrorizing her?

- During the six days Charlie and Caril spent at the Bartlett house, Caril was left alone many times when Charlie went to the grocery store. Why didn't she run away as soon as she was sure he was gone? Granted, they had no phone but she had the opportunity to run away. Although both Charlie and Caril testified she was tied up at least on one occasion that Charlie left the house, there were other times she was not. She went out to get the mail most every day. Could she have run away when doing that?

- When they arrived at the Ward house, Caril sat all alone in the driveway while Charlie went inside. He was inside for almost twenty minutes before calling for her to come in. Could she have run away and survived that time?

EPILOGUE

- Why didn't Caril say something to Juanita Bell (waitress at Brickey's Cafe) or write her a note asking for help? She was in a busy cafe; did she really think that Charlie would have blasted his way into the cafe to get at her if she asked for asylum?
- During the day Caril and Charlie spent in the Ward house, they were in different parts of the house on several occasions. Charlie was also asleep for a while. Why didn't she run out the back door or attempt to call the police? There were telephones all over the mansion, yet she never attempted a call.
- On the way to Wyoming, Charlie went to the restroom, leaving Caril alone in the car. He even left the guns with her. Why didn't Caril drive away? She knew how to drive.
- Speaking of Caril, Deputy Sheriff Bill Romer said, "she told me she had seen Mr. Starkweather kill ten people. She said she had seen him kill her mother, her stepfather, her stepsister and a boy and a girl, and a farmhand and three other people." This contradicts her story that she had not known about her parents' deaths until after her capture. The whole point of saying she couldn't run away because Charlie could go and kill her family if she left was no longer valid.
- Earl Heflin, sheriff of Converse County, Wyoming, testified he found several newspaper clippings in Caril's pocket when she was taken into custody. They were from the January 27 *Lincoln Star* and although there was no specific mention of the murders in the clippings, one did refer to "the slayings," and photographs of Mr. and Mrs. Bartlett and Betty Jean were included. How could she have said that she did not know her family was dead, that she was staying with Charlie because she was afraid he would hurt her parents, when all the time she was carrying reports of their murders in her pocket?
- When they left Bennet after killing the two teenagers, Charlie testified he thought about giving up but Caril wanted to keep going. He talked to her about it until she threatened him with a shotgun. I must point out that in many cases Charlie was not a very reliable witness, but it is a strange thing to say.
- Caril was her own worst enemy. Her testimony and court demeanor left the impression she was guilty. Was it because she was a scared fourteen-year-old girl who didn't know how to act? Or was it because she knew she was guilty?

There is only one person alive today who knows what really happened from January 21 to January 29, 1958. And it's more than likely the rest of us will never know.

Did the Nebraska law enforcement agencies do all they could to stop the murder spree?

This was a question of great concern immediately after Starkweather and Fugate were apprehended. In fact, a special investigator named Harold Robin-

CHAPTER SIXTEEN

son prepared a report as to the performance of the Nebraska Highway Patrol, the Lancaster County Sheriff's Department, and the Lincoln Police Department. Robinson was an ex-FBI agent who worked for the California Department of Justice at the time of the murders. Some of the concerns the public had included these questions:
- Did the Lincoln Police Department fail to take steps which might have prevented some of the brutal murders?
- Why didn't police find the Bartlett bodies in Belmont on Saturday, January 25?
- Were all the complaints voiced by the Starkweather family, Barbara Von Busch and Pansy Street fully investigated?
- How could Starkweather and Fugate possibly elude capture while fleeing the entire length of Nebraska?

Robinson spent the majority of his time focusing in on the Colvert murder investigation and the Bartlett murders. Obviously, the murder spree would have been prevented if Charlie had been arrested a month earlier for the murder of Robert Colvert. Could the Lincoln Police Department have done better in this investigation? Also, given the fact two different sets of police officers stopped at the Bartlett house, could they have done something that would have led to Starkweather's arrest?

Looking at the Colvert case, Mr. Robinson reported it was regrettable that persons who later proved to have important information concerning the Robert Colvert murder did not turn this information over to lawmen. The prime example of this was the comment made by Rodney Starkweather immediately after the Bartlett bodies were found: "I . . . own a 12 gauge shotgun that I loaned to my brother in November and he returned it to me after the Robert Colvert murder."

Robinson also said that "if only the personnel at the Crest Service Station had done what County Attorney Elmer Scheele had asked them to do—that is, tell authorities any fragment of information about persons who frequented the station no matter how unimportant it may have seemed—Starkweather might have been linked to the Colvert killing. Much further investigative work and tragedy could have been avoided if three Crest employees had only recalled that Starkweather frequented the station. One employee even remembered that Charlie looked over his shoulder late one night while he balanced the cash receipts.

Robinson said Starkweather and Fugate went into the Crest station about one week after the Colvert murder so Caril could examine a toy doll, yet once again no one had been able to recall this during the investigation.

It was different when Robinson commented on information given to the police by Mrs. Katherine Kamp, the clothing store operator, who said a youth,

EPILOGUE

later identified as Charles Starkweather, bought $9.95 worth of clothing after the Colvert murder.

It was not the police department's fault Mrs. Kamp identified the man who came in as a "male, unkempt individual, approximately 25 to 30 years of age." This certainly was way off on Charlie's age and failed to mention such characteristics as his bow-legs and short stature. In fact, fate played a hand when the police promptly followed up her report and brought Mrs. Kamp photographs of possible suspects, but none of the pictures were of Charlie. This was not surprising, as Charlie had never been arrested.

Robinson concluded his report about the Colvert murder by saying, "The investigation of the Colvert slaying by the law enforcement agencies wasn't inadequate in any material aspect . . . they took the necessary steps which were dictated by the meager information made available to them by residents of the area, who now find a deeper significance. It can be cited that until his apprehension in Wyoming, the name of Charles Starkweather didn't enter into the investigation of the Colvert murder."

There was much criticism directed at the Lincoln Police Department regarding the activities at the Bartlett house. The major concern was for the time that elapsed between 9:25 p.m. Saturday, January 25, when the Police Department investigated a suspicion complaint at 924 Belmont, and 4:30 p.m. Monday, January 27, when three members of the Bartlett family were found dead.

It's hard to find fault with the police officers regarding their investigation. Here's why:

- Caril was calm and collected when Officers Soukup and Kahler visited her. There was nothing said to make them overly suspicious of her. She was very sincere with her answers and showed no emotion that would have led them to have any reason to doubt her.
- The Lincoln Police Department investigated thousands of domestic complaints a year and this one didn't seem to be out of the ordinary. They had no legal right to use a forcible entry into the house and there was no evidence urging them to do so on that Saturday night.
- Regarding what happened the following Monday morning when the two detectives accompanied Pansy Street to the Bartlett house, Lancaster County Sheriff Merle Karnopp said, "While it might be hard to believe, there was no evidence in the Bartlett house to indicate foul play. There were no blood stains and no bullet holes."
- Police Chief Carroll was asked if the officers should have asked to see the sick people Caril kept talking about. "Not normally, unless they had reason to doubt the girl. Even the relatives were apparently satisfied with the investigation."
- Carroll was asked how the murder suspects could elude police for about 48 hours and make their way out of Nebraska and into Wyoming. He

CHAPTER SIXTEEN

answered that every lead was followed and that the suspects had a good start on an escape by the time each new killing was discovered.
- It was openly questioned why the two outbuildings weren't searched, and Robinson said this: "In light of subsequent developments it is regrettable that they did not, but it must be borne in mind that the primary reason for them going to the premises was not to conduct a search but to satisfy Mrs. Pansy Street concerning the subject matter of her complaint."

I think Mr. Robinson summed it up when he said, "Fate played its hand a number of times. This was one of the most unorthodox patterns of crime that I ever investigated. Charlie had the breaks all the way."

Police Activities
Monday, January 27
    4:20 p.m.   Bartlett victims found
    5:45 p.m.   Pick-up for Fugate and Starkweather broadcast
Tuesday, January 28
    3:15 a.m.   Missing persons broadcast for King and Jensen
    12:25 p.m.   Starkweather car found on Meyer farm
    2:30 p.m.   Meyer's body found
    3:00 p.m.   Jensen and King's bodies found
Wednesday, January 29
    9:00–11:00 a.m.   Circulars and pictures of fugitives distributed

Starkweather and Fugate
Monday, January 27
    9:30 a.m.   Left Belmont
    1:30 p.m.   Stopped at Tate's Service Station
    1:45–5:15 p.m.   At Meyer farm
    5:30 p.m.   Back at Tate's Station
    5:40 p.m.   Stuck in mud on Meyer farm
    7:45 p.m.   Got in Jensen car
    10:30 p.m.   Drove to Lincoln
    10:45 p.m.   Enroute to Hastings
    3:30 a.m.   Return to Lincoln
Tuesday, January 28
    8:00 a.m.   Arrived at Ward house
    7:00 p.m.   Left Ward house in Packard
    12:25 p.m.   Police find Jensen car at Wards'
Wednesday, January 29
    3:40 p.m.   Captured in Wyoming

EPILOGUE

Six Criticisms Offered by Harold Robinson:
- Inadequate appropriation in city and county budgets for operation of police and sheriff's office.
- Some individuals connected with the case had pertinent information which wasn't passed onto the authorities. This included those who discovered the Colvert body and personnel of the Crest Service Station.
- Need for mutual understanding between citizens and the law enforcement agencies.
- Need for higher salary adjustments.
- Large turnover with police department.
- Need for centralization of some records and identification files of the Lincoln Police Department, Lancaster Sheriff's Department, and the Nebraska Safety Patrol.

Seven-Point Commendation
- Complete cooperation and assistance by all law enforcement agencies and individuals while Robinson handled the investigation.
- Assistance by Lincoln Police Department to the sheriff's office the night of the Colvert murder, without request.
- Detailed search of Colvert murder case for physical evidence which might point to a suspect.
- Over 100 interviews handled by various members of the sheriff's staff in connection with the Colvert case.
- Law enforcement handling of Colvert slaying was not inadequate in any material respect.
- Law enforcement agencies took the necessary steps with the meager information that was available.
- Commendable actions by officers at the Bartlett home before the Bartlett bodies were discovered.

Recommendations
- More mutual understanding between citizens and local law enforcement agencies.
- Assigning one police officer to work in the sheriff's office and one deputy sheriff to work in the police department.
- Serious study by the City Council on the matter of police salaries, "which has such a direct relationship with the recruitment and retention of efficient personnel."
- Assignment of "a capable individual of superior rank" to improve operations within the present Lincoln police training organization.

APPENDIX A

Excerpts taken from the official statement of Caril Fugate, given in the Administration Building at the Nebraska State Hospital, Lincoln, Lancaster County, Nebraska, on Sunday, February 2, 1958, at 8:15 p.m., by Dale Farnbruch, Chief Deputy County Attorney, in the presence of Dr. E. A. Coats and Mrs. Merle Karnopp. Audrey Wheeler, Reporter.

D.F.: And how old are you, Caril?
C.F.: Fourteen.
D.F.: And where were you born?
C.F.: In Lincoln.
D.F.: Have you lived in Lincoln your whole life?
C.F.: Yes.
D.F.: And where do you live?
C.F.: 924 Belmont Avenue.
D.F.: Now, Caril, to start out, do you know Charles Starkweather?
C.F.: Yes.
D.F.: How long have you known Charles Starkweather?
C.F.: For about a year and a half.
D.F.: And where did you meet him?
C.F.: My sister brought him down.
D.F.: To your home?
C.F.: Yes.
D.F.: Have you been dating him since that time?
C.F.: Yes.
D.F.: And how old is Charles Starkweather?
C.F.: I think he is eighteen.
D.F.: Does he go to school?
C.F.: No.
D.F.: Have you been with him the last couple of weeks?
C.F.: Yes.

Regarding August Meyer's murder:
D.F.: Now, as I understand it, Caril, there was a man found dead out near Bennet?
C.F.: Yes.
D.F.: Do you know anything about that?
C.F.: Yes.
D.F.: What do you know about it, Caril?
C.F.: Well, I know who killed him.

APPENDIX A

D.F.: And what man are you referring to?
C.F.: Mr. Meyer.
D.F.: Is that August Meyer.
C.F.: Yes.
D.F.: What type of work did he do, do you know?
C.F.: No, I don't.
D.F.: Do you know where he lived?
C.F.: Yes.
D.F.: Where?
C.F.: I just know a farm; he lived on a farm.
D.F.: He lived on a farm near Bennet?
C.F.: Yes.
D.F.: And you say you know who shot him?
C.F.: Yes.
D.F.: Or who killed him?
C.F.: Yes.
D.F.: And who was that, Caril?
C.F.: Chuck Starkweather. Charles Starkweather.
D.F.: Do you know when that was done?
C.F.: It was done in the morning.
D.F.: In the morning?
C.F.: I think so.
D.F.: Well, now, how did you get out to the farm?
C.F.: In a black Ford.
D.F.: Who was driving the Ford?
C.F.: Chuck was.
D.F.: And did you go out with him?
C.F.: Yes.
D.F.: And where had you come from, Caril?
C.F.: My house.
D.F.: Now, after you go out to the farm, what happened out there, Caril?
C.F.: Do you want me to tell the story?
D.F.: Yes.
C.F.: I am all mixed up. I don't know if I can tell straight or not now.
D.F.: Just tell it as best as you remember it.
C.F.: Well, we went out there and pulled up in the drive, and we got stuck, and then we got out of the car and tried to get it out, but we couldn't, so we went down—what do you call that place, a bomb shelter or what?
D.F.: You are referring to what, Caril? What was it near?
C.F.: Well, we pulled up in the driveway, where the teenagers were found.
D.F.: Then you got stuck there?
C.F.: Yes.

D.F.: Was that on the way to the Meyer farm?
C.F.: Yes.
D.F.: And what happened?
C.F.: We got out of the car, and we couldn't move it because it was stuck, and then we went down into that place.
D.F.: When you say you went down into that place, you mean the bomb shelter?
C.F.: Yes.
D.F.: And what was down in the cellar?
C.F.: Some old school books.
D.F.: Did you take anything else with you at that time?
C.F.: Yes, we had Dad's shotgun, and while we was down there he loaded it.
D.F.: What kind of shotgun was it?
C.F.: I think it was a 45. It was my dad's gun.
D.F.: Did you have any other guns or weapons of any type?
C.F.: Yes, he had a knife and a little pistol.
D.F.: How long did you stay down in the cellar, approximately?
C.F.: About a half hour.
D.F.: Then when you left the shelter where did you go?
C.F.: We went up to the farm.
D.F.: Did Chuck have anything?
C.F.: Yes, he had the gun and pistol and the knife.
D.F.: When you walked up to the house, what did you do and what did Chuck do?
C.F.: Well, we walked up, and the dog—we started to go up to the house and the dog started barking and Mr. Meyer came out.
D.F.: And then what happened?
C.F.: Mr. Meyer came out. I don't know what he said, and we walked over to the red barn; that's the first barn; and Chuck said he needed the horses to pull the car out.
D.F.: Who did you see raise the gun?
C.F.: Chuck.
D.F.: And you saw Chuck raise the gun and fire it?
C.F.: Yes.
D.F.: Do you know where he was pointing it when he fired it?
C.F.: At his head.
D.F.: When he was shot, was he on the porch?
C.F.: Yes.
D.F.: Did you look at him, Caril?
C.F.: No, I didn't look at him. I knew he was face down.
D.F.: How did you know that?
C.F.: I seen the body. I didn't see his face or anything.

APPENDIX A

D.F.: Then what did you do after you walked around there?
C.F.: Well, I saw him, and then I stood away, and Chuck took him by the feet and drug him across and put him in that house there.
D.F.: Did Chuck say why he shot him?
C.F.: I don't remember.
D.F.: Did you help put Mr. Meyer in that little house?
C.F.: No. I picked up his hat.
D.F.: You picked up his hat?
C.F.: And threw it inside.

Regarding the Jensen-King murders:
D.F.: Then what happened when you were walking toward Bennet?
C.F.: Well, there was a car coming around a curve. We had walked about a mile or two, I'm not sure. There was a car coming around the curve and he stopped him.
D.F.: Who stopped who?
C.F.: Well, the car coming around the curve, and the car stopped. I don't know whether he flagged him down or not.
D.F.: Then what happened?
C.F.: And we got in the car.
D.F.: Both of you got into the car?
C.F.: Yes, and the boy said he would take the guns, and Chuck assured him they weren't loaded.
D.F.: Then what happened?
C.F.: Then we started off, and started to go to Bennet, and he asked what was wrong, and he said that the car had got stuck about a mile back, a little ways back. Then he asked him which way he was headed toward.
D.F.: Then what happened, Caril?
C.F.: Then we started going over there, and Chuck pointed the gun at him and told him to keep going.
D.F.: Then did he keep going?
C.F.: He said—he told him to keep going or he would blow his head off. I think that's what he said. The boy said, you wouldn't do that, or I don't think you would do that, and Chuck said, do you want to find out buddy. He said something about buddy, and then the boy kept driving.
D.F.: Then what happened, Caril?
C.F.: Then he told him he was going to take his car.
D.F.: Where were you going then?
C.F.: Going out to Mr. Meyer's place again.
D.F.: Was that before or after you had driven on through Bennet?
C.F.: After, when we started out to Mr. Meyer's.

D.F.: In other words, you were turned around again and going toward Mr. Meyer's farm?
C.F.: Yes.
D.F.: What did Chuck tell him again, Caril?
C.F.: He told him he was going to take the car.
D.F.: What did the driver say?
C.F.: He said he didn't care.
D.F.: What did you say?
C.F.: I didn't say nothing.
D.F.: And then what happened, Caril?
C.F.: And then the boy said he had to be careful, because the car pulled; when we slowed down and stopped the car pulled over to the right, and he told him all about the car.
D.F.: Then what happened, Caril?
C.F.: Then we started back again to Mr. Meyer's.
D.F.: Did you have a gun in your hands at that time?
C.F.: Yes.
D.F.: Which gun did you have in your hands?
C.F.: My dad's.
D.F.: Then what happened, Caril?
C.F.: Then we started back to Mr. Meyer's and pulled up in the drive. We didn't pull all the way because we got stuck before.
D.F.: And what was it stopped near?
C.F.: What do you mean?
D.F.: Well, was it stopped near anything? Is that where you got stuck before?
C.F.: Yes.
D.F.: And is that near the cellar?
C.F.: Well, the cellar is a little ways off.
D.F.: What happened when the car was stopped?
C.F.: Well, he told him to get out.
D.F.: Who told who to get out?
C.F.: Chuck told the boy to get out, and I pointed the gun at the girl. I put it on the back seat and told her to get out.
D.F.: You mean you pointed the gun at the girl and told her to get out?
C.F.: Yes.
D.F.: Why did you do that, Caril?
C.F.: Because he told him to get out.
D.F.: He told the driver to get out?
C.F.: He told them both to get out.
D.F.: Then what happened, Caril?
C.F.: Then they started walking back toward the cellar, and I got out of the back and got in the front.

APPENDIX A

D.F.: Then what was the next thing you saw?
C.F.: I saw all of them go down in the cellar.
D.F.: And how long were they all down in the cellar?
C.F.: Oh, about a half hour, or an hour.
D.F.: Then what happened, Caril?
C.F.: Then they started down the cellar and I heard two shots.
D.F.: They just went down the cellar?
C.F.: Yes.
D.F.: And you heard two shots as they were going down in, is that right?
C.F.: Yes.
D.F.: It could have been more?
C.F.: Yes.
D.F.: And what were you doing all that time?
C.F.: I was just sitting in the front seat of the car.
D.F.: Were you watching for anyone?
C.F.: No.
D.F.: You were just sitting in the car?
C.F.: Yes.
D.F.: And what happened, Caril, after those shots?
C.F.: Then Chuck went down into the cellar. I don't know how long he stayed down there, about a half hour.
D.F.: Then what happened after he came up?
C.F.: Well, he put the door over.
D.F.: Over what?
C.F.: Over the top of the place.
D.F.: Over the top of the cellar?
C.F.: Yes.
D.F.: Then what happened, Caril?
C.F.: Then he came back and got into the car and started to back out and backed the whole side of the car off in the ditch.
D.F.: Then what happened, Caril?
C.F.: Then we got out and started getting out.
D.F.: Now Caril, before we go any further, let's go back to the time just before you got this car from this driver and this girl and boy were shot. Was there anything else taken from them?
C.F.: Yes, there was $4.00.
D.F.: And did that come about?
C.F.: Well, Chuck asked them if they had any money, and the boy said yes, he had $4.00, and handed his billfold to Chuck, and Chuck handed his billfold and the boy's billfold to me. I took the money out of the boy's billfold and put it in Chuck's, and handed Chuck's billfold back to him, and handed the boy's billfold back to the girl, because she asked me to.

D.F.: Were those the only items that were taken from the boy and girl, the automobile and the money?
C.F.: Yes.

Regarding the Ward-Fencl murders:
D.F.: Now, Caril, did you go to the Ward house, you and Chuck?
C.F.: Yes.
D.F.: And was that on Wednesday, or Tuesday? Do you remember the exact date?
C.F.: No.
D.F.: And who was in the Ward house when you got there?
C.F.: Their maid and Mrs. Ward.
D.F.: And what did you do?
C.F.: I sat down in the chair there, she asked me if I wanted some coffee. Chuck asked me if I wanted some coffee, because the lady asked him. I said yes, and had a cup of coffee.
D.F.: Then after you had the coffee, what did you do?
C.F.: Then I went and laid down on the couch.
D.F.: Where was the couch?
C.F.: In the parlor, I guess.
D.F.: Now what did you do after you got in there?
C.F.: I laid down on the couch and went to sleep.
D.F.: How did you sleep?
C.F.: I don't know.
D.F.: Well, was it for quite a long time?
C.F.: Yes.
D.F.: While you were laying down there and sleeping, what is the next thing that happened?
C.F.: Well, Mrs. Ward brought me—brought some pancakes in to Chuck.
D.F.: Did you wake up at that time?
C.F.: Yes.
D.F.: Did you get some too?
C.F.: No.
D.F.: And what happened after Charlie ate the pancakes, Caril?
C.F.: I went back to sleep.
D.F.: And then what was the next thing that happened, Caril?
C.F.: Well, when I woke up and I was looking around and couldn't find Mrs. Ward, and he told me that she was dead upstairs in the bedroom.
D.F.: Did you hear any shots, Caril?
C.F.: No, I didn't, or nothing.
D.F.: Was the maid there at the time?
C.F.: Yes, she was alive.

APPENDIX A

D.F.: O.K., Caril. What happened after Charles told you that Mrs. Ward was dead upstairs?
C.F.: Well, I asked him how he killed her.
D.F.: What did he say?
C.F.: He said he stabbed her in the throat.
D.F.: And what did you say?
C.F.: I just said I didn't—well, I didn't say nothing.
D.F.: What did he do then after he told you that?
C.F.: He had a knife and he told me to go in the bathroom and wash it off.
D.F.: Where did you wash it off?
C.F.: Downstairs in the bathroom.
D.F.: Where was the maid at this time?
C.F.: In the kitchen.
D.F.: Now, what did you do after you washed the knife off?
C.F.: He told me to go upstairs and sprinkle some perfume around.
D.F.: What did you do?
C.F.: I went upstairs and sprinkled some perfume around.
D.F.: After you sprinkled this perfume around and put the bottle back, what did you do then?
C.F.: Then I went downstairs, and I think he asked me—I think he told me to go in the closet in the man's room and see if there was any coat or jacket.
D.F.: And did you find a coat?
C.F.: No.
D.F.: Now Caril, did you ever have a gun in your hands while you were in the Ward house?
C.F.: Yes.
D.F.: And what gun did you have in your hands?
C.F.: A .22.
D.F.: And was that loaded at the time?
C.F.: Yes.
D.F.: And what did you do with that gun, Caril?
C.F.: I pointed it at the maid.
D.F.: And why did you do that?
C.F.: Because he told me to.
D.F.: You say you were sitting in the living room watching for Mr. Ward.
C.F.: Yes.
D.F.: Now were you watching for him? What were you looking out of watching for him?
C.F.: Out a window.
D.F.: And how long did you sit there waiting?
C.F.: About a half an hour.
D.F.: And where was Chuck at that time?

C.F.: I don't know.
D.F.: And where was the maid?
C.F.: In the kitchen.
D.F.: Did something happen?
C.F.: Yes, he came home.
D.F.: And what did you say?
C.F.: I told Chuck he was pulling into the driveway.
D.F.: Did you holler at him, or was he beside you?
C.F.: I hollered.
D.F.: And then what happened, Caril?
C.F.: And then —
D.F.: Did Mr. Ward drive into the driveway?
C.F.: I don't know.
D.F.: All right. What happened after you hollered that Mr. Ward was coming?
C.F.: I went into the bathroom.
D.F.: Which bathroom is that?
C.F.: The bathroom downstairs.
D.F.: Then what happened as far as you know?
C.F.: Well, he told me, then Mr. Ward came home and he didn't get all the way in the house, and I think he said he came in a little ways, in the door, and grabbed hold of the gun.
D.F.: Mr. Ward grabbed hold of the gun?
C.F.: I think that's what he said, and they started fighting out there, and he was standing by the stairs, and he said he let go of the gun and Mr. Ward fell down the stairs and Mr. Ward started picking up the gun, and he said he picked up the gun, and Mr. Ward, I think he said, picked up a piece of steel or something, and he shot him, I think. I heard a shot. And then he told Mr. Ward to go upstairs nice and easy, and Mr. Ward started up the stairs, and he got a little ways up and started running, and I don't know what happened then.
D.F.: Were you in the bathroom all this time?
C.F.: Yes.
D.F.: What did you see when you came out of the bathroom, Caril?
C.F.: Well, the maid was sitting there where the large table is, sitting on a chair there against the wall, and Mr. Ward was laying on the floor by the door, moaning.
D.F.: What did you go into the bathroom for?
C.F.: I just went in there. I was scared.
D.F.: And Mr. Ward, when you came out, was laying by the front door?
C.F.: Yes.
D.F.: Then where was Chuck?

APPENDIX A

C.F.: He was—I think he was looking out the window.
D.F.: And what did he say to you?
C.F.: He told me to hold the gun over the maid.
D.F.: The .22?
C.F.: Yes.
D.F.: Let me put it this way, Caril. What happened in relation to the maid then, after Mr. Ward was laying there by the door, and after you had held the gun on her, and he went out to the kitchen and got some food, and then what happened in regard to the maid?
C.F.: Well, she sat down there.
D.F.: In the kitchen?
C.F.: No, in the living room.
D.F.: Now then, what happened to the maid after that, Caril?
C.F.: Well, before that she was downstairs, and Chuck told her to go upstairs and nothing would happen. When she got upstairs he asked her if she made a phone call and she said no, and he said, if you did, we'll leave, but if she didn't we were going to stay. He said there was supposed to be about fifteen or twenty guys supposed to come, and that's when he told her, he said if anybody came to the door, she would be the first one to get shot.
D.F.: In any event, then what happened, Caril?
C.F.: Well, then we waited for a few minutes to see if anybody was coming, and then we went upstairs.
D.F.: Who went upstairs?
C.F.: Chuck, I and the maid.
D.F.: Did you have a gun at that time?
C.F.: Yes.
D.F.: What did you do when you went upstairs, Caril?
C.F.: He said for her to sit down in the chair, and I was looking out the window.
D.F.: What room were you in at that time?
C.F.: One of the bedrooms.
D.F.: Then what happened while you were in that room? Was the light on?
C.F.: No.
D.F.: Did you have anything in your hands other than the gun?
C.F.: The light. The flashlight.
D.F.: And the maid was sitting in the chair in that bedroom?
C.F.: Yes.
D.F.: Then what happened, Caril?
C.F.: Well, he got a sheet and started tearing it, and then he started to tie her wrist, and I told him why didn't he let her lay on the bed, because she would get tired sitting up all night. I didn't know he was going to kill

her then, and then he made her lay down on the bed and started tying her wrists.
D.F.: How did he tie her wrists?
C.F.: With both hands together.
D.F.: And—
C.F.: And then he tied them to the bed post.
D.F.: Were her hands over her head or not?
C.F.: Yes.
D.F.: Then what else did he do?
C.F.: He tied her feet.
D.F.: And did he tie them to anything?
C.F.: To the end of the bed.
D.F.: And then what happened after that, Caril?
C.F.: She kept saying to turn on the light because she was scared of the dark.
D.F.: Did somebody turn on the light?
C.F.: No.
D.F.: Then what happened?
C.F.: I was looking out the window, and he started stabbing her, and she started screaming and hollering.
D.F.: How many times did he stab her?
C.F.: I don't know.
D.F.: Did she say anything while he was stabbing her?
C.F.: I don't know. He put a pillow over her face.
D.F.: Did he stab her more than once?
C.F.: Yes.
D.F.: Would it be more than twice?
C.F.: Yes.
D.F.: How do you know that, Caril?
C.F.: I heard it. Every time he stabbed her, she moaned.
D.F.: About how many times did she moan?
C.F.: Well, more than five.
D.F.: And then what happened after he got done stabbing her?
C.F.: He said he didn't think she was ever going to die, and then he said to shine the flashlight over there and he cut the strips holding her legs, and covered her over.
D.F.: What did he cover her up with?
C.F.: A blanket that laid on the bed.
D.F.: Did you see any blood?
C.F.: I seen the blood on the bed, but I didn't see the stabs.
D.F.: Then what did he do after he covered her up?
C.F.: He told me to shine the flashlight on his arm. There was blood stains all over his shirt; all over the cuff of his shirt.

APPENDIX A

D.F.: What did he do after that, Caril?
C.F.: I went and found a white shirt.
D.F.: And while you were in the Ward home, did you talk on the telephone?
C.F.: Yes.
D.F.: And when was that, Caril?
C.F.: Just as we started to leave.
D.F.: How did you come to talk on the telephone?
C.F.: The telephone rang, and I answered it. He told me to answer it.
D.F.: Where was this telephone?
C.F.: In the kitchen.
D.F.: Now, what did you say when you answered the telephone just before you left?
C.F.: I think the lady asked how Mrs. Ward was, and I said she was sleeping.
D.F.: And then what happened?
C.F.: That's about all.

Regarding the Bartlett Murders:
D.F.: Caril, what happened when you came home from school on that Tuesday?
C.F.: I came in, and I opened the door and walked in, and he was standing behind the door. I don't remember whether he grabbed me or not. He told me—he said for me to sit down on the couch, or chair, and then I asked him where my folks were, because they were out there and they were gone, and then he told me that story.
D.F.: What story was that?
C.F.: He told me my folks were over at that old lady's house where he had the hot rod. I guess that's what you call it, and he said if I done what he told me, then they wouldn't be hurt. I asked him how they got over there, and he said he had come in and my mother had told him to get out, and he asked them if they were going along peacefully, and he said my mother kept telling him to get out, and they grabbed my little sister, and then they asked him if he was going to peacefully and he said they would.
D.F.: What did you think about that?
C.F.: Well, I didn't believe him at first. I kept saying, I don't believe you. Then I went out into the kitchen and I either plugged in the coffee, or he did.
D.F.: And then what happened after you plugged in the coffee?
C.F.: I don't remember what went on in the house.
D.F.: What went on in the house?
C.F.: No.
D.F.: What do you mean, Caril?
C.F.: I don't remember it all.

D.F.: You don't remember it all?
C.F.: I don't remember it all.
D.F.: What do you mean you don't remember it all?
C.F.: I don't remember what went on.
D.F.: Then what happened after that, Caril?
C.F.: He told me to change my clothes at first, because I was scared to then, and then I went in and changed them.
D.F.: Then what did he and you do?
C.F.: Watched television.
D.F.: Did you and he talk back and forth?
C.F.: Talked about my folks.
D.F.: What did you say, and what did he say about your folks?
C.F.: I asked him if I could talk with them, and see them, if they were all right, and he assured me they were all right.
D.F.: Did you stay in the house?
C.F.: Yes.
D.F.: And how many times would you say, Caril, you stayed in the house while he went away?
C.F.: Almost every night.
D.F.: Now Caril, Chuck has told me he tied you up the second night and that is the only time, is that right?
C.F.: He tied me up when he left the house, and he didn't tie me up tight so it hurt.
D.F.: Could you get loose?
C.F.: Well, what do you mean?
D.F.: Well, what did he tie you up with?
C.F.: My mother's dishtowel.
D.F.: Now Caril, I have talked with the people that have interviewed Chuck, and they tell me that he told them that there was only one night he tied you up. Is he wrong when he says that?
C.F.: Yes.
D.F.: As I understand it, you do not have a telephone at your house.
C.F.: No.

APPENDIX B

One of Charlie's letters to Prosecutor Scheele

Charles Starkweather
Box 111
Lincoln, Nebraska
March 28, 1958

Dear Mr. Scheele:
   i'n writing this at ny own free will and well sign it when done. It would take to much paper to tell why i change ny mind of what happen in Caril f part of Killing of Carol King? i Know my folks can tell you why i'n writng this. When i kill the boy out at the cave by the school house, he drop on the steps and landed on the floor in the cave. the King girl never ran or said anything i told her to stay right where she was i gone on dowm into the cave and he was moving a little, show i got up out of the cave and Carol King was standing right where i left here. "i think she was Shock" i went to the car to get a flash light Caril fugate was siting in the front and with the 4.10, i gone down into the cave and was down there about 15 to 25 min. then i got scared and ran out of the cave and told King to go down into the cave, and not even stay intull she got down she was on about the 2'd step and ran to the car, i was so dan scared i back of into a dichd. we got out of car to see what happen, i and caril went on back up to the cave and i told carol King to come on up. i gave the 22 cal. to caril fugate and told her to watch her, gone on back down to the car and was on the side jacking the car body up, then i heard a shot and ran back to the cave, caril said that King started to run and had to shot her. caril went on to car and got it. i put the King girl in the cave, on about the 2 or 3 step from the top. the rest is in the statemind i gave you. when we got the car out i caril walk up to the cave and pass the door and some boards on the opening of the cave, if there is any details you would like to Know about the King case come out or asked ny folks to asked ne, and i'll tell you. and the nan that got Kill in wyoing, caril and i both shot hin! My writing is a little of a mess, but i hope you can read it.

APPENDIX C

Letter from Mrs. Guy Starkweather to the Lincoln Journal *published May 17, 1958*

To the interested parties of Lincoln

    I have heard there are comments on my statement of my "six problems and one catastrophe." I will admit what happened to Charles in that week was a catastrophe, few can deny that. I did not mean that I had raised six problems in the definition the dictionary gives of the word problem. What I mean was I had problems to be met. Every mother and father has. Each child at some time or other has a different problem and has come to me and his father for a solution. Sometimes the answer we gave was the same as far as the other children, sometimes different, according to how we felt we could best get the answer across to the child's understanding.

    At the pace this old world is set today one cannot deny there are numerous problems that children and youth find hard to cope with. What with the atomic bomb, the speed of our planes being faster than sound, Sputnik and our own Vanguard, I think we parents wonder what our world is coming to so we should see what our young folks are up against.

    Do you parents believe that you can always give an answer to your children and know that they have fully grasped the meaning? I don't think so.

    Every mother and father knows that each child is a separate individual, each with different ideas and thought. We love each and every one of our children, one no more than the other. There are problems for a parent to meet in the years of raising a family, sometimes small, other times large.

    We have taught our children that when they come up against something they do not understand not to dodge it but to face it to the best of their ability.

    I think all of us at some time in our life, probably mostly in younger years, met with something that was really an obstacle, but with the help and understanding of our parents we surmounted that obstacle and were better persons because of it.

    When one of my children came to me with a problem and were seeking the best explanation I could give, I hope they understood. My problem was, did they? Anything that needs thinking and working out is a problem, mathematics or diagraming a sentence for an English lesson. That is what I mean by six problems and a catastrophe.

    We all have a big problem on our hands sometimes in trying to understand our children. I truly hope everyone understands what I am trying to get across.

    I thank you all very much.

                                          Mrs. Guy Starkweather

APPENDIX D

Letter Charlie wrote to Mrs. Pansy Street (Velda Bartlett's mother)

Nebraska State Penn.
February 21, 1958

Dear Mrs. Street:
   i hope mrs. street that you will read this and not destroying it befor you do read it. i'n writing this to tell you, that i'n sorry for the sorrou we have gave you and there are a lot of others we hurt also. but i'n sorry for you cause you lost your daughter and i know hou you must lover her, So i'n not asking you to give in any way, but i had to tell you that "i'n sorry" and i would not blame you for hating. Someday i'n going to write you another letter, telling you what started and cause this to happen the way it did. i hope you well read it too, "if you do you nay hate some other people to and naybe you'll know then that i'n not the only one to blane for what happen. i wish there was a way to re-pay you for what has happen. "but there's not." Tell your daughter and some that i'n sorry.

Chuck Starkweather

APPENDIX E

List of admitted crimes committed by Charles Starkweather

Armed Robbery (Dec. 1 at Crest Service Station)
Attempted safe burglary or robbery (at Crest Station)
Assault (simple, common, felonious, aggravated, with deadly weapon; and battery, with intent to do great bodily harm)
Unlawful transportation of a dead body (Bartletts' bodies and others moved)
Forcible entry
Petty larceny and grand larceny
Mayhem
Inciting to riot, and disturbing the peace
Auto theft
Discharging firearms within the city limits
Carrying concealed weapons (knife and .32 cal. pistol)
Possession of shotgun with sawed-off barrel
Unlawful flight to avoid prosecution
Contributing to the delinquency of a minor
Accessory (before, after, and during the commission of a felony)
Perjury
Execution of a false document (conflicting confessions)
Destruction of private property
Destruction of evidence and mutilation of a body
Violation of Dyer Act (transporting stolen auto across state line)
Violation of Mann Act (woman across state line for immoral purposes)
Violation of Smith Act (gun across state line for illegal purposes)
Speeding (over 110 mph in Wyoming chase)
Resisting arrest
Reckless driving and running red light (Douglas)

APPENDIX F

Questions and Answers from Charlie prior to execution.

What is the most important message you want to tell the people of the United States at this time in the way of advice to other kids after your experiences?

Any advice to the young people today is to go to school, and attend Sunday school, and church every Sunday. Go to church and receive the Lord Jesus Christ as your own personal Savior. Our God is a kind God, he'll forgive, and accept you as one of his even if your heart is black and heavy with sin. With God there be peace within your soul, and in Heaven eternal life will be in your hands through all eternity. You can feed the mind with knowledge, and the body with food, but don't forget the soul; feed it with the love and the words of the Lord. So I advise young and old to attend their church of God and worship the Lord Jesus Christ, and pray that we can maintain the Christian faith that holds together the trust, the truth, the love, and the righteousness of the American people, and the people of the world.

Also I advise the young today to attend their schools, and take advantage of the free education our forefathers created, and that same education amongst many other acts of democracy America has fought so hard in bloody battles to have and maintain. Our country has fought and won again and again for the type of democracy that we want. Our soldiers have died in battle slain just so we could have a free land to live in, so we could have freedom of speech, the privilege of doing, going, and coming as we please, a church of our choice, and working where, when, and as we wish, and most of all so we could have free schools to attend—free from propaganda, and the teachers are not a unit of Colonels who wear armbands, and take you out and have you shot at sunrise if you don't read and learn just and only what they want you to. Our free schools provide us with the education that will make us the future Americans of tomorrow, but we don't realize it. The girls and boys who quit when they become of age are the ones who don't realize it. They don't realize how important education will be in their lives.

So don't make the mistake of quitting school—oh I know you might get a job, save some money to buy an automobile, and have a lot of money to spend on dates, but tell me what do you have in the long run?—Well, I tell you, you haven't a thing that amounts to anything. It's that High school and college diploma that takes all the gravy in the future. I have regretted this experience in the past. I quit school when I came of age, got a job that didn't amount.

Had you ever thought of committing any violence before the spree?

I had the reputation for fighting and raising cain all the time and you could even say there was a little of violence in it, but I never ever had any intentions or thoughts of committing such violence and unjustable crimes as that of the spree.

At the time you did the killings, why did you think that you were right in doing that? Have you changed your mind on your feelings that you were right? At the time you were running away from the police, were you scared? What did you have to gain from the killings?

The killings we committed—some of the victims were killed while we defending our own lives, and the others exactly did attempt to block our path of escape. It's unknown to me what Caril's that I was going to give up as we were driving back to Lincoln from Bennet. Caril then threatened out loud that she wasn't going to give up, and that I or no one else was going to make her, and with a shotgun laying across her lap with the barrel pointing directly at me, and with her fast talking she convinced me that we didn't have anything to gain by giving up. But now I'm sorry and regret that I ever listened to her, instead give up and just took the chance of being shot by her.

Do you feel sorry for the victims?

My feelings are of great sorrow and remorse for the people we have killed. And for the heartache, and sorrow and grief we caused to the people who lost their loved ones, my feelings are much deeper yet, and I pray that God will forgive us for what we have done.

How do you feel about Caril today?

My feelings toward Caril are of great regret for ever knowing her. In the past Caril and myself had a lot of good times and fun and excitement together. Our love in the beganing was very ardent and passionate. But as time went along our love tapered off to emotional passion and lust, and as time went on and on my love for Caril began to fade out, but it didn't fade out and die fast or soon enough and eventually led to my downfall.

Today as I put it, my love for Caril is completely dead. It took a long time to end, and wish it would have ended before now. I hold no grudges against Caril, and as far as caring for her, my feelings are none whatsoever.

What are your thoughts and feelings today as you face the date of execution?

The past year has been one of imprisonment. I have had a great deal of time for thought and to retrace back over my life. I am young, and under normal circumstances my life would still be ahead of me. Going to the electric chair will bring my life to an end. I hold no fear for the electric chair; it is the price I am paying for taking the lives of others. Bringing my life to an end does not answer why certain things took place. Going to the electric chair will bring to an end my search for answers that are hard to find. God alone knows how I have suffered and if he feels I have had enough, then with his help I'll go

APPENDIX F

unafraid to the electric chair. If for any reason the Lord feels that I haven't suffered long enough, then I'll go on living my tormented life.

Who was your favorite teacher and why?

My favorite teacher was one whom I had in my last year in school. She didn't act like she was better or smarter than the others, and this one teacher of all the other school . . .

APPENDIX G

Twelve jurors in Starkweather case

Mrs. George McDonald Jr., housewife, Rt. 6
Mrs. Mildred Fagerberg, department store employee, 3401 Pawnee
Anders H. Hallbert, carpenter, 5716 Madison
Mrs. Beatrice I. Volkmer, rubber plant employee, 7126 Thurston
Oliver E. L. Rosenberg, hospital employee, 735 S. 29th
Mrs. Adeline E. Muehlbeier, housewife, 1641 Pawnee
Mrs. Evelyn V. Russell, housewife, 4303 Hillside
Alvin M. Christiansen, electronics specialist, 1726 S. 23rd
Mrs. Ellen E. Heuer, bookstore employee, 2741 N. 48th
Raymond E. Swanson, salesman, 236 S. 27th
Mrs. Miriam F. McCully, housewife, 3619 Garfield
John Svoboda, railroad employee, 6404 Kearney

APPENDIX H

Chart of Charlie's confessions

Seven different confessions were introduced as evidence in the Charles Starkweather case. Two were long documents while others were letters and notes. The confessions, in chronological order, are:

1. A letter addressed "For the law only," which Charlie said he wrote Tuesday, January 28, while he and Caril were at the C. Lauer Ward house. This letter was taken from Charlie after his capture in Wyoming. It first appeared to have been written by both Charlie and Caril, but Charlie said later he wrote the note himself.

2. A confession Charlie wrote in longhand the night of Wednesday, January 28 while in a Douglas County, Wyoming jail.

3. A letter he wrote to his parents the same night.

4. A letter he wrote on the wall in the Gering, Nebraska jail on January 30 on the return trip to Lincoln.

5. A statement County Attorney Elmer Scheele took from Charlie February 1 at the Nebraska State Penitentiary.

6. A statement given to Chief Deputy Attorney Dale Farnbruch February 27.

7. A letter detailing the slaying of Carol King which Charlie wrote and mailed to Scheele April 9 from the prison.

The chart on the next page points out major conflicts in the seven confessions.

	Bartlett Family	Meyer	Jensen	King	Ward Family	Collison	Colvert
1.	In a portion apparently written by Caril from the wording of the letter, Caril said she hit Betty Jean Bartlett with a gun 10 times. The letter said "Chuck" killed Mr. Bartlett but was vague about who murdered Mrs. Bartlett.	No mention.	No mention.	No mention.	No mention.	No mention.	No mention.
2.	Starkweather said the family before Caril came home from school.	How Meyer was killed was not mentioned.	Admits the slaying.	Said he shot the girl.	Admits knifing Mrs. Ward but said she was alive when he left the house. Admits killing Mr. Ward but denies having anything to do with the slaying of Miss Fencl, the maid.	Said he shot him "3 or 4 times."	No mention.
3.	Says Caril helped him but had nothing to do with any of the slayings.	No mention.	No mention.	No mention.	No mention.	No mention.	No mention.
4.	Starkweather said he killed 9 men, Caril 3 women. But 6 men, 4 women and the Bartlett child were murdered. Note said Caril wanted to go to Washington state.	No mention.	No mention.	No mention.	No mention.	No mention.	No mention.
5.	Said Caril was at school when he murdered the family. Said Caril asked only once where her parents were and that he told her they were not at home.	Admits shooting the farmer.	Admits the murder.	Said he shot the girl.	Admits knifing Mrs. Ward, but says she was alive when he left the house. Admits shooting Mr. Ward but denies knifing the maid. Said he wrote the note addressed "For the law only."	No mention.	No mention.
6.	Said he murdered the family late in the afternoon after Caril returned from school.	Admits to the shooting.	Admits the murder.	Said he shot the girl and partially undressed her. Said he lied when he told Police Lt. Robert Henninger he had relations with the girl after she was dead.	Admits knifing Mrs. Ward once and knowing she was dead before leaving the house. Denies the knife-slaying of the maid but says Caril was alone upstairs with the woman part of the time. Admits shooting Mr. Ward and hitting him with a poker. Said Caril made several remarks on the trip to Wyoming about the maid "trying to get away."	Admits shooting Collison.	Admits robbing Crest station and shooting the attendant.
7.	No mention.	No mention.	No mention.	Said Caril Fugate shot Miss King, but does not explain the report the girl was the victim of an abnormal sex attack.	No mention.	Admits shooting Collison but said the salesman "had a lot of fight left in him" when Caril walked to the opposite side of the car and shot Collison several more times.	No mention.

ACKNOWLEDGMENTS

I would like to thank James McKee, who revived this project when no one else seemed to care. I would also like to thank the Nebraska State Historical Society for their professional attitude and willingness to help. Andrea Paul, Linda Wagaman, Marty Miller, Anne McBride, and Emily Levine were always willing to go the extra mile to help my research needs.

This book of "faction" is based primarily upon testimony given at Charlie's and Caril's trials during the spring of 1958. The Nebraska State Historical Society in Lincoln, Nebraska, has the trial transcripts on microfilm. If you wish to purchase the film or borrow it at your local library under the inter-library loan system, please contact them and reference the following:

- Lancaster County District Court of Nebraska—3rd Judicial District: *The State of Nebraska, Plaintiff vs. Charles R. Starkweather*, Case #34498, Roll 1 and Roll 2, #17,910 & #17,911.
- Lancaster County District Court of Nebraska—3rd Judicial District: *The State of Nebraska, Plaintiff vs. Caril Ann Fugate*, Case #34590, Roll 3 and Roll 4, #17,912 & #17,913.

Other sources which helped in writing this book were:
- *Starkweather—Portrait of a Mass Murder*, William Allen; Avon Books, 1976.
- *Caril*, Ninette Beaver, B. K. Ripley and Patrick Trese; J. B. Lippincott Company, 1974.
- Newspapers: *Lincoln Journal, Lincoln Star, Lincoln Sunday Journal-Star, Hastings Daily Tribune.*